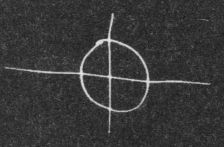

THE MOST DANGEROUS

ANIMAL OF ALL

SEARCHING FOR MY FATHER . . .
AND FINDING
THE ZODIAC KILLER

GARY L. STEWART
WITH SUSAN MUSTAFA

HARPER

NEW YORK · LONDON · TORONTO · SYDNEY

HARPER

A hardcover edition of this book was published in 2014 by HarperCollins Publishers.

THE MOST DANGEROUS ANIMAL OF ALL. Copyright © 2014 by Gary L. Stewart and Susan Mustafa. All rights reserved. Printed in the United States of America. No part of this book may be used or reproduced in any manner whatsoever without written permission except in the case of brief quotations embodied in critical articles and reviews. For information address HarperCollins Publishers, 195 Broadway, New York, NY 10007.

HarperCollins books may be purchased for educational, business, or sales promotional use. For information please e-mail the Special Markets Department at SPsales@harpercollins.com.

FIRST HARPER PAPERBACK EDITION PUBLISHED 2015.

Designed by William Ruoto

Library of Congress Cataloging-in-Publication Data has been applied for.

ISBN 978-0-06-231317-1 (pbk.)

15 16 17 18 19 OV/RRD 10 9 8 7 6 5 4 3 2

For the man who adopted
the abandoned baby on the stairwell
and raised him as his own

CONTENTS

This memoir is based upon my research over a twelve-year period, which I recorded in a journal as I went through the process of discovering the facts of my father's life. Through conversations with my father's best friend, family members and my biological mother, police records, newspaper articles, old Best family letters, marriage and divorce records, and other government records, I was able to create a timeline of my father's early life, which makes up Part One of this book. The narration of that period is presented in a novelistic manner of storytelling because this was the most coherent way to tell his story. I have taken some small liberties when re-creating dialogue in this section of the book, but even those conversations are based upon the memories of my father's family and friends and the facts of his life that were related to me. Likewise, dialogue in Parts Two and Three is based upon twelve years of investigation and the facts that investigation revealed. I should note that all of the conversations that took place between me and others, including my biological mother, my father's best friend, and detectives at the San Francisco Police Department, are related verbatim.

The details concerning my father's life span five decades and are complex. It seemed best to simply start at the beginning, in order to give the reader a real sense of how and why my father grew into a serial killer.

—GARY L. STEWART

The Zodiac case has been shrouded in mystery for almost fifty years. When I began my journey to find my biological father, I never envisioned that my search would lead me to a series of brutal murders that terrorized the residents of California in the 1960s and '70s. The very idea that my father committed these acts is repulsive to me, and I try hard to disassociate myself from the horrific crimes he perpetrated upon innocent young people. After I met my biological mother, I simply wanted to find the man responsible for giving me life. I wanted to know him, love him, and even forgive him for what he had done to me. I had been raised in an adoptive home and taught that love and forgiveness are tenets by which to live one's life.

I had been gathering information about my father for two years before I got the first suspicion that he could somehow be connected to the Zodiac killings. At the time, I did not want to believe what my instincts were telling me, so I set out to uncover the truth, to prove to myself that my father could not possibly have been a serial killer. As years went by and more and more telling evidence unfolded, there came a day when I could no longer deny that my worst fears were true. That realization prompted me to write this memoir. I felt it was my responsibility to share the truths that I had learned in a way that would leave no doubt as to the identity of this killer and the reasons why he had committed these murders.

February 1963

The sound of the baby's hungry cries
pierced the darkness. His father angrily
flung his covers aside and climbed out
of bed, hurrying to the footlocker that
doubled as the infant's crib. Furiously, he
slammed the lid shut.

Inside, the cries soon turned to gasps as
the baby struggled for air.

PROLOGUE

May 2002

Thirty-nine years. That's how long I had waited to hear the words. Thirty-nine years spent wondering about my name, my parents' names.

Finally, I knew.

My mother's name was Judith.

I could see that something was bothering my adoptive parents, Loyd and Leona Stewart, the day I found out the truth. I observed them surreptitiously as I stirred the crawfish, sausage, corn, and potatoes one last time before dumping out the huge pot onto the newspapers lining the table in my sister Cindy's backyard. Loyd wasn't laughing and cracking jokes in his Cajun French accent like he usually did, and Leona's pretty face was drawn tight, as though she had something serious on her mind.

It was hot, the Louisiana humidity already sucking any coolness from the spring air, but a light breeze made the heat bearable as we sat around the table pinching meat from the tails and sucking spicy seasonings from the heads of the tasty mudbugs. After I finished my pile, I began hosing out the boiling pot. I watched as Loyd and Leona nodded to each other and then began walking toward me.

Uh-oh. I could tell by the way they were so deliberate in their approach that something was very wrong. I wondered who had died.

"Hey, Geg," Dad said.

Loyd never called me Geg. That was a shortened version of my name used only by my grandparents. His use of that nickname, coupled with the fact that he looked like he was going to cry, made me even more nervous.

I flipped the towel in my hand over my shoulder and said, "What's the matter, you two?"

"There's no easy way to say what we have to say, so I'm just going to say it," Loyd said. "A couple of weeks ago, a lady in San Francisco called us and said she was your mother."

My mother? What?

Leona slipped her arm around my waist. "When we first received the package and picture she sent, I didn't want to believe she could be your mother, but your dad said how much you looked like the lady in the picture. I denied it with every ounce of my being. I even refused to look at the picture again for a day or two."

I tried to swallow the lump that had suddenly formed in my throat.

"But then I prayed about it," she continued, "and the Lord laid it upon my heart that this was your mother and that your daddy and I should be honest with you."

"When I first saw the picture, I just knew it was your mother," Loyd piped in. "I told your mama, and she just wouldn't believe it."

Seeing the tears that were welling in my eyes, Leona gave me a gentle squeeze.

I couldn't believe it. After all these years, I would finally have an identity, a name that was really mine. I could feel a wave of excitement flowing through me, and I reached for my father and mother and hugged them tightly. I promised them that no matter what happened, they would always be my parents. At that moment, I had no way of knowing how much this day would alter the course of my life.

Leona explained that she had received the call on May Day. She and Cindy had been in the living room, visiting with Loyd's mother, Evelyn, when the phone rang, and she went into the kitchen to answer it.

"Hello," Leona said in her sweet southern voice.

"Hello. Is this Leona?" the voice on the other end of the line asked nervously.

"Yes, it is. And who is this?"

"My name is Judith Gilford, and I live in San Francisco. I believe I am your son Gary's birth mother."

For a few seconds, Leona couldn't speak.

When she was able to catch her breath, she managed to say, "What makes you think that?"

"I have information from his placement file," Judith explained. "Look, I don't want to interfere in your lives," she rushed on. "I just want to make the information available to Gary, to give him an identity just in case he wants to know."

Leona listened as the woman explained some of the circumstances of her life and how she had come to give her baby up for adoption.

"I never wanted to give him up, and I've always wanted to find him," Judith said just as Loyd poked his head into the room. Leona waved him away and walked into her bedroom, closing the door behind her. She listened carefully while Judith told her everything she had gone through to find her son over the past few years. Leona, always attuned to the feelings of others, couldn't help but feel sympathy for the woman.

"Please just let me send you a package with a letter and some pictures for him," Judith begged.

"I'll discuss it with my husband," Leona said. "And I'll talk to Gary."

Judith cut her off. "Please don't make me any promises. I will just send the information and trust that whatever should happen will happen."

A few days later, when Leona received the FedEx box from Judith, she turned it over and over, afraid to open it, fearing the potential it had to change all of our lives.

All the birthday parties, the skinned knees, the boo-boos she had kissed. All of the memories she had shared with me flashed through her mind. Was this some kind of cruel joke? How dare this woman intrude into her life—her son's life—like this?

With trembling fingers, Leona opened the box. A picture clipped to a letter caught her eye. The woman who had called stared at her from the wallet-size photograph. Tears began to cloud Leona's vision and then rolled down her cheeks. She tried as she searched the picture to convince herself that the woman looked nothing like me. But try as she might to lie to herself, the truth stared back at her from the photo.

She brought the picture to Loyd.

He held Leona's hand as he scanned the photo.

"He sure does look like her," Loyd said. He wanted to tell his wife that this woman could not possibly be my mother, but he knew he had to be honest.

For the next few days, they talked about nothing but this unbelievable predicament in which they suddenly found themselves. Mine had been a closed adoption. This shouldn't have happened. Should they tell me? Should they keep this a secret? Holding hands, they prayed together, asking God to show them what to do.

Finally, one night Loyd got his answer. He turned to his wife and said, "He deserves to know who he is and then decide what he wants to do."

Leona knew her husband was right, but she was very afraid I would get hurt. For the next week, Leona and Loyd prayed harder than ever that God would give them the strength to be unselfish, that He would help them deliver this news in just the right way.

And now I knew.

I drove the twenty-eight miles back to my house that evening in a state of shock, remembering all the times I had fantasized about what my real parents might be like and wondering from whom I had inherited my reddish hair. Because I didn't know my real name or why my adoption birth certificate stated that I had been born in New Orleans, I had struggled with an identity crisis for most of my life. Excited and anxious to look through the package Leona had given me, I pressed my foot a little harder on the accelerator, holding the picture of the woman in my hand. I caught myself veering off the road several times because I couldn't take my eyes off it. As I drove, I thought about my son Zach's reaction to the photo.

"Hey, Dad, he looks just like you," Zach had naively said, looking at the man standing next to Judith in the photo she had sent. Everyone had laughed. The man was clearly of American Indian or Hispanic heritage, but Zach had assumed that if the woman was my mother, then the man had to be my father.

When I got home, I turned on the overhead light so I wouldn't miss a detail as I sifted through the letters in the box. Sitting in my favorite recliner, I stared at the picture of the woman who claimed to be my mother.

Her eyes.

Her nose.

Her mouth.

They were like mine.

I pulled out the letter Judith had written to all of the men she could find who had been born on my birth date in Louisiana.

Tears gathered in my eyes as I read.

In the letter, she explained that she had been fifteen and a runaway from California when I was born. She had been married to my father, but the marriage had been annulled by her mother because she was underage. Judith went on to state that she and her husband had been apprehended and sent back to California. The condition her mother had set for her daughter to eventually move back in with her was that I—two months old at the time—be given up for adoption. She said she had married again at the age of twenty-six and had another son.

I had a brother?

Then she said that she had loved me from the day I was born and that I had been with her every day since. "It would be the happiest day of my life if the phone rang and my son said to me, 'I believe you are my mother,'" she wrote.

I read the letter over and over and then reached for the phone. As I began to dial the number she had provided, my hand began to shake, and I hung up. What would I say?

My thoughts turned to Leona. I knew how difficult it must have been for her to share this news with me. The next day was Mother's Day, and I felt guilty even thinking about calling this woman when Leona had been such a wonderful mother to me. Throughout my life, I had spent that special day in church honoring her as she proudly wore the corsage that announced she was a mother. She had chosen to love me when she had no obligation to do so. She had happily taken me into her home and treated me as well as she had her biological child. She didn't deserve such disloyalty.

As I sat near her in the pew at church the next morning, I

felt such love for her, but as I squeezed her hand, I couldn't stop thinking about the other woman, the one who had given birth to me when she was only fifteen years old. I couldn't quite fathom that. I felt compassion for the young girl who had been faced with such an adult situation.

By the end of the day, I knew what I had to do. I had always believed that everything happens for a reason, and this could be no different.

When I got home, I walked into the living room and sat down in my favorite chair. Still holding the woman's picture, I reached for the phone and began dialing. My heart was pounding as I punched in the numbers. Holding my breath, I waited.

One ring.

Two rings.

Three rings.

Then I heard a man's voice on the answering machine. Speaking with a distinct accent, he said, "You have reached Judy Gilford and Frank Velasquez. Your call is very important to us, but we are unable to take your call at this time. Please leave your name and phone number, along with your message, and we will return your call as soon as we can."

Disappointment raced through me. I wanted so badly to hear her voice. I hesitated for a moment.

Taking a deep breath, I finally spoke. "This message is for Judith Gilford. This is Gary Stewart, and I think you may be my mother." I paused for a moment, steadying my voice. "If you are my mother, I would like to wish you a happy Mother's Day . . . for the first time. If you are not my mother, then I hope you have a happy Mother's Day as well. If you would like to return my call, you can reach me at . . ." And I left my number.

Not knowing if I had done the right thing, I sank into my recliner, drained. It had taken everything I had to make that call.

I reached over to turn on the lamp and then sat there for hours, staring at her picture.

Later that evening, Frank Velasquez decided to call home and check for messages. He and Judy, as she preferred to be called, were visiting relatives in Albuquerque, New Mexico. Although they were not married, Judy often referred to him as her husband. They enjoyed traveling together and had booked this trip as a short getaway.

Frank listened for a moment and then retrieved the message again.

"Honey, you have to listen to this one," he said, handing Judy the phone. She listened to the message over and over, crying uncontrollably as she heard my voice for the first time.

"You have to call him now," Frank insisted.

Judy couldn't. She was too overwrought.

"I can't. It's so late," she hedged. "And I don't think we have enough minutes on the phone card."

Frank took the phone from her hand and dialed a number, paying for an additional thousand minutes before handing the phone back to her.

Judy stared at it for a moment and then dialed the number I had left on the recorder.

I was still sitting in my living room when the shrill ringing of the telephone startled me out of my reverie.

"Hello," I said, my voice cracking as I tried to still my trembling hands.

"Hi," Judy whispered into the phone. "This is Judy Gilford."

The sound of her voice shot through me like an electrical current. I started crying. I couldn't speak.

"I know you may not believe me, but I love you. I've always loved you," Judy said, her voice quavering. Like a dam that had suddenly broken, we both started talking at once. "You have a grandson," I told her. "He's ten, and his name is Zach."

We talked for what seemed like hours, interrupting each other in our eagerness to share everything. It felt as though I were in a dream—that this was happening to someone else, that an impossible prayer was being answered. We agreed to leave the past behind us and make our new relationship whatever we wanted it to be. Excitedly, we began to make plans to meet.

When I hung up the phone, I leaned back in my chair, savoring this special Mother's Day. It was a day I would never forget.

I couldn't sleep that night, so I tried to put my feelings into words by writing her a letter:

Mom,

Today my world changed. When I first learned that you were searching for me, I was completely shocked. Then, when I spoke to you this evening, I knew once and for all that you are my mother. Words cannot describe what my heart feels now. There is so much more to motherly love than most people understand. For all my life, I have had an emptiness in my heart that was impossible to fill. The missing piece was something that I did not understand, something I didn't even know existed. When you spoke those words to me this evening, "Gary, I love you," the emptiness was gone.

On June 1, 2002, Zach and I drove to New Orleans International Airport and boarded an airplane bound for Oakland, California. I sat quietly, my stomach in knots, looking out the window at the fluffy white clouds below while Zach talked with Joe Dean, the athletic director for Louisiana State University, who was seated next to us. Zach sensed how nervous I was and left me to my thoughts. As the plane made its way across the country, I became more afraid and excited.

Although I had experienced unconditional love and acceptance in my adoptive parents' home, the knowledge that my biological parents had not wanted me had plagued me throughout my life. In my mind, I had always been John Doe, a boy who had been discarded and given a new name by adoptive parents. As a result, I had trust issues during my adolescent years and then later in my adult relationships. I lived with the fear that I could be rejected at any moment because I could never be good enough that someone would want to keep me around. Loyd and Leona did everything they could to make me feel loved and wanted, but all of my adult relationships with women were destined to fail as long as I remained John Doe in my heart. My fear of being discarded rendered me incapable of loving fully, because I felt like I didn't deserve to be loved. After all, how could anyone love me when I didn't even know who I was?

Although I was divorced from Zach's mother, my relationship with Zach was quite different. I might not know myself, but I knew my son deserved better from me than I had received from my biological parents. I dedicated my life to ensuring that he would never experience the horror of feeling unwanted and that he would always understand how much his father loved him.

Now that I knew that Judy had been a child when she gave me up for adoption, I had no residual bitterness as I mentally prepared for our meeting. My excitement began to build as I realized that I would finally have answers to the questions that had accumulated over my lifetime.

When the plane finally landed, I wiped the sweat that had beaded on my palms onto the legs of my pants. I had yearned for this moment my entire life, and now that it was here, suddenly I was torn.

I wanted to run away.

I wanted to meet my mother.

A few minutes later, I saw her at the far end of the terminal, standing with the man in the picture she had sent, and my heart began pumping furiously. She was tall—taller than the man next to her. Her hair was shorter and blonder than the picture had suggested. She was looking around anxiously. Even from a distance, I could see the same fear and excitement that I felt reflected in her face. I broke out in a cold sweat, but my steps quickened when our eyes met for the first time. From the moment I saw her eyes—clear blue like mine—I had no doubt. This woman was my mother.

When I reached her, I dropped my suitcase and gathered her into my arms, hugging her tightly to me.

"Mom," I whispered into her hair.

Judy stepped back, her hands on my shoulders, searching my face. Tears filled her eyes as she took in every detail of my appearance.

"Gary," she said, her voice trembling, "My son."

Those words sounded magical to me.

With one arm still around her, I turned to introduce her to Zach. While they got acquainted, Frank held out his hand and introduced himself to me, then ushered us outside to his car.

As Frank drove from Oakland to San Francisco, I couldn't stop stealing glances at my mother. At fifty-four, she was slender and youthful, her beautiful eyes and hair enhanced by flawless, tanned skin.

Before long, we arrived at Fisherman's Wharf. Zach marveled

at the huge Dungeness crabs that filled aquariums in front of Alioto's restaurant, where we were to have dinner. Men, mostly immigrants wearing white smocks, fired the cauldrons while tourists sampled crab cocktails served in paper cups.

"Can we get one, Dad?" Zach said excitedly. He had never seen a crab that big in Louisiana.

"Maybe later," I laughed. "Let's eat at the restaurant first."

Once seated, we looked out the window at the colorful fishing boats lined up along the dock, their hulls rocking back and forth to the rhythm of the bay. The menu, featuring seafood brought in on those boats, reminded me of home.

"What looks good?" Judy said.

"Everything," I laughed, "but we definitely have to order calamari. I bet it's much fresher here than in Louisiana."

"Sometimes squid will school into the bay, but mostly they're caught just beyond it in the Pacific," Frank said.

We kept the conversation light throughout dinner, each of us wanting to say so much but realizing we had to get to know one another slowly. After dinner, we walked along the wharf, peeking in shop windows and watching street performers dance and hula-hoop for passersby.

"It feels so good here," I told Judy, enjoying the cool breeze that swept along the bay. "At this time of year in Louisiana, you can't even breathe because it's so hot."

"It's like this all year round. We love it," she said, reaching for my hand. "I'm so glad you're here. I can't wait to show you San Francisco."

It was late when we arrived at the apartment Judy and Frank shared. After Frank and Zach fell asleep, Judy and I stayed up until three in the morning, sometimes talking, sometimes just staring at each other, neither of us really believing this was happening. Finally we could talk no more, and for the first time in my life, I kissed my mother good night.

The unfamiliar roar of city buses on the street below woke me the next morning. Zach was still sleeping on the couch when I walked into the living room, and I leaned down and kissed him on the cheek before walking to the sliding glass door of my mother's third-story terrace overlooking the city.

The view of San Francisco was beautiful. Straight ahead, I could see Noe Valley, a working-class neighborhood filled with Edwardian row houses colored in pinks and blues and greens. In the midst of the valley, the twin steeples of St. Paul's Catholic Church climbed high into the sky. Just across San Francisco Bay, I spotted the hills of Oakland. To the right, Candlestick Park carved an oval into the landscape, and to my left, cars moved quickly across the upper and lower decks of the Bay Bridge. Between the Golden Gate Bridge and the Bay Bridge, Alcatraz appeared hauntingly serene. I stood there for a moment, taking it all in before getting dressed.

Judy and I had agreed to attend church that morning, and later that afternoon we drove to Benicia, a tiny fishing village that had grown into a thriving city thirty-five miles northeast of San Francisco, to see the corporate headquarters of a company that had recently offered me a position.

My seventeen-year career as an electrical engineer had been an unsteady rise up the ladder of success. I graduated from Louisiana State University with a bachelor of science in 1985, and over the years I'd advanced with one company and then another, working my way into management before becoming vice president of industrial services for a large company. As often happens in the boom-and-bust industrial cycle in Louisiana, that company started showing signs of downsizing, and I began to worry about my job security.

A month before Judy called my mother, Delta Tech Service, in Benicia, had contacted me. The company was looking for someone to open an industrial service location in Baton Rouge. Fatigued by the ups and downs of the oil business, I turned the offer down and accepted a job as plant manager at a plastics manufacturer. I was supposed to start that job the Monday after Mother's Day, but then Judy entered my life and everything changed. I accepted the position with Delta Tech, excited about the prospect of being able to travel in and out of San Francisco. It seemed like divine intervention that the job offer had come so close to the time I needed to be in California as often as possible. It was perfect. I could visit my mother whenever I was needed at our company headquarters.

Judy and I rode together in her sporty red Grand Am while Frank, wanting to give us some time alone, followed with Zach in a blue Mercury Sable. As we rode, I absorbed the landscape—the colorful Victorian houses climbing one after another up the hills, the unfamiliar shrubs and trees, the golden wild grass. It all seemed so surreal—a lifetime of emotions and experiences being crammed into a few short days. For a while we rode in silence, Judy wondering when I would start asking the tough questions and me trying to figure out what to ask first.

"Isn't this where the bridge collapsed during the 1989 earthquake?" I said.

"Oh, yes. In fact," Judy said, pointing overhead through the windshield to the bottom of the upper deck of the Bay Bridge, "right here where the red markers are is the exact spot the bridge failed."

"I remember seeing that on TV like it was yesterday," I said, before spitting out the question I had been dying to ask. We had been dancing around it since I arrived.

"So, Mom . . . who is my father?"

Putting both hands on the steering wheel, Judy cleared her throat and straightened in her seat. I could see she was nervous.

"You remember when we first talked on the phone, and you asked me to be completely honest with you?"

"Yes."

"Well, I promise you that I will always tell you the truth. We have to build our relationship on love, truth, and honesty. But, honey, it's been so long now, and you have to realize that I was forced to forget everything about your father and about you. My memory of that time is severely repressed."

Judy began sharing with me some of her recollections of my father, which were sketchy at best. "His name was Van. I don't remember his full name," she said, before explaining that they had met when she was very young and had run away together.

"Anyway, we ended up in New Orleans, and I ended up pregnant. One day, I think when you were about three months old, your father took you to Baton Rouge. I remember he took you by train, because we still didn't own a car. He took you to a church. When he returned without you, I left him," Judy continued. "Your father got mad at me for leaving and turned me in to the authorities."

I struggled to comprehend what I was hearing. *I had been brought to a church?*

"So my father took me to Baton Rouge and turned me in to the authorities at a church, and then he turned you in to the authorities?" I queried, wanting to be sure about every detail.

Judy hesitated and then nodded her answer. "Yes."

I sat quietly for a moment, taking it all in. Finally I said, "You know what, Mom? I really don't think I want to know any more about my father. I have a wonderful family back home in Baton Rouge, and my dad is the best father in the world."

Judy's relief was visible. She obviously didn't want me to find him, either.

I wish that would have been the end of it for me, but over the next few months, the more I thought about my biological father, the more I wanted to meet him, to learn his side of the story, maybe even forgive him and begin a relationship. My mother's memories were limited. Maybe his memories would be better, and he could give me a reason why he had brought me to Baton Rouge and left me there.

I decided I would try to find him after all. I wanted to learn the truth about him—what kind of man he was, why he didn't want me. I know now that sometimes things should be left in the past, that knowing isn't always better. Sometimes the truth is so horrible that it must be uncovered in bits and pieces, snippets here and there, absorbed slowly, as the whole of it at once is simply too shocking to bear.

And sometimes the truth changes everything . . .

— PART ONE —

THE ICE CREAM ROMANCE

1

October 1961

Earl Van Best Jr. sat on a bench in front of the bookstore across the street from Herbert's Sherbet Shoppe. He was waiting while the owner of the store tallied up his earnings for the antique books he had brought back from Mexico City. While he sat there, he watched intently as a beautiful young girl came bouncing off the school bus that had just stopped on the corner of Ninth Avenue and Judah Street. As she walked, her blond hair shimmered, reflecting the afternoon sun. He stood up and stepped directly into her path, stopping her before she could cross the street.

"Hi," Van said warmly, flashing the charming smile that made him a good salesperson.

"Hi," she responded, smiling back before turning to walk toward the ice cream parlor.

He followed her.

"I'm Van. What's your name?"

"Judy."

Van opened the door for her, and they made their way across the beige mosaic-tiled floor to the glass-framed counter. Judy scanned the selections of sherbet before deciding on a plain vanilla ice cream cone. My father paid for her ice cream and asked if they could share a table. He looked like a nice fellow, very neat and polished, and Judy nodded her agreement, flattered by the attention from such a well-dressed, older man. They walked to a table in the corner, near the black-and-white-checkered wall.

Van sat down and gazed into the clear blue eyes that stared back at him so innocently. He loved beautiful girls, the younger the better, and this one was prettier than most.

Employing the British accent he liked to affect, he asked, "How old are you?" She looked like she was about twenty, but he was aware that she had just gotten off a school bus.

"Almost fourteen."

Van didn't believe her. She was much too mature, too pretty to be that young.

"Impossible," he murmured.

"Yep," she giggled, licking her ice cream, before adding, "My birthday is October eighth."

He sat there for a moment, wondering if he should stay, but one look into her smiling eyes convinced him that her age did not matter. Although he was twenty-seven, it was, for my father, love at first sight, total and complete. He had to have her. She was young, innocent, malleable.

To Judy, Van seemed worldly and wise as he told her stories about trips to Mexico, about growing up in Japan. He talked about music and art and literature, things the adults in her life didn't talk about.

"Where do you live?" Van asked.

"By the park," Judy replied, "on Seventh Avenue."

"With your parents?" Van pressed.

"My mom and stepdad, but I don't like him. He's mean," Judy said.

"I have a mean stepfather, too," Van said, adding softly, "I would never be mean to you."

Judy giggled and stood up. "I'd better get home before I get in trouble."

Van followed her out the door and watched her walk up the hill until she was out of sight before he headed back into the bookstore to collect the money owed him. Satisfied with the store owner's estimation of the value of his books, he headed back to the Castro District, just around Mount Sutro, where he lived with his mother and stepfather.

The next afternoon, Van stood in front of the ice cream shop waiting for the school bus that hopefully would again deliver to him the loveliest girl he had ever seen. He watched as some pedestrians walked out of an Asian market and into a nearby Irish pub. Others stopped at the sidewalk cafés, enticed by the aroma of coffee streaming from their doorways. The Sunset District was always filled with pedestrians, mostly young college and high school students and older locals, businessmen who had helped develop the area, believing America's promise of a better life for hardworking immigrant entrepreneurs.

My father wanted that entrepreneur lifestyle, and he was smart enough to have it. He had graduated from Lowell High School, a school that catered to gifted children, and attended City College of San Francisco, but his grades belied his intelligence. B's and C's lined his transcripts, except in English and ROTC, where he excelled. Those were the only subjects that really interested him. He had spent much of his life reading everything he could find, but he especially enjoyed literature—the kind that bores the presumably less intelligent.

He soon spotted the school bus coming up the street and watched as several children climbed down the steps. Then there she was again . . . beautiful and sweet.

He called out to her when she turned to walk up Judah Street. When she saw him, she smiled a big, happy smile.

"Hey, what are you doing?" she said.

"Waiting for you. Let me walk you home."

"Oh, no. My mother would be mad if she saw me walking with a boy."

"Well, then, we won't let her see us," Van grinned, taking Judy's arm and steering her across the street. "We'll cut through the park."

Judy felt a quiver of excitement as they walked past her street and into Golden Gate Park. Her experiences with men throughout her life had not been good ones, but this man seemed different. Her mother, Verda, had divorced her father a few years before, because he was a strict disciplinarian and had treated his daughters cruelly. He had spanked Judy and her sister, Carolyn, often, leaving red welts on their backsides that made sitting down unbearable. Those spankings had finally ended with the divorce, but sometimes Judy missed her father.

Verda had moved with her girls to San Jose, where she had tried to pick up the pieces and make a new life, but things had not been much better there. Her first date resulted in rape, and Verda soon discovered she was pregnant with her rapist's child—a boy she named Robert, who was born May 28, 1961. Verda knew she could not keep the child. He would be a constant reminder of what she had suffered, and she already had two mouths to feed. She put her son up for adoption immediately after his birth.

Rebounding from that experience, Verda moved back to San Francisco and married Vic Kilitzian, a marine electrician who worked at Hunters Point Naval Shipyard. An Armenian from Greece, Vic did not speak English well. Judy could barely understand the words he spoke, except when he hurled insults at her mother. Although he did not hit the children, he made sure everyone knew that he thought Verda was stupid. In its own way, that was as bad as the spankings for Judy, who couldn't bear to see her mother treated that way. For Verda, life had become worse than ever. She worked hard at Crocker Bank to help support the family and then returned home each afternoon for another round of belittling. Depressed and hopeless, she had little affection to give her daughters.

At thirteen, my mother was starving for love, and Van was eager to give the innocent girl the attention she sought. Judy smiled happily, feeling special and grown-up when Van tucked her arm into his. Her smile widened when he kissed her hand before leaving her at the edge of the park, six houses from her home.

She hoped he would be waiting when she got off the bus the next afternoon.

He was.

Van watched as Judy looked around for him. He saw that beautiful face light up when her eyes met his, and he moved toward her, taking her hand.

"Where are we going?" Judy said, not really caring. She had no fear. Van made her feel safe.

"It's a surprise—one of my favorite places," Van replied, steering her toward a nearby bus stop.

"We're going to church?" Judy exclaimed when the bus let them off on California Street and Van pointed to Grace Cathedral.

"Have you ever been inside this church?"

Judy shook her head, staring at the majestic building, with its high towers and tall steeple that jutted up toward heaven.

Once inside, Van pointed out his favorite works of art hanging on the cathedral's walls, including murals by Jan Henryk de Rosen, and impressed her with his knowledge of the history of various pieces.

Judy was fascinated—not just with the art but with the man who seemed to know so much about the church. No grown-up had ever talked to her like this, like she was an equal, like her opinion mattered. Van proudly showed her the cathedral's organ, pointing out the long tubular pipes suspended on the walls. "I play the organ here sometimes," he informed her.

They had made their way to the stained-glass windows depicting Adam and Eve when my father decided it was time for Judy to go home. As they headed back toward the Sunset District, Judy suggested that he meet her mother.

"I don't think that's such a good idea," he said. "It would be different if you were seventeen. She won't like me. She'll say I'm too old for you."

Judy nodded and agreed that they would keep their friendship to themselves for a while. She liked the thought of Van being her very own secret.

"I'll see you tomorrow?" he asked when she turned toward her street.

"Yes," Judy said breathlessly. "I can't wait."

Swinging her book bag over her shoulder, Judy almost skipped up the steep hill. She had never felt so happy. The young girl didn't question why a man Van's age would be interested in her. She didn't know to ask questions about his past. In her mind, their relationship seemed perfectly natural. She felt giddy when he touched her, when he smiled at her. That was all that mattered.

Soon she would discover there was much more to Van than his charming exterior, that he had a dark side, a past cloaked in pain that he kept carefully hidden.

2

Van's father, Earl Van Best Sr., was born October 16, 1904, into a loving Christian family. By the time Earl was born, the Best family name had become synonymous with love of God and country. Earl's ancestors, beginning with his grandfather, John James (J. J.) Best, had fought hard for their beliefs, right or wrong. J. J. had been a Confederate captain in the Civil War, assigned to the South Carolina 9th Infantry Battalion, known as the Pee Dee Rifles. On April 1, 1865, J. J. was shot and captured at the Battle of Dinwiddie Court House and taken as a prisoner of war to Johnson's Island, Ohio. On June 18, 1865, two days before the last shot of the war was fired, the Confederate captain signed an oath of allegiance to the Union and was released.

Prior to the war, J. J. had been a tobacco farmer and a registered slave owner. After the war, he returned to his farm, in Galivants Ferry, South Carolina, and reunited with his wife, Winnifred, and his two children. Because of the injuries he had sustained in the war, some of his slaves stayed on the farm to help him, despite the fact that they had been freed.

The year after the war ended, J. J.'s third child, Earl Van Dorn Best, was born, named after Major General Earl Van Dorn. Dorn, J. J.'s hero, had fought gallantly in the war but had suffered defeat at the Battle of Pea Ridge, in Arkansas. This battle had been a turning point, because it was here that the South lost control of the Mississippi River to the Union soldiers.

In 1880, J. J. donated some of the Best land for the construction of a new Methodist church and then more land across the dirt road to be used as the church cemetery. That cemetery is known today as Old Zion Cemetery, but back then the locals referred to it as the Best Cemetery.

Like his father, Earl embraced the southern tradition of tobacco farming, and he spent his childhood working the fertile land. As an adult, his knowledge of farming and his business acumen made him one of the wealthiest citizens in the small community of Galivants Ferry. In the late 1800s, Earl served as his pastor's right-hand man and confidant, and in 1902 he was elected Horry County superintendent of schools.

Earl eventually married Anna Jordan, and the couple had eleven children, among them my grandfather Earl Van Best.

Then tragedy struck.

Earl Van Dorn Best was shot and killed by a former slave in 1907, when my grandfather was two years old, and Anna suddenly found herself a widow with a brood of children to feed.

The stories told to him about his father steered my grandfather into the ministry, and he would remain committed to God for the rest of his life. As a teenager, long before he had any formal training in the ministry, Earl became one of Bishop Francis Asbury's circuit riders, who traveled from town to town on horseback preaching to anyone in Horry County, South Carolina, who would listen to their message of salvation. Earl later left his family home to attend the University of South Carolina, putting himself through school on a preacher's meager salary. When he met the pretty Miss Gertrude McCormac, from Mullins, South Carolina, Earl fell in love with the talented girl, who could play the piano so well he knew the angels in heaven must be singing along. But Gertrude was not an easy girl to understand. She said she loved him, and Earl believed her, but when he could not be at her beck and call, Gertrude would replace him without a thought. It was a lesson she would teach him over and over again during the years they spent together.

On November 9, 1929, my grandmother wrote my grandfather a letter, explaining how grateful she was that he had recently traveled to visit her. She mentioned that she would soon be attending an oyster roast and she wished he could be there, but she understood how difficult it was for him to make the long trip to see her every day. "I want you to understand me now beforehand and know that my intentions will always be for the building up rather than the breaking down," she wrote, before adding a post-script on November 10 that read, "Had a very good time at the oyster roast. Nick was kind. He brought me back. Wish you could have been with me instead."

Her ploy worked.

Earl hurried back to Mullins to ask Gertrude's father, Duncan, for her hand in marriage. Duncan gave the earnest young man his blessing.

"Will you marry me?" Earl implored, kneeling gallantly before Gertrude in the parlor as she reclined on a sofa.

Gertrude pouted prettily and thought for a moment. "I would love to," she said, smiling into her fiancé's eyes.

Gertrude was impressed by the minister's intelligence. He was the most motivated and educated man she knew, even if he was a bit boring. The young woman was aware of the respect she would gain as the wife of a minister. It was a very appealing prospect.

Everything had gone well in the marriage for a few years, until Earl's brother Austin Haygood Best died in 1931, and his wife, Betty Wilmoth Best, died in 1933, both having contracted consumption from the sanatorium where Betty worked. The couple left behind four children—Louise, Mildred, Aileen, and Geraldine ("Bits"). Mildred was sent to live with Earl's sister Nan. Aileen and the youngest child, Bits, went to live with Earl's sister Estelle. Gertrude, at Earl's insistence, unwillingly took in Louise, who was fourteen.

My grandfather didn't make a lot of money, and my grandmother had to stretch every nickel now that they had another mouth to feed. While moving from college town to college town had seemed exciting at first, being tied down with no money and a child did not fit in with Gertrude's plans. "Why can't Nan raise Louise?" Gertrude complained.

Earl, who attended the College of Charleston, looked up from a paper he was writing and sighed. "Because she can only afford to raise one," he explained again.

"But it's not right. Mildred is always saying that the Best family split them up like a litter of kittens. Sisters need to be together."

"Well, maybe we should bring Mildred here," Earl said, watching Gertrude's reaction with smiling eyes.

She shut up and stomped out of the room.

Earl laughed as he went back to his writing. Sometimes his spoiled bride begged to be put in her place.

For the next year, Gertrude suffered in relative silence, fearful that Earl would get the notion that raising all the girls together was the right thing to do. But she wasn't nice to her niece. Earl, who had grown up without a father, was a strict disciplinarian, because he was determined to raise Louise right. As the years passed, Louise came to hate her aunt and resent her uncle for letting his wife treat her like the orphan she was.

Toward the end of 1933, Gertrude missed her monthly cycle and feared she might be pregnant. She and Earl were living in Wilmore, Kentucky, while Earl studied at the Asbury Theological Seminary, on his way to earning another certification that hopefully would bring more income into the family.

"How will we support two children?" Gertrude whined after sharing her news with Earl, hoping this would force him to send the girl away.

"We'll manage just like we do with one," Earl reassured her.

Gertrude decided she wanted a girl—a girl of her own. Maybe when Earl held his own daughter, he would realize that the other one didn't belong. She began sewing dresses for the baby from yards of lace and cloth, never once entertaining the idea that her baby could be a boy. That just wouldn't do.

On July 14, 1934, Gertrude gave birth to a son, Earl Van Best Jr. Earl decided to call him Van.

When the midwife tried to place my father in Gertrude's arms, her cheeks turned red and tears streamed from her eyes.

"Look, dear. He's a fine, healthy boy," Earl cajoled, trying to get Gertrude to hold her son.

Gertrude wouldn't look at him. "Take him away," she insisted, turning over in her bed to face the wall.

Earl didn't understand. Mothers were supposed to love their children.

A few days later, Gertrude was still in bed when her husband brought the baby to her again.

"I'm not well," she said when Earl moved toward her with the child in his arms.

"Just look at him," Earl begged. "Hold him for just a minute. He's a sweet fellow."

"No. Leave me alone. I don't want it."

Every day for weeks, Earl brought the baby to her, and every day, she refused to hold him. Finally he could take it no more. He was tired of washing diapers, feeding his son every four hours, listening to him cry for the comfort of a mother's arms, doing all the things Gertrude should be doing. Enough was enough.

"Get up," he ordered after another sleepless night. "Get out of that bed and take care of your child like a good Christian mother. I will not allow you to act like this. Get up!"

Gertrude knew she had pushed him as far as she could. She got up and reluctantly assumed her role as a mother to the boy. She fed him. She changed and washed his diapers. She bathed him. But she didn't mother him any more than was absolutely necessary.

Happy that his wife was better, Earl left her to her duty. In a letter to his mother, he explained that he and Gertrude had very definite ideas about rearing a child. "When he cries, we let him whoop it out," he wrote. "If he is comfortable, we try to forget about him and let him alone. I believe to walk them around and humor them when they get blue from crying is one of the worst things that can be done for them. He will be a fine boy if we don't coddle and fondle him into being a regular sissy."

In 1935, my grandfather became an ordained Methodist minister and accepted a missionary assignment to Japan, taking his wife and their one-year-old son with him. Louise happily joined her sisters at Estelle's house. Earl's assignment was to help create a universal Christian church in Japan that incorporated all denominations. As a representative of the Methodist Board of Missions, my grandfather had been invited to meet with Emperor Hirohito (the Mikado), along with representatives from other Christian denominations, to discuss bringing more American missionaries to Japan. Earl would later write about his efforts in his master's thesis. It took five years to accomplish, but in 1941, church union became a reality in Japan.

Earl was very proud to have been a part of this effort, but the highlight of his time in Tokyo was meeting the Mikado, and he liked to impress Van with stories of the meeting. He took his son to see the Gilbert and Sullivan opera *The Mikado*, among others, and sent the playbills back home to his nieces.

By 1940 Van had grown into a six-year-old who was already showing signs of becoming a polymath, much to my grandfather's delight. He had picked up Japanese effortlessly, as easily as he had acquired the German that Earl often spoke with him. While other American children were learning to write from the left side of the page to the right, Van was learning to write in three Japanese scripts—kanji, hiragana, and katakana—going from right to left in columns. Earl insisted that Van take advantage of the unique opportunity living abroad afforded him. Gertrude fed his artistic side, teaching him to play piano and organ, teaching him to draw—more to keep herself occupied than out of any affection for the boy. There were no kisses on the cheek or affectionate hugs. There was no sympathy when Van got hurt. "Dust yourself off. You're a man. You have to be tough," Earl would say. Perversely, Gertrude would decorate Van's clothes with lacy collars and ruffles, doing her best to turn him into a "regular sissy."

Van tried to be tough. He tried to please his father, but Earl's philosophy of "Spare the rod, spoil the child" resulted in whippings for minor infractions. And when Van cried, the rod became more vicious.

Van understood early on that learning was paramount to his well-being, and so he studied to stay out of trouble. He learned. And he made his father proud.

Earl had equally high expectations of Gertrude, but she needed constant attention and strained against the restrictive bonds of her marriage. My grandfather had suspicions about her activities when he wasn't around and occasionally voiced them, but Gertrude always assured him that he was being silly. Wanting to believe the best, Earl allowed himself to be consoled. Not many men could resist when Gertrude turned on the charm, and her husband was no exception.

Between his wife's flirtations and the instability in the region, my grandfather knew it was almost time to send Gertrude and Van home. Japan had formed an alliance with Italy and Germany, and Earl realized that did not bode well for any peaceful resolution to tensions that were building around the world. My grandmother couldn't wait to go home. She had not bargained for the strict lifestyle she endured as the wife of a missionary in Japan. For five years, she and Earl had lived at Aoyama Gakuin, a university established in 1874 by the Methodist Episcopal Church. Her life might have been more bearable, but she was an artist and musician, a free spirit, and Earl and his Christian ideals were much too rigid for her creative soul. Gertrude liked to have fun.

Earl had responsibilities, which he took very seriously—namely, saving heathen souls from the fires of hell.

On October 28, 1940, Earl waved good-bye to his wife and son from a dock in Kobe as they boarded the ocean liner *Tatuta Maru*, bound for the United States. By January 1941 they would be back in Japan, their return spurred by Earl's family, who had no problem informing him that he needed to keep a closer eye on his wife.

3

On December 7, 1941, the Japanese Imperial Navy bombed Pearl Harbor. Two thousand four hundred and two Americans lost their lives in the attack, and more than twelve hundred people were wounded. The United States responded with a declaration of war the next day. My grandfather sent my father and grandmother home on the first ship out of Japan. Gertrude and Van anxiously waited for Earl to meet them in San Francisco and were relieved when he finally arrived a few weeks later.

Earl didn't waste a second thought on the six years he had spent in Japan. His country had been sneak-attacked by the Japanese, and he wanted to pay them back for their treachery. "I've decided to attend the U.S. Army Chaplain School," he told Gertrude. "You and Van can move back to South Carolina and stay with Estelle until I finish. I'm going to join the military."

Gertrude pleaded with Earl to let her and Van stay in California, but he refused. "No. We don't know what's going to happen. They might attack again. I want you with my family, where you'll be safe."

The next day, the three of them rented a car and left California, heading for Estelle's home in Conway, South Carolina. Earl kept up a steady stream of conversation with Van, who relished the attention, while Gertrude pouted the whole way across the country. Her mood worsened a few days later when they pulled into Estelle's driveway and she saw Bits and Aileen playing outside. It dawned on her that she would have to help take care of them.

"I am not taking care of those brats," she informed her husband.

"Calm down, Gertrude," Earl said. "Estelle can't continue to care for three children by herself. She was kind enough to take Louise while we were gone. We're Christians. These girls are family. We must behave like Christians and help her."

"Christians be damned!" Gertrude shouted, marching into the house and slamming the door behind her.

After getting their bags from the car, Earl put his arm around his sister.

"Don't pay any attention to Gertrude," he said. "She'll be fine."

Estelle wasn't so sure. She loved her brother and wanted to help, but she was well aware that Gertrude was spoiled and petulant. Louise had often complained that Gertrude had treated her poorly when she lived with her.

Once his family was settled, Earl submitted his application to the Corps and waited eagerly for his acceptance letter. While he waited, Earl acquainted himself with his new parishioners, many of whom were happy to turn to him for guidance and prayer as they proudly and fearfully watched their sons go off to war.

Earl soon received his letter of acceptance and headed off to Williamsburg, Virginia, where he would eventually earn his degree from the U.S. Army Chaplain School. He then joined the Navy as a chaplain, determined to give spiritual guidance and counsel to young soldiers who were putting their lives on the line for America. He moved up quickly, earning the rank of lieutenant, and was assigned to the USS *Altamaha*, an escort aircraft carrier, under the command of Admiral "Bull" Halsey. His primary role was to give comfort and inspiration through his message of hope and salvation.

When he wasn't ministering, Earl worked as an intelligence officer, tasked with tracking and deciphering the enemy's coded messages. Because he could read and write Japanese and German, Earl soon became an asset to his unit. During World War II, the U.S. Navy and Army utilized a complex cipher machine called SIGABA to write American codes. This machine proved to be a valuable asset, because SIGABA codes were unbreakable, whereas Japanese codes, called PURPLE, and German codes, written with a machine called Enigma, could easily be deciphered by the Americans. The U.S. military had another advantage when passing along secret information not meant for enemy eyes: American Indian Code Talkers, comprising Navajo, Cherokee, Choctaw, and Comanche Indians, among others, who used the arcane language of their forefathers to create intricate codes. There were so many dialects in the languages that no one in the Axis forces could crack the codes.

Earl loved serving his country, but back home, angry that her husband had left her with his sister and the children, Gertrude fumed. Like Louise had years before, Aileen and Bits quickly learned to stay out of her way. So did Van. He hid in his small room at the back of the house, wishing that his father would hurry back. He didn't like his cousins. They laughed at his books, his music.

My grandmother, desperate for some fun, began concocting this reason or that for why she needed to be away from the house in the afternoons. Estelle wasn't fooled when she saw Gertrude's hair swept up in a bow and the pretty dresses she wore. Word soon got to Earl that his wife was fornicating with members of his congregation, but he had God's work to do. He would deal with her as soon as he had fulfilled his obligation to the military.

A few months later, Earl traveled back to South Carolina to straighten out his errant wife.

"Look, Gertrude," Earl yelled, placing his Bible in front of her, "right there in Hebrews, chapter thirteen, verse fourteen, it says, 'Let marriage be held in honor among all, and let the marriage bed be undefiled, for God will judge the sexually immoral and adulterous.' Do you want to be judged as an adulteress?"

Gertrude tearfully shook her head. "I don't know what comes over me," she cried.

Earl didn't know, either.

"I'm a minister, for God's sake. My wife is supposed to be a pillar of the community."

He begged and pleaded with his wife to be faithful, and when that didn't work, he screamed at her. Nothing he did mattered. Gertrude craved more attention than her husband could give her.

Things got so bad that Gertrude would weep when Earl pulled up in the driveway. It was a strange dichotomy. On Sundays, he would stand in the pulpit preaching the gospel, and Gertrude would sit at the piano, playing hymns beautifully, smiling as she praised God. They looked like such a happy family, but no one was fooled. Earl didn't have to ask which men who sat in the pews of his church had slept with his wife. He knew. He could tell by the way they averted their eyes when he looked at them and spoke about sin. He struggled to forgive Gertrude for her transgressions, but she just transgressed some more.

To take his mind off his problems, Earl focused on my father. Back then, most children did not have a television to occupy their time, so they either stayed outdoors playing ball or inside playing board games, word games, tic-tac-toe, and checkers. When my grandfather was home on leave from the Navy, he began teaching Van how to write and solve simple codes using numbers, Japanese symbols, and German and English lettering. Van was a good student, often deciphering his father's encrypted messages quickly. Earl was impressed and endeavored to make each new one more difficult than the last. Before long, Van was creating his own codes and asking his father to break them. Van would watch from a corner of the room while Earl worked his way through the letters, numbers, and symbols. What had begun as a learning game became a competition as father and son tried constantly to outwit each other. Van enjoyed the challenge and the attention he received from his father during this pastime.

Earl had no way of knowing that one day Van would employ their game to do the devil's work and to gain attention on a much larger scale.

4

After the war was over, when he could take the embarrassment no more, Earl moved with Gertrude and Van to San Francisco, hoping that his wife would be happier there and would mend her ways. But San Francisco offered Gertrude a host of new men with whom to carry on her flirtations, and Earl, well aware that divorce was unacceptable in the Methodist religion, did the unthinkable. He asked his wife for a divorce.

"I want you to file the papers, because I don't want my son to grow up thinking I abandoned him. I'll let him stay with you, though," Earl said. "A boy needs his mother. You can send him to me during the summer months."

As unhappy as she was, Gertrude did not relish the idea of being a divorced woman. She liked having the best of both worlds—all the men she wanted and the security and respect that came with being a preacher's wife.

"I'll be better. I promise," she cried, as she had so many times before. "Please, Earl, think of the embarrassment," she said, placing her arms around him.

"I *am* thinking of the embarrassment," Earl retorted, removing her arms. "I've tried to forgive. I've tried to forget. It keeps happening. God forgive me, but I cannot live like this."

When my grandfather refused to bend, my grandmother filed for divorce.

Van begged his father to let him stay with him, but Earl insisted that it was best he live with his mother. "You'll be fine," he told his son.

Van knew he would not be fine. So did Earl, and his heart was heavy as he boarded the train that would take him back to South Carolina, more than two thousand miles away from his nine-year-old son.

Gertrude and Van moved to 514 Noe Street, located on a steep hill in the heart of the Castro District. Their home, a two-story, turn-of-the-century Victorian, was divided into two apartments—one upstairs and one downstairs. Gertrude and Van occupied the first floor. The house was one of the few that had not been destroyed during the 1906 earthquake. Noe Street, unlike many streets throughout San Francisco that were built on sand dunes, had a solid rock foundation, which spared all of the houses on the hill from destruction.

Van's room soon became his refuge and his prison. He filled it with his beloved books, and when he wasn't in school, he hid there while his mother gave piano lessons to the neighborhood children. He could hear the sounds of the children laughing in the living room beside him and his mother laughing with them as they banged away on the keys of the piano.

Gertrude did what she had to do for Van—she made sure he ate and went to school. Other than that, she ignored him. She embraced her newfound freedom, and soon a bevy of men were steadily making their way to her home.

Van could hear, sometimes, the banging of the headboard, the moans and gasps permeating the walls. He let the sounds of his music—flutes and violins and clarinets—swirl around him as he turned up the volume of his phonograph to drown out the banging. As he listened to *The Mikado*, the tale of lust and deceit captured in the opera mimicked his own life, and he listened over and over, memorizing every word.

Other times he occupied himself with writing codes, wishing his father were sitting across from him trying to decipher the meaning. Van missed his father. Even though he was strict, my grandfather had given him attention, had challenged him, had made him feel like he was important. In San Francisco, Van felt like he was nothing more than a nuisance, invisible.

Nobody.

Earl would spend the rest of his life regretting his decision to allow his only son to live with his ex-wife, but at the time, he had been convinced that a child was better off being raised by his mother.

5

On the day his divorce from Gertrude became final, Earl married Eleanor "Ellie" Bycraft Auble, a widow twelve years his junior. He had met Ellie two years earlier, when he was tasked with informing her that her husband, George Coleman Auble, had been killed in an explosion while loading depth charges on the USS *Serpens* on March 10, 1943. Ellie had appreciated the comfort the chaplain had given her, and when Earl returned from San Francisco, these two souls searching for comfort in an unfair world were drawn to each other immediately. Neither of them had deserved their fates, but together their wounds could heal. Earl fell in love with Ellie's genteel manners and steadfastness. She was a woman who would be faithful, a woman who would be a role model for Van.

After they married, the couple moved to Indianapolis so that my grandfather could teach military intelligence and business at the U.S. Army Finance School at Fort Benjamin Harrison. He had been excommunicated from the Methodist Church because of his divorce, but the preacher was soon welcomed into the Disciples of Christ ministry in Indianapolis.

The following year, Earl flew Van from San Francisco to Chicago for summer break. When he got off the plane, Van ran into Earl's arms, excited to see him after so long.

"Van, this is Ellie, your new mother," Earl said, prying Van's arms from around his neck. "She's my wife now, and you are to listen to her and give her the respect you give me."

Van turned slowly and looked at the pretty young woman standing next to his father. The smile that had lit up his face when he saw Earl disappeared into a trembling frown.

Ellie reached out her hand.

Van hesitated, then shook it when Earl urged him forward.

"Hi, Van. It's so nice to meet you. Your father has told me so much about you."

Van didn't respond.

"Are you ready for the beach?" she asked.

Van nodded and turned to walk with them to the waiting car.

Each year, all of the Bests gathered in the family-owned beach house at 302 Ocean Boulevard in Myrtle Beach, South Carolina, for summer vacation. Van had looked forward to this trip for months, and now this woman had ruined everything. Van slumped into the backseat and stared out the window, occasionally stealing glances at the woman who held his father's attention.

"How do you like San Francisco?" Ellie inquired.

"I don't," Van said.

"Watch yourself, young man," Earl warned.

"Well, she asked. I don't like it."

"Why not?" Ellie pressed.

"Mother has too many boyfriends," Van said, hoping the shock value of his words would make them leave him alone.

It worked.

Ellie gave up and spent the next fourteen hours on the road ignoring Van, who spoke to his father in Japanese so Ellie couldn't understand him. When Earl insisted he speak in English, Van stopped talking.

By the time they reached the beach house, the animosity my father felt for his new stepmother had reached a fever pitch. Grabbing his bag, he stomped up the stairs into the house, ignoring Louise, Aileen, and Bits when they said hello. He ran into his usual bedroom, slammed the door, threw himself on the bed, and cried. He was still crying when Earl walked in.

"I had hoped you would have grown up some and learned how to behave yourself properly, but apparently your mother has not been disciplining you," Earl said, pulling off his belt. "You will treat my wife with respect. Now bend over," he added sternly.

Aileen and Bits were listening and giggling down the hall. "He just got here. What do you think he did?" Bits said.

"I don't know, but it must have been bad. Uncle Earl sounds real mad," Aileen replied.

The next morning, Aileen was waiting for him in the hall. "How's your backside?" she said, laughing. Van punched her in the arm. Hard.

It didn't take long for Van's cousins to pick up where they had left off when he moved. At breakfast, the girls began making fun of him for reading a book at the table. When Aileen accidentally spilled milk on his book, Van exploded.

"Don't cry over spilt milk," his cousins jeered.

"You have no idea. This is a first edition," Van cried, grabbing his book and running into the kitchen to tenderly dry each page.

The girls spent the summer teasing him mercilessly. One afternoon, as Van sat alone on the handrail of the second-floor porch, reading, Ellie asked him to go to the car and fetch her sunglasses. Startled from his book, Van fell over the railing, landing on his head in front of the whole family. Ellie screamed when Van hit the sandy ground with a thud. For a moment, everyone thought he was dead. Embarrassed, my father lay there stunned for a moment, then got up, brushed the sand from his clothes, and disappeared into a far room in the back of the house to cry. He knew this was more ammunition for his cousins. He was different and could not fit in. And he didn't care enough to try. He preferred rummaging through an old trunk he'd found in the attic, looking at the crinkled papers and yellowed christening gowns someone had tucked away years ago, rather than playing silly games. He didn't want to run on the beach with them or swim in Withers Swash. He wanted to be left alone with his books, his escape from his family.

His cousin Mildred had already escaped.

She had disgraced the Best family the year before when she gave birth out of wedlock to a baby girl named Joyce. Mildred promptly ran off to Hollywood with an aspiring Cuban actor, leaving her child to be raised by her aunt Estelle.

Joyce would be raised to believe that her aunts—Bits, Louise, and Aileen—were her sisters, and her great-aunt, Estelle, was her mother.

As the summer wore on, Van began longing for San Francisco. His dark, lonely bedroom was more tolerable than this.

Earl realized early on that it was fruitless to try to force Van and Ellie's relationship. Van made no bones about his hatred for his stepmother, and he constantly tried to make Earl see that she was mean to him, hoping his father would send her away.

On the way home from the beach, things finally came to a head. Ellie was talking with Earl, and Van interrupted, smiling because he knew it would make her mad.

"Van, has anyone invited you to this conversation?" Ellie said.

"I didn't need an invitation to speak before you came along," Van said smartly.

Earl slammed on the brakes and pulled over to the side of the road. He grabbed Van, yanked him from the car, and spanked him in front of his cousins and everyone driving by. Humiliated, Van huddled in the corner of the backseat, ignoring his laughing cousins, staring daggers into the back of Ellie's head. He dreaded the coming weeks he would have to spend with his stepmother and cousins, who Earl had decided should spend the remainder of their summer vacation in Indiana.

Once back on the road, my grandfather stopped in every state along the way—North Carolina, Tennessee, Kentucky, Indiana—and let each of the children drive a few feet, just so they could tell their friends they had driven in different states. Van wanted to refuse to participate, but one look at Earl's face when his turn came convinced him otherwise. He drove slowly, sitting in the driver's seat next to Ellie, his knuckles white on the wheel.

From the backseat, Bits watched Van and almost felt sorry for him. Almost.

6

After that first miserable summer with Ellie, Van was almost happy to see his mother when he returned to San Francisco. He ran into the bedroom that housed his most precious possessions, feeling lighthearted for the first time in months. Here he was safe from the outside world, safe from the teasing of other children. His feelings of happiness were fleeting, however.

Gertrude had met a new beau while Van was away. Within months, she married John Harlan Plummer, a man who had little tolerance for Van and who was jealous of any attention Gertrude paid to her son. Van learned quickly to stay out of Harlan's way. The only times Van saw his mother were at the dinner table and when he played the piano. Sometimes when she heard him playing, she would come into the living room, sit beside him, and give him pointers. It was during these times that Van felt a bond with her, but then Harlan would call her name and she would disappear. Left alone again, Van pounded his heartache into the piano keys.

Then he met William Vsevolod Lohmus von Bellingshausen and everything changed.

Fear had raced through Van's body when he first walked through the double doors of Lowell High School. He observed the pretty girls laughing and joking with boys who seemed unconcerned with the enormity of high school, knowing it wouldn't be long before they uncovered his secrets, their whispers reverberating down hallways between classes. *His mother's a whore. Did you see those glasses he wears? What's wrong with him, anyway? He thinks he's so smart.*

"*Guten Tag,*" Van said in German when a boy sat next to him in the cafeteria on the first day of school—his way of saying hello and establishing superiority with anyone he met.

"Guten Tag," the boy unexpectedly responded. *"Wie heißt du?"*

"My name's Van. You speak German?" Van said, stunned that this ordinary-looking kid had caught him at his game.

"My name is Vsevolod von Bellingshausen, and I am German. And Chinese. Half and half. But in the States, I go by William Lohmus. Just makes it easier," the boy informed Van, smiling at the look on his face.

William and my father became fast friends, and they soon began scheduling their classes together. In ROTC, they befriended Bill Bixby, who would later rise to fame for his work in the television series *The Courtship of Eddie's Father* and *The Incredible Hulk*. The three boys went through drills three times each week, and on Mondays and Fridays they studied military history, tactics, and theory. During summer maneuvers, they were Company C and took on the role of the enemy, hiding under brush until the single guard passed by and then swooping in like lightning to claim the flag and victory. Van occasionally called Earl to discuss what he was learning, confident that his gaining military knowledge would impress his father.

After school, Van volunteered at the de Young Museum, in Golden Gate Park. In the Ancient Arms room, he honed his skills cleaning, maintaining, and preserving medieval weapons. It was in that museum filled with relics from the past that Van became fascinated with weaponry and the art of killing.

William and Bill realized that Van was different, but that he was also very intelligent, and they enjoyed listening to him pontificate on this topic or that. He knew a little something about almost everything. They were also impressed with his musical talent.

"Where did you learn to play like that?" William asked one afternoon when Van was showing off on the piano in his living room.

"Mother taught me," Van replied. "I also listen to a lot of classical music and operas. I'll show you."

Van introduced William to Giacomo Puccini's *Tosca*, another tale of lust and murder that Van particularly liked. "Puccini adapted 'Miya Sama, Miya Sama' from Act II of Gilbert and Sullivan's *Mikado*," Van explained. Before long, William became a fan, and the two boys spent their evenings reciting the words from *The Mikado* to each other until William knew them as well as Van.

At school, they mostly spoke to each other in German, which annoyed and alienated the other students. But when Van joined the English-Speaking Union, an organization with the charter to preserve the language and culture of the motherland, he began to cultivate a proper English accent and called everyone by their surname, which was similarly annoying to his classmates.

"You know, Bellingshausen, my family roots trace back to England and royalty," Van bragged. "My father told me I am a distant relative of Queen Elizabeth."

William didn't know whether to believe him, but he let him have that one, because you never really knew with Van. And when his friend's assumed accent sounded like someone caught in the middle of a conversation between Sherlock Holmes and Dr. Watson, William just smiled. He let Van have that, too.

But whenever Van turned the conversation to an Asian slave box, a four-inch cube made of dark wood that William had once shown him, William got a little nervous. Van believed that some cultures collected the souls of their slaves for the afterlife in boxes like that one, and Van had become fascinated with the notion of killing one to put in the box. Walking together down the hallway between classes, Van would often point out a pretty girl. "She'd make a good one, don't you think?" he would say, and laugh.

William knew what he meant and worried sometimes that Van wasn't joking.

7

After graduation, in 1953, William left San Francisco to spend several months in Mexico, sailing away on a sixty-eight-foot yawl. Van had other plans. He had befriended Alexander Victor Edward Paulet Montagu, a member of British Parliament, at an English-Speaking Union meeting. Montagu, commonly known as the Viscount of Hinchingbrooke, had been impressed by Van's knowledge of England and amused by his stiff British correctness. He took a fancy to Van and invited his young American friend to England for a stay at his father's home, Hinchingbrooke House, with the promise of meeting the queen. Excited about the prospect, Van convinced my grandfather to buy his passage to England as a graduation present.

On May 4, 1953, the RMS *Ascania* safely sailed into the port in Liverpool, England, and Van disembarked to begin his adventure.

The viscount had arranged for a car to bring Van to the family estate, just outside Huntingdon, Cambridgeshire, some three hours southeast of Liverpool. Although Victor maintained a residence in London, he had arranged for Van to have the pleasure of experiencing high country living. Originally, the massive house had been built as a church, around 1100. It had later become a nunnery before coming into the possession of Richard Williams (also known as Richard Cromwell) in 1536. Cromwell and his sons added numerous rooms, a medieval grand entrance, and the Great Bow Window that gave Hinchingbrooke House its distinct character. Debt forced the Cromwells to sell their prized possession to the Montagu family in 1627. The Montagus continued with improvements, and when it came into the possession of the fourth Earl of Sandwich, John Montagu, Hinchingbrooke House became known for its lavish parties, hosted by the earl and his mistress while his wife lived her life tucked away in a sanatorium.

When they pulled onto the grounds of the manor, Van noticed the family's coat of arms. The words *Post tot naufragia portum* ("a haven after so many shipwrecks") served as the family motto.

Once inside the majestic home, my father was struck by the smell—a mustiness that had seeped for centuries into every crack and crevice of the dwelling. Immense portraits lining walls, elaborate draperies, exquisite furnishings, scented candelabras—nothing could overcome that first impression. Van sniffed and covered his nose.

"My American friend," Victor Montagu said when he greeted Van as he emerged from a shadowy hallway. "How was your trip?"

"It was good, Sir Montagu," Van said, looking up at the man approaching him.

At forty-six years of age, the viscount was a striking figure—tall, with broad shoulders and a slender build. "Welcome to my family's home," he said, instructing the manservant to show Van to his room.

Over the next few weeks, Van received a thorough education in English history and politics as he and the viscount alternated their time between Hinchingbrooke and London. Victor Montagu had become very involved in politics as a young man and had a wealth of knowledge to bestow upon his guest. He had served as the private secretary to Stanley Baldwin, a well-respected lord president of the council, and had written several books by the time Van met him. He had also served in World War II before being elected to Parliament. Van absorbed every word the viscount said, storing each new bit of information in his memory, to be revisited later with William, especially the fact that Queen Elizabeth and King James I had slept within these walls.

But Van had trouble sleeping within those walls. Each night, he listened intently to the sounds of old boards creaking, cracking, as if someone or something was walking the halls. The sounds would get closer and closer, louder and louder, until Van huddled under a blanket in the corner of his room. Watching.

Waiting.

For hours.

And then morning would dawn and the sun would cast its reassuring light across the room. Van would finally close his eyes and sleep until breakfast was served, where he usually ate only a piece of bacon or two with his tea.

"Aren't you hungry?" Victor asked as he wolfed down baked beans, sausage, bacon, eggs, and fried bread.

"Mother rarely cooks breakfast, so I'm not used to eating a lot in the morning."

"Americans," Victor said, laughing. "You don't know what you're missing. Well, at least the tea will keep you going."

Van nodded. He liked English tea, if for no other reason than that it was part of the culture he so desperately wanted to adopt.

"I've got something special in store for you," Victor announced. "We're going to London for the queen's coronation."

Van was delighted. The Montagu family, through its royal connections, fed his Anglophile appetite and emboldened him to model the walk, talk, and style of dress of his blue-blooded hosts. And on June 2, 1953, my father stood in Trafalgar Square, amid the throngs of fawning people who had gathered to watch Elizabeth II ride by in the spectacular horse-drawn coach that would take her to Westminster Abbey, where she was crowned in the coronation theater in the same chair in which kings had been crowned since Edward, in 1274. For Van, this was the thrill of a lifetime, but he would later express his displeasure to William that he had been stuck outside with the commoners instead of seated with the viscount's family. After all, he was related, he insisted.

Upon their return to Hinchingbrooke House the following month, Montagu resumed his tutelage of his American friend.

"I need to sort through some of the old letters and documents that my father stored away. Would you like to help?"

"Yes, sir," Van said. "I'd love to."

Van followed the viscount into an office furnished with heavy wooden desks and bookshelves lining the walls. He reverently searched the titles, drawn to the bound leather covers and the parchment paper inside.

"You can touch them," Victor said, noticing Van's expression.

Van pulled one from a shelf. Carefully, he opened it, letting his fingers run across the texture of the pages. He noticed everything—the print, the binding, the yellowing. Victor let Van browse while he placed stacks of letters on a desk and began looking through them. "Look at this," he said.

Van walked over and took the letter Victor handed him. It was written by Captain James Cook and addressed to John Montagu.

"John was the fourth Earl of Sandwich. You know, they named the sandwich after him," Victor said, with a laugh. "He was a nefarious fellow, but it was his sponsorship of Captain Cook's explorations that brought him the most notoriety. Do you know there are islands named after this house and John Montagu off the Australian coast?"

Van nodded. He had read everything he could about the family before he arrived.

"Was he really a member of the Hellfire Club?" Van ventured, turning the conversation to the subject he most wanted to discuss. He had come across this tidbit in his readings.

Sensing Van's interest and enjoying his fascinated audience, Victor stood up and closed the door. He and Van talked for hours, discussing the club's history and the rumors that had swirled around its members. "No one really knows what is true and what is not," Victor said.

Over the next two months, Van learned everything he could about the club, and grew excited about sharing his newfound knowledge with William when he returned home. He quizzed the viscount relentlessly, tucking away each detail to be savored later. Amused, Montagu fed Van's fantasies, unwittingly inspiring in his young friend a greater interest in the occult. The club allegedly comprised eighteenth-century English gentlemen who made sacrifices to Venus and Bacchus, animals, and sometimes nymphs. Van loved the rumors of orgies, debauchery, and sacrifices by noblemen such as Sir Francis Dashwood and the fourth Earl of Sandwich. Their motto, *Fais ce que tu voudras* ("Do what you will"), meant nothing was off-limits. Everything Van heard was the antithesis of his father's teachings, and Van knew that Earl would have been none too pleased had he known how his son was utilizing his time in England.

The days passed by rapidly, and Van hated the thought of returning to the United States.

But then one night, as Van lay in his bed, unable to sleep once again, he listened to whispers of the past echoing through his room. Chilled by the damp air that pervaded the house and fearful of spirits that he was sure lurked nearby, he pulled his blanket tightly around him. When he heard the ominous sound of boards creaking in the hallway, he tensed. It sounded louder this time, more defined. He jumped from his bed and ran into the corner of the room. Using his blanket as a shield, he sank to the floor, hoping the sound would stop.

It did. Right outside his door.

Van watched in terror as the door opened slowly. An eerie orange glow from the lantern on the wall in the hallway spread into the room, illuminating a shadowy figure.

The next morning, he abruptly decided to cut his trip short and return home.

Before he left, Victor showed Van his family's collection of ancient weaponry. He presented Van with a bronze mace, shaped like the head of a bull. Its mouth opened into a menacing grimace, and Van detected a pungent odor when he tried to look inside. My father politely thanked the viscount for the unusual gift and for inviting him to stay at Hinchingbrooke, but he couldn't wait to get away from the castle and its dark secrets.

In early September, my father boarded the RMS *Franconia*, bound for Quebec, with mixed emotions—sadness at leaving behind a royal lifestyle he enjoyed and relief at being away from the ghosts that haunted him at night.

In 1962, upon his father's death, Victor Montagu sold Hinchingbrooke to the Huntingdon and Peterborough County Council, ending five hundred years of private family ownership, and in 1964 he renounced his position as the tenth Earl of Sandwich, after only two years. In the ensuing years, Victor would lose his prominence in government and earn a reputation for being eccentric.

Back in San Francisco, William noticed a change in Van. His friend had become obsessed with spirits. Van talked incessantly about the fourth Earl of Sandwich and the Hellfire Club. "A lot of devil worshipping and satanic ritual went on in those meetings. I heard they also sacrificed slaves. I wish I could have been there for just one meeting, just to get one slave."

"Your father would have a heart attack if he heard you talking like that," William said.

Van laughed. "Yes, he would. And he paid for the trip."

"Have you heard from Montagu since you've been back?"

"No, and I don't think I will."

"Why not?"

Van looked uncomfortable, hesitating before he spoke. "He made a move on me while I was there," he confessed.

"What did he do?" William asked.

"I don't want to talk about it," Van said.

William didn't ask him about the incident again, but he didn't quite believe his friend. Van had a way of twisting the imagined into reality.

"What happened to your head?" William asked, suddenly noticing a large bump protruding from Van's forehead.

"That damned mace," Van said, shifting his weight from foot to foot uncomfortably. He had shown William the mace earlier. Van had hung it over his bed at an angle, supported by a metal bracket, the handle resting in a makeshift support. "Last night, while I was sleeping, something hit me in the head. It hurt like hell, and when I sat up, the mace was in the bed. This isn't the first time it's happened. I'm telling you, William, there's something evil about that mace. It's possessed by medieval spirits. I know it is. Here, look at it and tell me what you think," Van insisted, handing the offending weapon to his friend.

William gave the mace a thorough inspection, then lifted the bull's mouth to his nose and grimaced at the foul odor. "Smells like old blood," he said.

"I have to get rid of this thing. It's going to kill me," Van said, fear evident in his eyes. "Do you want it?"

"No, thank you," William said adamantly.

Van spent the next months searching for someone, anyone, who would take the mace off his hands. Finally he found a collector and rid himself of the evil spirit that had attacked him at night.

8

The Korean War had provided a disturbing threat during my father's high school years. While William, Van, and Bill had enjoyed playing make-believe war in the ROTC, none of the boys had any interest in heading overseas after graduation to fight in a real war. They had decided early on that they would enroll in City College of San Francisco, a two-year preparatory college that did not offer ROTC but would keep them out of the draft if their names were to be called. Fortunately for the boys, the war ended in 1953, but they enrolled in the school anyway. Van and William opted for criminology, while Bill pursued drama—he had already decided he wanted to become an actor and was determined to achieve that goal. William wanted to become a private investigator, while Van simply liked the idea of studying forensics. His real interest was music, but he was already far beyond what a college could teach him and found music classes boring and repetitive. Gertrude had made sure of that.

By this time Van was an accomplished organist and a classical music aficionado, partial to Bach. He sometimes spent his spare time playing the pipe organ at Grace Cathedral, a French Gothic Episcopalian church on California Street. It had taken thirty-six years to build the church, but when it was complete, an architectural masterpiece awaited sinners who walked through its doors.

Stained-glass windows, depicting Jesus and his disciples, Mother Mary, and other biblical characters, radiated a spectrum of color across the arched ceiling over Van's head as he sat at the organ, caressing the keys. To his left, a circle with a cross in the middle graced the marble floor.

When Van played, passersby would stop, lured into the beautiful church by the magical sounds echoing from the vast open space. Built in 1934, the organ featured approximately 7,500 pipes, each contributing to the magnificent sound of the instrument. Even Van felt humbled when he heard the music his fingers created.

Although he had asked her more than once, Gertrude refused to come to the church to hear him play, and she no longer allowed him to play the piano in their living room, because Harlan no longer wanted Van in the house. Eager to be rid of Gertrude's son, Harlan was doing everything he could to make Van's home life as miserable as possible.

In need of an outlet other than the church, Van discovered the Lost Weekend tavern, at 1940 Taraval. The bar itself seemed ordinary enough, long and cylinder-shaped, with tables and chairs that lined the walls to the right. A mirrored bar surrounded by deep mahogany dressed the wall to the left. The blond-and-black mosaic-tiled floor, so common in buildings built in 1930s San Francisco, gave the bar a familiar appeal. But it was the Wurlitzer organ jutting out from the center of the bar that caught Van's attention. Raised on a platform, the organ's pipes stretched upward to the edges of a circle of wood on the ceiling.

"Do you need an organ player?" he asked the bartender one afternoon, eyeing the massive organ appreciatively.

"Got one," the bartender said. "Some guy named LaVey. You should come by and hear him on Friday nights. It's a different scene, man."

The following Friday, Van and William sat at the end of the bar, nursing a drink, waiting to hear how the Wurlitzer would sound. Van's fingers itched to touch the ivory keys. When the bar began filling with people, he guessed he wouldn't have long to wait. He watched curiously when patrons began gathering in a circle on the floor around the organ while the tables and chairs remained empty. He could feel an air of excitement building in the room.

And then he walked in.

The organist bowed slightly to the crowd before taking his place behind the Wurlitzer.

"Welcome. I'm Anton Szandor LaVey," he said, his voice reverberating through the microphone. "Remember, *evil* backwards spells *live*."

His minions, crowded together on the floor, clapped enthusiastically.

Van listened intently as the first notes began flowing through the pipes. Modern classical. Not what he had expected. LaVey was good. Van knew he was better.

He sat quietly through the first set, hearing every chord breathing through the pipes.

He hoped to meet LaVey when he took a break, but that didn't happen. When the music stopped, the organist began speaking, and Van observed as the room became deathly silent except for the sound of LaVey's voice. His audience was mesmerized.

Van was impressed. This unusual man, dressed all in black, held the crowd in the palm of his hand as he explained that they should indulge themselves in all things.

Van listened and watched for what seemed like hours. No one left the bar.

Finally LaVey stood up, the mirrors behind the bar replicating his image as he bowed before stepping down from his throne.

Van flagged the bartender.

"Do you mind if I play for a minute?" he said, handing him a five-dollar bill.

The bartender shrugged. "Go ahead, but I don't think anyone will pay attention. They come for him."

Van waited for the crowd to thin before he moved toward the organ. LaVey, sitting at a table along the wall, was surrounded by the remainder of his admirers, each trying to get closer to him. No one paid attention when Van sat down in front of the organ. The crowd didn't turn when he launched into Bach's Toccata and Fugue in D Minor.

But LaVey did.

Van could feel LaVey's eyes staring, questioning. When the final note trailed away, Van got up and returned to his seat at the bar.

LaVey stood up, pushing the crowd aside as he walked over to Van and William.

"Who are you?" he said, looking at Van.

"Van."

"Where did you learn to play like that?" LaVey queried.

Van smiled. "My mother."

LaVey laughed, his dark eyes crinkling under his pointed brows. "I'm Anton LaVey."

"I heard," Van said.

LaVey handed him a card. "Come by and see me sometime, but call first."

Van looked at the card after LaVey walked away. It listed 6114 California Street as the address.

A few weeks later, Van knocked on the door of the inconspicuous house at the address LaVey had given him. Later, the house would be painted black, its windows shuttered and its interior turned macabre, but LaVey had not progressed to that point yet.

The door opened, and a young woman directed Van down the hallway, into a sitting room. Van's gaze was immediately drawn to two bookcases that stood against deep purple walls. He walked toward them, then stopped, noticing a sign that threatened amputation if the books were disturbed. Van laughed.

He understood.

His eyes scanned the titles housed on the shelves.

"Not bad," he said aloud.

"Glad you approve," LaVey said, walking into the room.

Van turned to find the organist again dressed in black.

"I enjoyed your show," he said.

"Care to sit in with me sometime?" LaVey offered.

"Yes," Van replied, pleased.

That afternoon, the two men discussed music, literature, even criminal behavior when LaVey learned that Van was studying forensics. At the time, LaVey's philosophy was still developing, but Van appreciated his rebellious attitude toward societal and religious norms. LaVey enjoyed the fact that Van's father was a preacher, and Van liked that everything about this charismatic man was the antithesis of his father's ideology. Each was attracted to the other's mind and talent. While Van never really became a member of the Magic Circle—a group of LaVey's core followers who would later form the Church of Satan—he came to understand the man's teachings better than most and would often sit in with him at the Lost Weekend. Van would relate these conversations to William, who would caution my father to be wary of such unorthodox thought.

9

While he was attending college, Van decided to pursue a new interest. His experience in the library at Hinchingbrooke had fueled his appetite for old books, and he made a trip to Mexico to see if he could find anything of historical value from book dealers there. The bookstores he visited, many located in outdoor markets in Mexico City, were filled with precolonial documents and books dating back centuries, and Van reverently ran his fingers across their thick, yellowed pages. He chose several that he could afford and returned to San Francisco eager to discover what kind of profit he could make from his purchases.

He contacted a man named Henry von Morpurgo, who, being an alumnus of Lowell High School, promised to help Van sell his books.

Van called William to tell him about Morpurgo.

"This guy is hiding from the law," he told William. "He was

indicted for embezzling funds from the Sister Kenny Foundation and charged with federal mail fraud. He has assured me he can sell some of my books and wants me to meet him in Los Angeles. Do you want to come along?"

"Sure," William said. "I'm not real comfortable with you dealing with this guy by yourself. He sounds like a shyster."

Van and William drove to Los Angeles a few days later and checked into a room Morpurgo had booked for them at the Roosevelt Hotel, where many celebrities of that era stayed. When they met with Morpurgo that evening, he informed Van that he had been unable to generate interest in the books.

"Let me make it up to you," Morpurgo said, handing Van a piece of paper. "She'll take care of you."

William went back to his room, and Van went to another room in the Roosevelt, listed on the paper Morpurgo had given him. A high-priced call girl, paid for by Morpurgo, awaited him.

The next morning, noting his friend's disheveled appearance, William asked Van what had happened.

"I don't want to talk about it," Van said, obviously upset.

William, taken aback by Van's demeanor, did not dare broach the subject again.

The following year, 1956, Gertrude, desperate to rid herself of her son, decided it was time for Van to get married. She enlisted the help of her best friend, Ruth Williamson, whose daughter, Mary Annette Player, was beautiful, meek, and impressionable. Ruth agreed that Van and Annette would be a perfect match.

Ruth and her husband had divorced when Annette was a young child, and Annette had spent her life being shuttled back and forth from her mother's home, in San Francisco, to her father's home, in Stockton. Her parents fought constantly, and Annette was often caught in the middle of their disagreements. She wanted to live with her father, but Ruth was a domineering woman who refused to turn over control of her daughter to her ex-husband. As a result, seventeen-year-old Annette suffered from bouts of melancholy brought on by the disharmony in her life. By the time Ruth and Gertrude decided to introduce her to Van, Annette was ripe for the picking.

Gertrude and Ruth arranged the first meeting carefully. Gertrude knew that if she told Van she was bringing home a girl for him to meet, Van would refuse to be there. Instead she waited for the right moment, finally deciding that she would invite Ruth and Annette over on a night Van had to play at the Lost Weekend. She wanted him to look his best, and Van always dressed sharply when he had a gig.

The two women picked the date, and Ruth showed up promptly with her daughter, who had no clue that she was being set up. Gertrude and Ruth chatted with Annette in the living room, waiting for Van to emerge from his room. Finally they heard his door open.

Van stopped abruptly when he walked into the room. Sitting on the sofa was the prettiest girl he'd ever seen. He stared for a moment at her thick, dark eyebrows, arching high over deep brown eyes that were slanted to perfection. He noticed the hint of red tinting the wavy brown hair that framed her sculpted face. She looked like Audrey Hepburn.

Annette fidgeted under Van's bold inspection but smiled shyly while Gertrude made the introductions.

On August 19, 1957, Earl Van Best Jr. and Mary Annette Player were married. The plan had worked.

Ruth had insisted that Annette's father not be told about the wedding, and he was livid when he discovered that his under-age daughter had married without his consent, but he held his tongue, because his daughter seemed so happy.

Van spent the first few months courting his young bride. They rented a small one-bedroom apartment at 415 Jones Street, on Nob Hill, and set about furnishing it using money Annette had saved. Van made a little money playing the organ but did not make enough to pay all of the bills. He convinced Annette to invest the rest of her savings—$1,090—in a trip to Mexico.

"When I was in England, there were all of these old books at Hinchingbrooke that had to be worth a fortune," he told her. "I know I can go down to Mexico, find old books and documents, buy them cheap, and bring them back here to sell for a profit. I've done it before. All I need is capital to get me started."

At first Annette resisted, but eventually my father wore her down.

He went to Mexico City and found an old book dealer who would sell him precolonial documents by the pound. Van sorted through them, choosing this one and that, and bought as many as his funds allowed. When he returned to San Francisco, he walked into Holmes Book Company, on the corner of Third and Market Streets, and sold some of his books for a substantial profit. Pleased with himself, he hurried home to tell Annette.

Before long, Van began making frequent trips to Mexico, his love of old literature suddenly becoming a successful business venture. He bought everything he thought could turn a profit— British first editions, rare comic books, old scrolls. He enjoyed not only hunting for rarities, but also haggling for the best prices he could get. He was finding his marriage, however, not so re- warding.

Upset by the tension the marriage had caused with her fa- ther, Annette had become more melancholy than ever, but Van had little sympathy for her emotional state. She was ignoring him just as his mother had ignored him all of his life, and to him that was a betrayal. Instead of comforting his wife, he belittled her, screamed at her, and eventually began physically abusing her.

Over the next year, any minor infraction was rewarded with a slap, a punch, and soon beatings that would leave the young girl bruised for weeks. Fearing for her life, Annette finally told Ruth and Gertrude what was happening, but they, too, were unsympathetic and insisted that she should try harder to make her marriage work.

Annette tried to be brave. She tried to please Van. Nothing worked. Van had so much anger buried inside of him, and she was available.

Annette toughed it out for as long as she could, but after a particularly brutal fight on New Year's night in 1959, her fear of dying became greater than her fear of disappointing her mother. Annette called her father when Van left to go play music at one of his familiar haunts.

H. S. Player was furious when he saw the bruises and cuts on his daughter's face. He helped her pack her things and hurried her from the apartment. The next day he called the law office of Felix Lauricella and arranged for a meeting.

On January 4, Mary Annette Best filed for divorce on the grounds of extreme cruelty and inhuman treatment. Her marriage to my father had lasted one year, four months, and sixteen days. She had barely escaped with her life.

Van was enraged when he found her gone, but there was nothing he could do.

The divorce was granted April 8, 1960, and Annette was awarded the furniture and the money she had invested in Van's business. He was ordered by the court to pay her seventy-five dollars each month until his debt was repaid.

Annette remarried in 1961.

Van moved back to his small bedroom on Noe Street.

10

Van sipped on a Zombie while he waited for William at the Tonga Room, in the Fairmont Hotel. The bar, famous for its exotic drinks as well as its unusual decor, had become one of his favorite hangouts.

As the orchestra set up its instruments on a barge that floated back and forth across a seventy-five-foot lagoon in the center of the bar, Van stared at the document he had brought with him.

"Sorry I'm late," William said, pulling out a chair. "Where's LaVey?"

"Couldn't make it," Van said, flagging a waiter. "He can't seem to get away from his flock these days."

"So how have you been?" William asked, wondering what Van wanted to show him. He had sounded excited on the phone and insisted that they meet that day.

"Wait until you see this." He held up the document for William to see. "Look, it's the Spanish coat of arms. And look here," Van said, pointing to the signature. "King Philip II."

"Where did you get that?"

"Mexico City. There's a run-down bookstore in La Lagunilla Market, near the old Santa Catarina Church. The owner is an old man who sits outside all day waving customers in. I walked by one day, and we started talking. He brought me into the back room of his store and let me go through everything he had. I got this for a pittance."

"What's its significance?" William asked.

Van put his drink on a nearby ledge and wiped the table off with his napkin before spreading the document across it. "It authorizes a young lieutenant to go to Nueva España to recruit soldiers from the native Mexican Indians in the sixteenth century. Apparently this lieutenant was of noble lineage, judging by his name and the care with which the scribe prepared this order. And look here: the king's own coat of arms in addition to the Spanish coat of arms. You don't come across documents like this every day. I can sell this for a tidy sum."

William was impressed. He had thought my father was crazy when he first started foraging in Mexico. "It's no way to support a family," he had informed Van then. "It's not stable income." William had developed a lucrative business as a private investigator and had hoped Van would join him. Van had refused, preferring to traipse across Mexico searching for treasure.

"I'm happy for you," William said.

"Thanks. I need this right now."

William sensed something was wrong. "How's Annette?" he said.

"Gone."

"Gone?"

"Yes. She took off to her father's months ago and filed for divorce. Said I was cruel to her. Can you imagine?"

William could, but he shook his head. "She was a little too young for you anyway."

Van smiled. "That's the way I like them."

The two men ordered their dinner as the orchestra struck its first notes. As the evening progressed, rain poured into the lagoon, and thunder and lightning accompanied the band. It was all part of a show designed to transport guests to the South Seas. Menacing totems towered over guests, creating an ambience of mystery and excitement in the room as couples danced to the music in the orange glow of lanterns and hanging globes.

Van enjoyed the Tonga Room because of its Asian cuisine, the menu reminding him of the succulent dishes he had eaten in Japan as a child. He and William talked as they ate, catching up on what had happened while Van was in Mexico.

"Have you noticed what's going on in North Beach?" William asked.

"What?"

"The beach is filling up with beatniks. They're everywhere. I hear they're coming from all over the country."

"Oh, yes. I remember Herb Caen wrote an article about them in the *Chronicle* a few years back. He seemed to be making sport of them."

"I think it's interesting," William said. "These kids are spouting poetry and quoting Kerouac like they know what they're talking about. I can see where this is going, but at least they're reading something. And the music there has gotten better. Lots of jazz being played in the bars."

"We'll have to check it out one night," Van said.

William nodded his agreement as Van flagged their waiter again.

"I'll get this," Van said when the waiter brought the check.

"Big money," William joked.

"I'll let you know how it goes."

Van would eventually collect a tidy sum for his document. He wasn't as fortunate on other trips, though, and soon found himself in dire straits, his bedroom cluttered with old papers and books that had no value in San Francisco's antiquities market.

Van decided he should branch out and began traveling up and down the California coast, stopping at libraries along the way that might be interested in purchasing his books. He was able to make a living of sorts, but it wasn't ever enough.

Seeking an alternative way to make money, he bought some ink and a quill and set about copying the handwriting from one of the documents in his collection onto some old parchment paper he had lying around. He dated it 1629. When he got to the signature, he pulled an old book from his personal collection and flipped through the pages until he found what he was looking for. He practiced for a few minutes before signing the document: *King Philip IV.*

He sold it the next day, and my father was back in business.

He continued his travels to Mexico looking for authentic documents, but when he couldn't find anything of value, he became adept at forgery. Bookstore owners trusted him; his finds had always been good before, so they didn't check what he brought them as carefully as they might have otherwise.

By the fall of 1961 things were looking up for Van. He had taken a job as an IBM clerk but was still selling legitimate antiquities and some forgeries on the side. He met up with William at Schroeder's Restaurant, on Front Street, in late September for lunch. Established in 1893, the restaurant had a menu that included staples of traditional Bavarian cuisine, such as Wiener schnitzel, bratwurst, sauerbraten, and potato pancakes, and it appealed to William's German side. Van liked it because no women were allowed inside during the lunch hour. It was a gentlemen's restaurant, where men were free to laugh and talk without the restrictive presence of ladies. Businessmen, dressed in business suits, would sit at the rosewood bar and smoke big cigars. Van felt important when he walked into Schroeder's, like he belonged at the bar with these fine gentlemen. He often stared over the lip of his tall beer stein at the Hermann Richter murals that dominated the walls, admiring Richter's use of color. In one, a tasty blond wench with an overflowing bosom playfully sat on the lap of an eager young man clad in shorts, a white-collared shirt, and a red vest. In another, a group of gentlemen sat around a table, gesturing grandly as they argued the politics of the day.

Van ordered an exotic German beer on tap and watched as the bartender tried to stem the head. He handed William a cigar.

Unwrapping it carefully, William noted its Cuban insignia. "I'm going to enjoy this one," he said. Van often brought him cigars and other gifts from Mexico.

Van smiled, lighting his own. "This is the life, huh?" he said in German. Usually he and William were the only two in the bar who could speak German, and they liked the feeling of superiority they experienced from speaking the language there.

"Yes, it is," William said. "Did you find anything of value on your last trip?"

"A few things. Some seventeenth-century letters that might be of interest," Van replied, omitting the fact that he had created them in his bedroom. William was a private investigator, a moral man. He wouldn't understand.

"When are you going back?" William asked.

"I don't know. Maybe next month. I'm getting bored around here. I need some excitement," Van said.

And then my father met Judy Chandler.

11

Van waited impatiently behind a tree at the edge of Golden Gate Park, his eyes trained on Hugo Street. Judy lived about six houses down on Seventh Avenue, where the road dead-ended, and from his vantage point at the top of the hill, Van could see when she came outside. He hoped her mother wouldn't follow her. Judy had told Verda about their relationship, and her mother had been doing everything she could to keep her daughter from seeing him. Judy liked the excitement of sneaking around and met Van whenever she could, mostly for hamburgers after school or an occasional movie.

He watched as the front door opened and his girlfriend walked outside. Judy liked it when he called her his girlfriend. It made her feel grown up. When he saw the suitcase in her hand, he let out the breath he had been holding. He hadn't been sure she would go through with it. He wanted to run down and help her carry it up the hill, but he couldn't risk Verda spotting him, so he waited until she reached him.

"Come on. We've got to hurry," he said, kissing her quickly before grabbing the suitcase from her hand.

Skirting the edge of the park, the couple half-ran to a nearby street where William had parked his car, waiting to drive them to the airport.

"Get in," Van said, throwing her suitcase on the backseat.

"She looks kind of young, Van. She's not like the other one, is she?" William asked, referring to Van's former wife.

"Oh. No. She's nineteen," Van said, lying.

"I'm so excited," Judy said, bouncing up and down in her seat, unaware that William was looking at her suspiciously. "I can't believe we're really going to do it."

They had planned it a few days before. Van had been walking her home when he pulled her behind a tree. "I don't want you to go home," he said. "I hate every minute you're not with me."

"Me, too," said Judy, "but I don't want to get in trouble."

Van wrapped his arms around her, pulling her close. "Kiss me," he commanded.

Judy snuggled closer and did as she was told.

"Run away with me," Van said. "Let's get married."

Judy pulled away, stunned.

"Are you serious?" she said.

"Dead serious. I love you. We should be together, and once we're married no one can stop us. Will you marry me, Judy?"

"But when? How?"

"Don't worry. I'll take care of everything. Meet me Friday morning about seven. I'll be waiting in the park. Pack a suitcase with a pretty dress and as many clothes as you can fit into it. We're going on an adventure. Are you in?"

Judy thought about it for a moment and then threw her arms around his neck. "I'm in. I'm in," she said, laughing. "Oh, my mother is going to be so mad. She doesn't like you."

"Don't worry about her," Van said. "I'll see you Friday?"

"Yes," Judy nodded.

Van had kissed her soundly one more time and then watched as Judy skipped down the hill.

Early on the morning of January 5, 1962, nervous but even more excited, Judy tucked her favorite dress into a suitcase and headed off for her adventure. She had known Van for only three months, but she was sure he loved her. She wasn't sure if she loved him, but she enjoyed the feeling of being in his strong arms, of being protected. He was nicer to her than any man had ever been, and the young girl had no doubt she was leaving her family for a better life.

At the airport, excitement and anticipation fluttered in Judy's stomach as Van guided her up the steps to the plane. After take-off, Judy stared in amazement at the fluffy clouds, first above her, then below. She had not flown before and could barely sit still, because she did not want to miss a thing. Van laughed at her antics, enjoying her excitement.

When they landed in Reno, Nevada, he whisked her off to the church, eager to be joined in holy matrimony to this delightful girl who had brought such beauty and light into his life. When they arrived, Judy excused herself and went into the bathroom to change into her bright pink dress and brush her hair, while Van filled out the marriage certificate and other necessary documents, lying about Judy's age, as they had planned.

"How old are you, young lady?" the minister asked.

"Nineteen," the fourteen-year-old informed him, just as Van had instructed her.

The Reverend Edward Fliger did not question her again. She looked old enough, and he had no reason to be suspicious.

The witnesses Van had hired—Birdie M. Nilsson and A. S. Belford—stood silently as my father and my mother said their vows in St. Paul's United Methodist Church on January 5, 1962.

"Do you take this woman to be your lawfully wedded wife, to have and to hold, in sickness and in health, until death do you part?" the reverend said.

"I do," Van said, holding Judy's hand tightly.

"Do you take this man to be your lawfully wedded husband, to have and to hold, in sickness and in health, until death do you part?"

"I do," Judy said, taking a deep breath and smiling up at Van.

"By the power vested in me by the state of Nevada, I now pronounce you husband and wife. You may kiss your bride."

Van pulled Judy into his arms.

With their arms still wrapped around each other, they left the church, anticipation growing as Van hailed a taxi.

Van and Judy spent that night consummating their marriage—the twenty-seven-year-old man initiating his innocent teen bride in the art of lovemaking.

They spent the next day in Reno—Judy enjoying her new-found freedom, and Van enjoying Judy—before flying back to San Francisco to face the music. Judy was very relieved when she called her mother to tell her she was married. Verda, for some reason, seemed unusually understanding.

The couple moved into an apartment on Clay Street, excited about the prospect of sharing their lives together, but on January 9, Judy awoke with severe stomach pains. Unsure what to do, Van called her mother.

"Call an ambulance," Verda said furiously, hurriedly jotting down the address of the apartment. As soon as she hung up the phone, Verda dialed the number for the San Francisco Police Department, to file a complaint against the man who had married her underage daughter.

"You could get into a lot of trouble for being with a minor," an officer warned Van after Judy was settled into the back of the ambulance. "Her mother has filed a complaint against you."

"We're married," Van informed him before climbing into the ambulance. "We've got to go. Can't you see she's sick?"

The officer let him go.

While Judy was having her appendix removed, Van moved to 765 Haight Street, hoping Verda wouldn't be able to find him there. Verda kept a watchful eye on Judy while she was in the hospital, and as soon as her daughter recovered she had her placed in the Youth Guidance Center—a section of the Juvenile Justice Center on Woodside Avenue—hoping to teach her wayward daughter a lesson.

"Mother, you can't do this. I love him!" Judy wailed when she was given the privilege of a phone call. "He's my husband."

"He is not your husband. He's a child molester," her mother countered.

On Valentine's Day, Verda had the marriage annulled.

Van was furious, but Verda had the law on her side.

Judy was desolate. She curled up in a ball on her bed and cried hysterically, like only heartbroken teenage girls can cry.

A week later, an unsuspecting Van was arrested for the rape of a female under the age of eighteen.

He soon posted bail, packed a bag, and took off for Mexico City, determined to make some quick cash. He was successful this time, and when he returned to San Francisco, he snuck into the Youth Guidance Center to visit Judy. She giggled as he told her his plan.

"I can do it," she assured him.

On the evening of April 28, 1962, Judy tied her bedsheets into a makeshift rope, climbed out of her upstairs room, and shimmied down to the ledge below. Van was waiting to catch her when she jumped the remaining few feet. Together the couple fled undetected into the gathering darkness.

"Where are we going?" Judy asked, once they were settled in Van's car.

"To the airport to catch a plane to Chicago," Van said, taking her hand in his. "My father's a minister in Indiana. I'm going to ask him to meet us there to marry us."

Judy giggled. "My mother is going to be so mad."

"We're not going to worry about that. You're mine, and I'm not going to let her take you away from me."

My mother snuggled closer to the man she was about to marry for the second time.

When they reached Chicago, Van called his father, but Gertrude had beaten him to the punch, informing Earl on the telephone that Van had been arrested for marrying the fourteen-year-old and warning him that they had run away again.

"Take her back to her parents," Earl barked into the phone before Van could say anything.

"But Father, I need you to marry us. We're in Chicago."

"That is not going to happen. She's fourteen. Have you lost your mind?" Earl yelled.

Earl had spent the past twenty years building a reputation and career of which any man could be proud, and he wasn't about to let his misguided son mess that up because he had taken a fancy to a young girl. As national chaplain of the Veterans of Foreign Wars of the United States, Earl was accountable to the government and to the public, and he was acutely aware that Van's actions could reflect badly on him.

"Please, Father. I don't want to live in sin," Van said, hoping the mention of sin would persuade the reverend.

"Take her home, Van. Now. Before it's too late," Earl urged.

"That's not going to happen. I love her, and I'm going to marry her with or without your help," Van retorted.

"What happened to you?" Earl said quietly. "You know this is wrong."

"I love her. What's so wrong with that?"

"She's fourteen!" Earl yelled. "That's what's wrong with it."

"As usual, I can count on you," Van said, knowing the effect his words would have on his father.

"Take her back," Earl begged, "before you get into more trouble."

"No. I won't."

"Please, son. Nothing good will come of this."

Van hung up the phone.

"Let's go grab a bite to eat," Van told Judy. "I know a place," he said, ushering her out of the airport and into a taxi.

"What happened?" Judy said when they were on their way.

Van shook his head. "I don't want to talk about it."

Seeing the tears welling in her eyes, he patted her leg. "It'll be okay. We'll figure it out."

After they were seated at Gene & Georgetti, one of Chicago's finest steakhouses, Judy tried again to get Van to tell her what his father had said, but he ignored her.

"Use this fork for your salad and this one for your entrée," he said, placing her napkin in her lap. "I'll order for you. You've got to have the beef. There's only three places in the world where you can get beef of this quality—Chicago, Kansas City, and Kobe, Japan."

Throughout dinner, Van was quiet, contemplating his next move.

"We're not going back," he said. "They can't take you away from me."

"Where are we going?" Judy inquired nervously.

Van smiled.

"Mexico. We can get married there."

12

Mexico City was everything Van had promised. Judy followed along happily when he dragged her from one market to another, searching for books and documents he could resell, taking in the sights, sounds, and smells of a world that was foreign to her. Van seemed quite at home as he skimmed through stacks of paper and scrolls of writing, seeming to understand the hieroglyphs from the precolonial period of Spanish occupation of the great city on the island in the lake.

When he wasn't working, Van took her to visit the Catedral Metropolitana, on the Zócalo, where Judy watched in awe as a boys' choir raised their heavenly voices in praise, emitting the most beautiful sounds she had ever heard. And when Van brought her to see the Teotihuacán pyramids, constructed around A.D. 300 just north of Mexico City, my mother thought she had never seen anything so amazing.

"Look at the way they are laid out," Van said, pointing from one pyramid to the next. "The Aztec people who came later believed that the gods were born here. There's the Pyramid of the Sun, and look, there's the Pyramid of the Moon. The Teotihuacáno warriors hunted people, sacrificing them to the gods because they thought the end of the world was coming. They hoped their sacrifices would save them from the earthquakes they feared would kill them all."

"What happened to them?" Judy asked.

"They just disappeared one day. The whole city. No one really knows why."

"How do you know this?" Judy asked.

"I know lots of things," Van said, smiling.

The next morning, Van decided it was time to get married.

"Pack your bags," he told her. "We're going to Acapulco. There's a resort there, the Las Brisas, where they pick you up in pink jeeps and take you around the city. You'll love it. I know a little church nearby where we can get married."

Judy, enjoying the adventure of it all, quickly packed the few items of clothing Van had bought her and was soon ready to go.

When they got to Acapulco, Van rushed Judy to the church but was disappointed to learn that he could not marry her without parental consent.

"What do we do now?" Judy asked.

Undeterred, Van said, "We go on our honeymoon."

Because the Las Brisas was fully booked, they had to settle for a high-rise complex nearby on Acapulco Bay. They spent the next few days acting like they were on their honeymoon—sunning on the beach during the day, making love at night.

On May 11, 1962, a slight shaking stirred Van and Judy from their slumber. It was a little more than the usual early-morning rumble of the city buses, to which they were already accustomed, having lived their lives in San Francisco. As Van reached for his glasses on the nightstand, it happened. A 7.1-magnitude earthquake knocked him off balance. Judy screamed as Van fell onto the floor, and the bed began to move on the rolling tile. Pictures on the walls crashed to the floor. Judy tried to reach Van as the building swayed for what seemed like an eternity but was actually less than a minute.

When it was over, they walked onto their balcony and surveyed the damage. Some of the balconies above them swayed dangerously, hanging on by only a piece of rebar. Van hurried Judy back into the room, lighting a candle so she could see. While Van went out again to assess the damage, Judy cleaned broken glass from the floor.

For the next few days, they were forced to stay at the hotel, because the rubble covering the city's streets made travel impossible. While Van sorted through the documents he had bought in Mexico City, Judy sat on the beach, gazing at the beautiful bodies of the bronzed young men surfing and playing volleyball. There was nothing else to do. Van, distracted by the thought of Judy being alone at the beach, watched jealously from a window high above.

On May 19, an aftershock with a magnitude of 7.0 struck the city. My father decided it was time to return to the States. He needed no more signs from the gods. He and Judy packed their things and boarded a plane, blissfully unaware that the seed of their undoing had been planted in Mexico.

13

Shortly after they arrived in Los Angeles, Van became ill and checked into a hospital for treatment. He was diagnosed with infectious hepatitis, a virus that was common in Mexico and frequently spread through the consumption of contaminated food or water.

"I'll be okay," he reassured Judy, who sat by his bedside, refusing to leave.

"Do you want me to call your parents?" she said, worrying.

"No. Absolutely not," he said. "The doctor said I won't be here long."

When Van recovered, they headed back to San Francisco and rented an apartment in a five-story building at 585 Geary Street, on the southern slopes of Nob Hill. The one-bedroom apartment featured a big bay window that overlooked the Hotel California, across the street. A fire escape climbed up all five stories on the front of the building. On either side of the entrance, a circular white light fixture trimmed in black depicted the shape of a cross in the center.

Van didn't bother to tell Judy that he had lived a block away on Jones Street with his last wife. He simply led his lover through the foyer and up the steps to their new home.

They spent the next month pretending they were married and hoping Verda would not find them. In July, Judy became ill, too. Worried that she had contracted hepatitis from him, Van brought her to San Francisco General Hospital on July 30.

Judy was diagnosed with hepatitis, but the physician also informed the fourteen-year-old that she was pregnant.

When she was released from the hospital, she nervously called Verda.

"Mother, I have to tell you something," she said.

"What now?" Verda snapped, irate that Judy had not contacted her since she had run away. "Where have you been? I've been worried sick."

"We went to Mexico, but there was an earthquake and we had to come back," Judy said nervously. "And I'm pregnant. Three months. Mother, I'm scared."

Verda's tone became reassuring, persuasive, as she asked Judy to come home so they could talk about it. "Bring some things for an overnight stay. We have to figure out what to do."

"Okay," Judy said. "I'll have Van drive me."

When Judy and Van pulled up to the house at 1245 Seventh Avenue, Verda was waiting. Although Van had scanned the area, he had not seen the police cars hidden around the corner from the house. The officers waited until Van got out of the car before they confronted him.

"Earl Van Best, you are under arrest for child stealing," one officer said, grabbing Van and pulling his arms behind his back. Judy struggled with the officer as he clamped the handcuffs tightly around my father's wrists.

Crying, she watched the police take him away.

"How could you do this?" she screamed at her mother as Verda herded her into the house.

"How could *you*?" Verda answered.

My mother was sent back to the Youth Guidance Center.

My father was placed in a cell on the sixth floor of the Hall of Justice. He was sitting on his bunk, contemplating his next move, when a handsome young man walked up.

"Mr. Best, might I have a word with you?"

Van looked at him questioningly, wondering if he was a lawyer. "I'm Paul Avery, with the *San Francisco Chronicle*," the man said. "Do you mind if I ask you a few questions?"

Van shook his head.

Avery pulled out his notebook. "Where did you meet Judy?" he asked.

"At Herbert's Sherbet Shoppe. She was there . . . beautiful and sweet," Avery would later quote Van as saying.

"But she was only fourteen," Avery said.

"That didn't matter."

Over the next half hour, Van told Avery the whole story.

"He Found Love in Ice Cream Parlor," read the headline of the *San Francisco Chronicle* on August 1, 1962. Pictures of Van and Judy were splashed across the page, accompanied by an article depicting their romance. "At the moment, several sets of steel bars and more than a mile in distance separate Van and his one-time wife, Judy Chandler," Avery wrote before describing how the now twenty-eight-year-old man had fallen in love with a teenager.

When Van saw the article, he was furious. He didn't like the way Avery had portrayed him as if he were some old, balding child molester. Avery would later dub their love affair "The Ice Cream Romance." Van would never forgive him for mocking his love for Judy.

Other newspapers followed suit.

The *San Francisco Examiner* reported that "the mild-mannered, bespectacled son of a Midwest minister sat in his cell at city prison yesterday and wept for his bride—blonde, 14, and pregnant."

On August 7, 1962, Van was indicted for child stealing, rape, and contributing to the delinquency of a minor.

Verda testified before the grand jury first, indignantly telling jury members how Van had taken her daughter to Reno and married her. She stated that she'd had the marriage annulled, but then Van had kidnapped Judy from the Youth Guidance Center.

William Lohmus was called to testify about how he had driven Van and Judy to the airport when they had first eloped.

Judy was also forced to testify, but when she came out of the jury room, she had a big smile on her face.

Those who saw her wondered why.

The whole country would soon know why.

Sitting in the lobby of the courthouse, my grandfather, who had flown to San Francisco as soon as he received Gertrude's call, bowed his head and prayed for his son when he heard the news that Van had been indicted.

Van had already been released on bail and was unconcerned.

The next day, Judy escaped from the Youth Guidance Center again.

Van was waiting.

On August 9, San Francisco police officers caught up with them, and Judy was sent to the maximum security ward at the Youth Guidance Center. Van was taken in handcuffs to the sixth floor of the Hall of Justice for the third time. This time the charges were more severe: criminal conspiracy, enticing a minor from home, and rape of a female less than eighteen years old.

Two days later, Earl posted his son's bail.

By August 24 Judy was sick again, the hepatitis she had caught from Van causing her to be hospitalized. She was placed in an isolation ward at San Francisco General Hospital.

On August 31, Van was back in a San Francisco courtroom for a hearing on his case. As would later be revealed in a video of the proceedings, Van, dressed in a white shirt with sleeves rolled up to just below the elbow, a beige sweater-vest, and pressed tan pants, confidently walked up to the podium, his face showing no expression as the judge set his trial date.

He left the courthouse and went to Crocker Bank to withdraw all of his money and close his account. Then he paid William an unexpected visit.

"What are you going to do?" William asked. He didn't like the determined look on Van's face.

"I can't tell you," Van replied, handing William five hundred dollars. "Hold this for me in case I ever come back or if I ever need some money in a hurry."

"Van, you've got to stop this," William begged. "She's not worth it."

"Yes, she is," Van said. "Please don't tell anyone I was here. I don't want you involved."

That same night, around midnight, my father, disguised as a doctor, walked into San Francisco General Hospital looking for my mother. He was not going to let anyone keep her from him. A few minutes later, doctor and patient walked nonchalantly out of the hospital, without attracting attention. Once outside, Judy and Van ran to the rental car he had waiting.

At 3:40 a.m., the floor nurse noticed Judy's empty bed and sounded the alarm, notifying Dr. L. N. Swanson of the escape. The doctor telephoned the police, who immediately put out an all-points bulletin for the couple.

"Sundae Bride Hunted," the headline in the *San Francisco News–Call Bulletin* read the next morning. "Guards on the Mexican border have been alerted to watch for San Francisco's 14-year-old ice cream bride and interrupt—if possible—her third elopement."

"The girl vanished early Friday from San Francisco General Hospital, and less than 12 hours later, a blood-stained auto was found abandoned near King City," reported the *Examiner*.

Newspapers across the country picked up the story, jumping on the illicit romance of it all. A nationwide manhunt ensued, but Judy and Van were long gone.

When they left the hospital, they had driven south on Highway 101, heading for Mexico, but Van had fallen asleep at the wheel and careened off the road.

Judy screamed as the car crashed into a ditch.

Van, jarred awake, jumped out of the car. "Let's go!" he yelled, ignoring Judy's concern about the blood covering the spot where his head had hit the steering wheel. "We've got to get out of here before the cops come."

Judy followed him onto the road. "What are we going to do?"

Van stuck out his thumb as a car approached.

It took them only two hitched rides to reach Sacramento. By that evening they were sharing a chocolate milk shake at a root beer stand in Williams, north of Sacramento. They spent the night in a roadside hotel, making plans. Van knew the police would suspect they were going to Mexico, so he decided to head for Canada instead.

The next day, another article appeared in the *Examiner*: "Judy Chandler, the missing 15-year-old ex-bride, was seen sharing a chocolate milkshake with her former husband Friday night in the Sacramento Valley town of Williams." The newspaper got it wrong—Judy was still fourteen.

The article went on: "When the owner of a root beer stand on Highway 99 and his two employees saw a picture of the missing couple on the front page of *The Examiner* yesterday, they called the newspaper. Police questioned the three last night and said they had positively identified the couple."

On Sunday morning, my fugitive parents stopped at a diner for breakfast. Van noticed his picture staring back at him from a newsstand and hustled Judy out of there fast. He realized they would not make it to the border without being recognized.

"I'm hungry. Why can't we eat?" Judy asked him.

Van did not answer as he steered them toward a Longs drugstore behind the diner. He told her to wait outside.

Van headed for the cosmetics aisle, studied the products for a moment, and then slipped a box of women's hair dye under his sweater. He walked up to the counter and bought a pack of Lucky Strikes. Judy nervously waited outside.

When they got back to the motel, Van insisted that she dye her hair.

"I don't want to, Van," Judy cried.

"Our pictures are everywhere. You have to do this," he insisted. "Do you want to go to jail? Someone will recognize you."

Tearfully, Judy watched in the mirror as her beautiful blond hair turned black. The person looking back at her was a stranger—a pregnant, black-haired stranger. She noticed Van's crooked smile of approval through her tears. For the first time, she realized they were in big trouble. She swallowed back a lump of fear in her throat.

Van decided to double back, confident that no one would recognize Judy now. He worried about his own appearance but thought that his glasses would suffice as a disguise. Most of the newspaper photos had been taken when he was not wearing them. He was right: no one recognized them as they hitchhiked to Los Angeles, where he hoped they could go unnoticed in the big city.

Van soon rented an apartment in an industrialized area near Torrance and insisted that Judy get a job, because he couldn't risk being recognized. Covering up the bulge in her belly as best she could, she got a job at a nice restaurant on the north side of Los Angeles near Hollywood. When the manager realized she could not even mix a Bloody Mary, she was fired within a week.

In late September, Van and Judy headed south to San Diego. There was no hiding Judy's growing belly now, and her chances of getting a job were becoming slimmer. The money Van had brought was running out, but he convinced a gullible woman to cash a bad check for three hundred dollars. He knew they had to get out of California. At a bar, he persuaded a drunken patron to give them a ride to Tucson, Arizona. He still held on to the thought that if they could get to Mexico they would be safe. He had crossed the border many times—at Tijuana, Tecate, Mexicali, and El Paso. He thought El Paso would be the safest route. They could travel to Ciudad Juárez and be home free.

Sympathetic drinking buddies provided transportation along the way. The Rescue Mission of El Paso provided lodging.

Judy was miserable. Each morning, in order to be able to eat breakfast for free, she and Van were required to attend church service and prayer sessions. Their daily breakfast, consisting of eggs with blood visible in the yolks, made the already nauseated girl sicker. After forcing herself to eat one morning, Judy experienced pains in her back and began having trouble urinating. When she doubled over on the floor, Van called for an ambulance.

Judy was diagnosed with a kidney infection, and Van, with no way to pay her hospital bill, befriended a woman named Belle and asked her to cash a check for one hundred dollars. Belle gave him her money, and he gave her a worthless check, signed by one of his growing list of aliases, John Register. Before Judy could be discharged, Van whisked her away from the hospital without paying the bill.

Worried about his love, Van spent the evening cooking a meal that Judy would always remember: ground beef with a baked potato. It wasn't that the meal was that special; it was the sweet way he'd tried to take care of her, the fact that he had cooked for her. Since their escape, Van had not been as nice as he'd been in the days they'd spent walking home from the sherbet shop or playing tourist in Mexico City. He had become short-tempered. Snappish.

Mean.

That night restored her faith in the man who had swept her off her feet.

In her befuddled state, and experiencing pain from the infection, it was only later that Judy realized what Van had already known.

The date was October 8, her fifteenth birthday.

14

My father's plan to cross the border near El Paso was nixed when someone at the hospital put the pieces together after the couple left without paying, and identified them as the Ice Cream Bride and her fugitive husband. Evening news reports announced that the runaway couple were planning to cross the border at El Paso.

Troops at the border were ramped up as U.S. Border Patrol and local law enforcement agencies vied to catch the runaway couple.

Van's father was determined not to let that happen. He had been in San Francisco when Van took off with Judy again, and he had returned home to Indiana with a heavy heart.

When two gentlemen in suits showed up at his home and produced their badges, he wasn't surprised.

"We'd like to monitor your telephone," one of the men informed Earl, who had no choice but to agree.

The minister listened politely while they explained how the bug worked. When they were finally gone, Van's father, tears rolling down his face, got into his car and drove to his pastor's home. Suddenly, the minister needed some ministering of his own.

After his confession, the pastor allowed Earl to use his phone. Earl called his family in South Carolina. He informed them that Van was in a lot of trouble and on the run. "Spread the word," he said. "If Van and the girl show up, I will pay for any help they are given."

Out of options in Texas, my father offered to write a check to anyone who would give him and his pregnant wife (as he called her) a ride to Mississippi. It wasn't difficult. Judy's condition elicited sympathy.

Earl's brother Rufus, having gotten the message, was not surprised when Van and Judy showed up at his door in Meridian, Mississippi, hungry and disheveled. He agreed to help the couple on a temporary basis.

Rufus's dilapidated farmhouse was located on a few acres in the woods outside of town. In mid-November, the temperatures were dipping into the mid-forties, but there was no central heat in the house, only a cast-iron wood-burning stove and a few space heaters scattered about. An outhouse served as the bathroom, and Judy, who was six months pregnant, had to make the trek to the smelly, rickety old building often.

From left: Anna Jordan Best and her husband, Earl Van Dorn Best, with their children in 1905. Earl Van Best Sr. is sitting on his father's lap.

From left: A business card showing my grandfather Earl Van Best Sr.; my father, Earl Van Best Jr. (known as "Van"); and my grandmother Gertrude Best when they were missionaries in Japan.

TARRY   PRA.

REV. AND MRS. E. V. BEST

Methodist Missionaries to Japan

Home Address: Cades, S. C.

Foreign Address:
   Aoyoma Gakuin,
   Shibuya Ku,
   Tokyo, Japan

GO   SEN.

My father, Van, as a boy in Japan.

From left: Carolyn Best, Katherine Broadway, Geraldine "Bits" Best, Bob Best, and Van on summer vacation at Myrtle Beach in 1948.

Van and his friends William Lohmus and Bill Bixby
in an ROTC photo in their high school yearbook.

Training Corps

"C" COMPANY

FRONT ROW: (L to R)—J. Piro, T. Rankin, D. Miskel ,R. Green, R. Wilson, L. Sutherland, J. Schwabacher, T. Palmer, W. Louie, D. Sherman, V. Best, C. Smith. ROW 2—H. Tietler, R. Martin, G. Green, W. Brady, R. Baker, N. Faix, R. Felicia, C. Blank. ROW 3—M. Orloff, W. Lohmus, C. Mallins, F. Reed, W. Bixby, R. Thein, R. Forst, E. Benton, J. Bishop, D. Yu.

The house at 514 Noe
Street in San Francisco,
where my father grew up.

Judy Chandler as a teenager, at about the time she met Van.

Van and Judy's apartment in New Orleans when I was born.

EARL VAN BEST
"Love at first sight"

JUDY CHANDLER
"Beautiful and sweet"

He Found Love in ice Cream Parlor

An accidental meeting at Herbert's Sherbert Shoppe on an Indian summer afternoon was the way in which Earl Van Best found love.

There was only one roadblock to the romance: his love was 14 years old.

"I can't help the difference in our ages," said the balding, 28-year-old Best. "I love Judy and she loves me."

At the moment several sets of steel bars and more than a mile in distance separate Earl Van Best and his one-time wife, Judy Chandler.

Best, who says he supports himself by selling rare books and documents he brings

See Page 20; Col. 1

The first in a series of articles by *San Francisco Chronicle* reporter Paul Avery, mocking my father.

Van holds up one of his swords in another *Chronicle* article by Paul Avery.

Love on the Run

Ice Cream Romance's Bitter End

New Orleans police yesterday picked up the pieces of the shattered, fugitive romance of Earl Van Best and his 15-year-old former wife, Judy Chandler.

The couple's reckless love, that began in a San Francisco ice cream parlor, ended bitterly in New Orleans' French Quarter.

Blonde Judy has been taken to Baton Rouge to talk with welfare authorities there about the future of the baby she abandoned two months ago.

Van Best, 28, a minister's son, waited in the New Orleans jail for the return trip to San Francisco, where he faces charges on a Grand Jury indictment of child stealing, statutory rape and conspiracy.

To be together, Van Best jumped $5000 bail last August and Judy slipped away from San Francisco General Hospital where she was being treated for infectious hepatitis.

On Thursday, after eight months living as fugitives, Van Best telephoned San Francisco police to say Judy "has cleaned me out of money and clothes."

New Orleans juvenile division officers picked up Judy with another man outside a French Quarter apartment.

Van Best was arrested yesterday morning as he talked with a priest in the rectory of St. Louis Cathedral in New Orleans.

He told police that Judy had his baby in February. He took the infant to Baton Rouge and abandoned it in an apartment there.

Van Best, a book salesman, met Judy in an ice cream parlor in the Sunset district in October, 1961. She was 14, but Van Best said she looked 20.

They married in Reno the following January, but the marriage was annulled a month later.

Two months later they left San Francisco on a long trip that took them to Chicago, El Paso, Mexico and Los Angeles. When they returned to this city, Judy was found to be pregnant.

EARL VAN BEST
Minister's son

JUDY CHANDLER
Married at 14

Paul Avery reports the end of the "Ice Cream Romance."

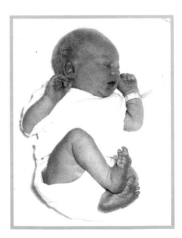

My baby picture, taken at Southern Baptist Hospital, February 12, 1963.

The apartment building at 736 North Boulevard in
Baton Rouge where my father abandoned me.

The stairwell on which I was found.

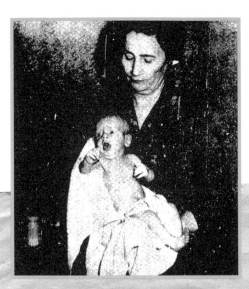

My baby picture, as it appeared in the *Morning Advocate*.

DAILY

Vol. XXII   Opelousas, Louisiana, Sunday

TWO PERSONS WERE KILLED in the head-on collision Saturday morning of these two cars, which smashed together 1 1/2 miles east of Port Barre. The victims were Sheryl Lynn Stewart, 13-months-old daughter of Mr. and Mrs. Harry L. Stewart of Baton Rouge, a passenger in the car at left, and James K. Reasonover, 52-year-old New sole occupant of car at right. The ba adopted grandchild of Mr. and Mrs. A of Krotz Springs. The crash happene Hwy. 190 during a drizzling rain. — Capt. Lonnie Rogers of state police)

A report in the local newspaper of the wreck that took the life of Sheryl Lynn Stewart.

Sheryl Lynn Stewart.

Leona and Loyd Stewart on their way
to pick up their new son.
(Courtesy of Boone Stewart)

My second birthday.

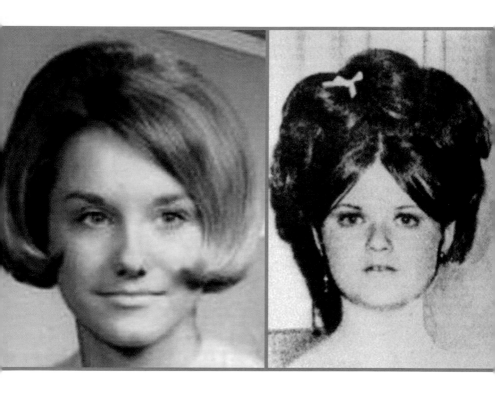

Above left: Zodiac victim Cheri Jo Bates.

Above right: Zodiac victim Betty Lou Jensen.

Above left: Zodiac victim David Faraday.

Above right: Zodiac victim Cecelia Shepard.

Above left: Zodiac victim Bryan Hartnell, who survived the attack.

Above right: Zodiac victim Darlene Ferrin.

Above left: Zodiac victim Michael Mageau, who also survived the attack.

Above right: Zodiac victim Paul Stine.

Alta Plaza Park

June 19, 1974

Judy Chandler and Rotea Gilford's
wedding announcement.

My mother, Judy Chandler, and I share our first hug.
(Courtesy of Frank Velasquez)

From left: My dad, Loyd; my son, Zach; me; and my mom, Leona, at Zach's graduation.

(Courtesy of Francesca Pandolfi)

My mother and father, Leona and Loyd Stewart.

"I want to go home," Judy told Van on the first night of their stay, trying to get comfortable on the lumpy sofa bed Rufus had folded out for them.

"Stop whining and be still," Van said. "We're lucky to be here. At least we're safe."

Judy didn't see it that way.

Although Rufus allowed them to hide out there, he was not comfortable with the idea. He worried that others would find out that he was harboring fugitives and constantly made the couple aware of the trouble he was courting on their behalf. He had promised Earl he would take care of them. He had not promised to make their stay a pleasant one.

"If you want to eat, you hunt your food," he told Van. "I can't be feeding the whole damn family."

"You can come with me," Van told Judy. "I'll teach you how to hunt."

"No," Judy cried. "I don't want you to kill anything."

"You want to eat? Let's go." Van grabbed a rifle from beside the door, checked to make sure it was loaded, and headed out the door with Judy in tow.

"Just aim and shoot," he said, positioning the rifle along her shoulder.

"I don't want to," Judy begged, tears glistening in her eyes.

"Shoot the damn thing. Just aim and pull the trigger," Van said.

She got off one shot and handed him the gun, trying to hide her trembling hands by rubbing her shoulder where the gun had kicked.

She watched in horror as a squirrel appeared from the brush and Van took aim and fired.

"Look," he said, holding the bloody rodent triumphantly for Judy to see. "One shot. And he was running."

Judy didn't want to look, but Van held the squirrel close to her face and then laughed when she retched.

At dinner, Judy begged him not to make her eat it, but Van insisted, the tone in his voice inviting no argument. Judy put the meat into her mouth and tried not to vomit.

Every day, her body burdened with the weight of her child, Judy hesitantly followed Van into the woods, praying he wouldn't shoot another animal. Van's bullet always met its mark.

Three weeks later, Van decided it was time to move on. Judy couldn't have been happier. The Van she saw in the woods was not the charming man she knew. She didn't like this Van.

Rufus gave them some money and an old family footlocker in which to pack their things. Van recognized it from his childhood. "Where did you get that?" he asked.

"Your father gave it to me years ago," Rufus told him.

Van opened it reverently, but the christening gowns and family documents it had once housed were gone. He inhaled its familiar cedar scent before filling it with the few items he and Judy had brought with them.

Rufus silently wished them good riddance as my parents headed off to Jackson, Mississippi, where Van rented a cheap room in a motel frequented by prostitutes. It was a far cry from the hotel in Acapulco, where the balcony overlooked the Pacific Ocean, and room service brought baskets of fresh fruit each day.

When their money ran out, Van got desperate.

"You know, we could earn some easy money at this motel," he told Judy. "All the girls do it. It's quick cash, and I don't think it will matter that you're pregnant. Some men really like that sort of thing."

Judy couldn't believe what she was hearing. "You want me to sleep with men for money?"

"It's just until we get enough cash to get out of here," Van persuaded her.

"No," Judy yelled. "I won't do it. How could you even ask me that? I'm pregnant!"

"I know," Van retorted. "That's what got us into this mess." He stormed out of the room, slamming the door behind him.

Judy threw herself on the bed, crying. She hadn't bargained for any of this. Van had promised her excitement. He had said he would take care of her. She thought about calling her mother, but she didn't want to go back to juvenile hall, and she was afraid of what Van would do.

Van was in a better mood when he returned. He had gotten a man he met to cash a bad check for forty-five dollars.

"Get packed," he told Judy. "We're going to New Orleans."

15

America's most wanted couple arrived in New Orleans a few days after Christmas 1962, the gloomiest time of the year for outsiders in the City that Care Forgot. Van, using the alias Harry Lee, wrote a bad check to a man he encountered named Morris Stark, swindling enough money from the kindhearted gentleman to rent a run-down apartment at 1215 Josephine Street, two and a half blocks from St. Charles Avenue, in the city's Garden District. This area, once home to New Orleans aristocracy, had experienced a decline during the Great Depression when wealthy landowners were forced to sell their side yards for enough money to maintain their positions in society. Cheap apartments, poorly built because money was scarce, sprouted up along all of the streets bordering St. Charles Avenue, their design a startling contrast to the architectural masterpieces next door. Poor working-class people and vagrants flocked to the area, attracted by the inexpensive rent and cheap transportation afforded by the St. Charles streetcars.

Staying in their cramped apartment as much as possible during the day and going out for short stretches only at night, Van and Judy managed to attract little attention in this busy section of New Orleans. Once in a while, strangers would comment on Judy's growing belly or ask when the baby was due, but Van brushed them aside, not interested in chatting with anyone unless he was trying to scam them.

Judy tried to be happy about her pregnancy, but Van was having none of it. He could not have cared less about the impending birth of his child. Still, Judy tried to please him, cooking and cleaning and not asking too many questions when he went out alone at night, his face hidden beneath a hat. Nothing she did worked. Although he repeatedly vowed his love for her, Van belittled her swollen belly, offended somehow by its very presence.

Less than two months after arriving in New Orleans, on February 12, 1963, I was born Earl Van Dorne Best. (I'm not sure why my father added the *e* to Dorn—or whether that was a mistake made by the hospital.)

Van called William.

"I need the money I gave you," he said. "Judy had this damn baby, and I need to pay the hospital bill before they'll let her go. Can you wire it?"

"Of course," William said, "but Van, I need you to get back here as soon as possible."

"Why? What's going on?"

"I got arrested. They charged me as an accessory for bringing you and Judy to the airport when you eloped. I have to stand trial, and I need you to testify that I didn't know how old she was."

"You know I can't do that," Van said. "They'll arrest me the minute I get to San Francisco."

"Van, please. This could ruin my career if I'm found guilty."

"Sorry, man. I can't do it."

William hung up the phone. He wired Van the money, but he was angry that his friend would not help him.

Van paid the hospital bill.

The nurses at Southern Baptist Hospital, on Napoleon Avenue, did not know how young my mother was or they might have provided her with some instruction about child care before sending her home. After elementary guidance to a girl they thought was nineteen, they had smiled and waved good-bye, saying, "You take care of little Earl now." That had been it.

Two weeks later, my father, out of money and finding no one he could persuade to take his checks, talked my still-healing mother into taking a job as a cocktail waitress in a bar in the French Quarter. Van befriended the owner of the Ship Ahoy Saloon, on the corner of Decatur and Toulouse Streets, across from Jackson Brewery, and lied about Judy's age to get her the job. The bar was a favorite of thirsty sailors who arrived at the Port of New Orleans on the Mississippi River, a block away.

In addition to the bar on the ground floor, with seven French doors that were always kept open, the establishment featured a hotel on the three floors above, where sailors could conveniently retire with the girl of their choice after a rowdy night of drinking. Loud music streaming from the open doors attracted passersby, and the bar never wanted for patrons. It was notorious for its violent clientele, with bloody noses the predictable ending to each raucous night.

One evening after work, Judy stepped out of the St. Charles streetcar a few blocks from her home, shivering as the breeze off the Mississippi swept through her. It was early March and still cold—forty-three degrees and rainy. The skimpy outfit she wore beneath her coat, a requirement at the Ship Ahoy, did little to protect her from the cold. Judy hid her fear of the sailors well, smiling and flirting and lightly slapping overzealous hands to earn enough money to buy me formula and to keep Van supplied with the gin he needed for the Tom Collinses he now loved to drink.

This was survival, and my mother had learned a lot about survival from Van.

As always, Judy kept her head down as she walked. The police were still looking for them, and she worried about being recognized from photographs in the newspapers. Relief washed through her when she turned the corner onto Josephine Street. Our neighbor Charlie was outside, braving the rain to make sure she arrived safely, his fragile body silhouetted by the porch lamp. Van would never think to wait up for her—she could take care of herself. The old man, his face rutted from years spent working at the port, smiled and took Judy's arm, leading her toward the small courtyard in the center of the building.

"How'd you do tonight, girlie?" he asked, stopping her before she turned to walk up the stairs.

"I made enough to buy the baby some formula, but those sailors are rough," Judy said. "I think I have some bruises on my backside to prove it."

"You shouldn't be working there, child," the old man said. He worried about Judy. He had worried since she moved into the building with the man she said was her husband. He didn't like Van, didn't trust him. He could see the devil in his eyes. Charlie had lived in New Orleans all his life, had been raised with the voodoo traditions passed down through his family for generations. He knew evil when he saw it. Van scared him, and the old man did not scare easily. He had known from the minute he met them that he had to look out for my mother.

"The baby needs to eat," Judy responded, hugging the old man before she turned to walk up the stairs.

When she reached our apartment, she gingerly turned the knob. She didn't want the squeaky door to awaken my father. Hurrying over to Van's old family trunk, which now served as my makeshift bed, she quickly pulled the heavy lid open to find me lying inside with blue-tinged lips.

Barely breathing.

This happened almost every night.

She picked me up and cradled me in her arms, anxiously rocking back and forth to keep me quiet while I gasped for air, grateful that I would make it through another night.

Awakened by the sound of the lid opening, Van watched jealously.

Judy had dared to ask him a few nights before why he kept shutting me up in the trunk at night. "I'm sick of hearing him cry," Van had informed her. Judy kept silent. She knew better than to talk back to him. Van's temper had become increasingly worse since they arrived in New Orleans, and she had seen the signs of his cruelty to me more than once.

Blood on my nose.

A cut on my head.

She was petrified that Van would kill me, but he insisted she had to work. It was her responsibility to earn the money if she wanted me to eat.

"We've got to get rid of this kid," Van suddenly announced from his perch on the bed. "I'm going to bring him somewhere."

"You can't do that! Bring him where?" Judy cried.

"I don't know yet, but I can't take his constant screaming. It drives me crazy."

Judy ran into the hallway, still holding me in her arms, afraid of what Van might do. She knew she had to figure out a way to keep me away from my father. She wished things were different, like they had been before. She tried to be a good mother but had no knowledge of how to take proper care of an infant. She knew nothing about colic or burping a baby, nothing about how to prevent diaper rash or about trying different types of formula to learn what worked best. And with no money, even buying formula had become a problem. Being hungry only made me cry more, but whenever my mother reached out to comfort me, Van became angry. He couldn't stand it when her attention was directed toward me.

Slowly, she made her way downstairs, hoping Charlie was still by the fountain in the courtyard.

"You okay?" the old man said when he saw her.

Judy brushed the tears from her eyes with the back of her hand.

"Yeah, I'm okay."

"That's a fine boy you got there."

Judy smiled through her tears. "He's beautiful, isn't he?"

Charlie nodded, putting his finger out for me to hold. "You got your hands full, huh, *cher*?"

"Sometimes I just don't know what to do about things," Judy said.

"Well, my mama always tol' me, 'Just do what's in your heart.' Dat's all you can do."

The old man turned and walked up the stairs, leaving Judy alone with her thoughts. She sat in a chair by a doorway, staring mindlessly down the street as she rocked me back and forth. In the drizzle, beautiful flowers and foliage poked through the lamplit balconies along Josephine Street.

At first Judy had liked New Orleans, had felt safe there, hidden among so many people. It was a lot like San Francisco—edgy and beautiful, yet ugly, too. The Vieux Carré, or French Quarter, was a striking contrast between intricate French, Creole, and Spanish architecture, with balconies dressed in lacy wrought iron, and dark alleyways where winos drowned their sorrows in bottles wrapped in brown paper bags. Scantily clad prostitutes paraded up and down the narrow streets, earning meager wages for their talents, while wealthier ladies dressed in the latest styles perused antiques stores. The stench of urine from the alleys mingling with the tantalizing aroma of spicy seafood streaming from open restaurant doors permeated the Quarter. Beauty and degradation weaved together in a splendid cacophony thirteen blocks long and six blocks wide.

But the homes lining St. Charles Avenue, only blocks away, were part of a different and more gracious past in which huge mansions, many built in majestic Greek Revival, Italianate, or Colonial styles, with massive Corinthian columns and sprawling porches, had ostentatiously displayed the wealth of cotton moguls, politicians, and industrial tycoons. St. Charles Avenue was paradise plastered on the fringes of hell, the same hell that was filtering into Haight-Ashbury, back home in San Francisco. Judy could handle that sort of thing, even at her age. It was the hell inside her apartment that she couldn't handle. She dared not defend me against Van's rages, for fear that he would turn on her or, worse, leave her all alone.

When I began stirring, Judy hurried back to the apartment to boil water to warm my bottle. Van walked up behind her, wrapping his arms around her waist. "You're not mad, are you, baby? You know how much I love you."

Judy squeezed his hand. "Of course I'm not mad. I can't stay mad at you."

She checked to make sure my formula was not too hot. "Just let me feed Earl and put him to sleep. Then I'm all yours."

"That's my girl," Van said, slapping her on her behind.

Judy winced, the night's bruises still fresh. She fed me as fast as she could and laid me in the trunk, covering me with the receiving blankets the hospital had given her, leaving the lid open.

"Come get in bed," Van commanded. "I've got a busy day planned for tomorrow, and I can't sleep without you."

Judy quickly shucked her clothes and climbed into bed. Van pulled her into his arms and nuzzled her hair. "I'm going to make everything better soon," he whispered.

The next morning, Van got up and dressed while Judy was still asleep. Fumbling through her purse, his frustration rising, he jolted her awake. "Where's the money you made last night?" he demanded.

Judy looked at him without understanding.

"I need cash for the train. I'm taking the baby to Baton Rouge. It's the closest big city to New Orleans, and the capital of Louisiana," he informed her, as if these facts were of importance.

My mother looked around anxiously and saw me wrapped in my blanket on the floor next to the bed.

"He will be given a good home there," Van cajoled when he saw the stunned look on her face.

Judy jumped out of bed and grabbed for me. "Please, can't we keep him? I'll keep him quiet, I promise."

"No. I'm sick of him. All he does is cry," Van said, picking me up and jerking me out of her reach. "I want my life back."

My mother was no match for him. She knew she wouldn't win this fight. She had known since the day I was born that something bad was going to happen. Van hated me, and that was that. She was a fugitive dependent on my father to keep her safe, and there was nothing she could do except let him take me.

Judy turned to hide her tears as she handed him my bottle. Van refused to take it. "He doesn't need to eat right now," he said firmly, walking toward the door.

My mother grabbed my pacifier and put it in my mouth, fervently hoping that it would keep me from crying. When she tried to kiss me good-bye, Van pushed her aside.

The bang of the closing door reverberated through the room, and Judy sank to the floor, crying.

16

"All aboard!" the conductor of the Southern Belle yelled as people from all walks of life hurried toward the train bound for Baton Rouge. Part of the Kansas City Southern Railway, this passenger train, with its brightly colored yellow-and-red engine, traveled from New Orleans to Kansas City, Missouri, between the 1940s and the 1960s, with stops at cities like Baton Rouge and Shreveport, Louisiana.

Van hurried with the others to reach the train station on time. It was a short walk from the apartment, about ten minutes. Charity Hospital, known to the locals as "Big Charity," was only a few minutes' walk past the train station, but in the early 1960s, there were no "safe haven" laws that allowed parents to leave unwanted children at hospitals, police stations, or fire stations. If you wanted to dispose of a child at that time, you had to get creative.

"That'll be nine dollars even, four-fifty each way," the ticket master said. "The little guy rides for free."

Van paid for the round-trip ticket to Baton Rouge and boarded the train, which had been designed for passenger comfort, making his way down the spacious aisle to his seat. Other passengers had no clue that the nice-looking gentleman holding the infant was on such a dastardly mission. A few minutes later, the train pulled out of the station, and the rocking motion and the rhythmic sounds of the steel wheels upon the rails lulled me to sleep. Van held me while I napped, by all appearances a loving father as he settled further into his seat.

As the train rolled alongside Highway 61 toward its destination, it paralleled the Bonnet Carré Spillway, built in 1937, after the Great Mississippi Flood of 1927. Its purpose was to divert water from the Mississippi River into Lake Pontchartrain whenever the mighty Mississippi threatened to overspill its banks and flood the soup bowl that is New Orleans. In the distance, Norco Refinery, with its smoky plumes billowing into fluffy clouds, cast an eerie glow on the dreary, misty horizon.

Once we were past the swampland that borders Lake Pontchartrain, sugarcane fields, rice fields, and tall willows lined the tracks. As the Southern Belle approached Gramercy, the train's horn sounded, signaling drivers to beware its massive strength. Before long, passengers could see wooden shotgun houses fronted by rickety porches where families and friends often gathered to drink beer and feast on large, simmering pots of gumbo or jambalaya.

Our journey was almost over when the train passed the towns of Gonzales and Prairieville, the landscape here turning to marsh filled with huge live oaks whose branches, weighted with moss, hung low.

About twenty minutes later, a voice over the intercom announced, "Baton Rouge Depot" as the train squealed to a stop.

Van stood up, pulled me close to him, and exited the train on the west side of the station. He walked across the tracks and made his way up South River Road. My father could not help but notice the Old State Capitol, a neo-Gothic structure located on a hill overlooking the Mississippi River that is so memorable Mark Twain once wrote, "It is pathetic enough, that a white-washed castle, with turrets and things—pretending to be what they are not—should ever have been built in this otherwise honorable place."

A light wind began to swirl as Van turned right onto North

Boulevard. My thin blanket did little to shield me from the cool air. Looking for the perfect spot, my father passed by the State Library of Louisiana and then the police and sheriff's departments, housed together in one building. Fallen leaves and acorns from the plentiful live oaks that decorated downtown Baton Rouge crunched beneath his feet as he walked. Reaching the top of a hill, Van could see a needle-like structure that resembled the spaceship NASA was planning to send to the moon one day. Built by Huey P. Long, the Louisiana State Capitol stretched upward 450 feet and housed thirty-four floors, making it the tallest state capitol building in the country. To his right, the Old Governor's Mansion, home to Louisiana's singing governor, Jimmie Davis, who had risen to fame with his song "You Are My Sunshine," bore a strong resemblance to the White House.

Bells sounded out a chorus of the traditional Westminster chime from an old Anglican church. It was 11:00 a.m.

Just a little farther up North Boulevard stood an apartment building bordered by St. Joseph and Napoleon Streets. Built in a Georgian Colonial style, the redbrick building housed eight single-family dwellings. White-tile steps with the number 736 inlaid in blue tiles led the way to the front door. Crape myrtles and azalea bushes decorated the yard with brilliant splashes of color.

It was perfect. Because there were no spots allotted for parking on the busy street, Van knew there must be a back entrance. He carried me around the corner to St. Joseph Street, searching for the gate in the wrought-iron fence that he guessed would be there. Opening it, he stepped into a courtyard behind the building that featured beautiful oaks, an old sugar kettle with a fountain, and seclusion. He scoured the parking lot to the left to be sure he was alone and unobserved.

Climbing up two steps, Van turned the knob on the back door and walked into the building unseen.

He stepped onto a black-and-white checkerboard floor and noticed two apartment doors on either side of a foyer. A staircase straight ahead beckoned to him. He climbed three stairs and then walked onto a landing. Looking up, he saw more apartments. He hurried up the stairs, noted the apartment numbers, and went back down to the landing, determining that it would be the best place.

Van wrapped me tightly in the dirty blue blanket and laid me there on the floor, making sure the pacifier was in my mouth so I would not cry before he was able to make his escape.

My father turned away, leaving me alone in the stairwell, clad only in a white towel that served as my diaper.

Decades later, I would realize that the day my father abandoned me was the luckiest day of my life.

Others Earl Van Best Jr. encountered would not be so lucky.

17

Mary Bonnette was in no particular hurry as she strolled along North Boulevard on her way home from her job at Ethyl Corporation on March 15, 1963. She had no plans for the weekend other than enjoying the St. Patrick's Day parade that would roll in front of her apartment that Sunday. Mary liked living in downtown Baton Rouge, where politicians, lawyers, and judges mingled easily with more common folks who frequented area restaurants or sat on the levee watching boats traverse the Mississippi River. The hustle and bustle in this capital city seemed less frantic than in other, larger downtowns across the country, partly because of the beauty that enveloped the area. Although senators and representatives did indeed hurry toward the capitol steps, they were never too busy to talk with passersby who recognized them. Even Governor Jimmie Davis was never too busy to stop and sign an autograph for a fan.

Mary, the Jewish daughter of first-generation immigrants from Poland, had recently divorced. As she approached 736 North Boulevard, at about 4:30 p.m., and walked around the side of the building, she smiled, relieved that the weekend was finally here and she was home. She enjoyed her work at Ethyl but always looked forward to her weekends. Climbing the brick stairs at the back entrance, she reached into her mailbox, retrieving a single piece of mail before opening the door.

Mary had taken a few steps across the small lobby that led to the stairway to the second floor when she heard the sound of a baby crying. When she reached the landing, her heart stopped for a moment.

There, lying on the cold marble floor, was a naked infant. I was crying and kicking my feet. My soiled receiving blanket and pacifier had fallen next to me.

Mary looked around to see if she could find my parents. She knew that none of the residents in the building had children and wondered if someone had just left me there for a minute. She didn't see anyone. Just then, I let out a scream, snapping Mary into action. She stepped around me and ran up the stairs to apartment number 8.

When she got inside, Mary dialed the number for Judge C. Lenton Sartain. She and the judge had become friends after her divorce, and Mary was certain he would know what to do.

"Lenton, there's a baby on my stairway landing," she told him. "I found him there when I got home from work. It looks like someone just left him."

"I'll get help," the judge calmly said. "You go check on the baby, but keep your door open so you can hear the phone. I'll call you right back."

When he hung up with Mary, the judge double-clicked the receiver on his rotary phone and was immediately connected to the operator.

"Get me Chief Wingate White of the Baton Rouge Police Department," he said.

"I'll get Captain Weiner over there," Wingate said when the judge explained the situation.

Robert Weiner, the first appointed captain of the BRPD's newly created juvenile division, sent Officers Essie Bruce and J. Laper to the address on North Boulevard the judge had given him.

Judge Sartain called Mary and told her that help was on the way. "Keep an eye on the baby," he said.

"Oh, I hear the sirens now," Mary said, with relief. She went downstairs to keep an eye on me, but she didn't pick me up. She was afraid that she might disturb some evidence the police would need.

While Laper questioned Mary, Officer Bruce picked me up. Feeling the comforting warmth of a human touch, I stopped crying. The two officers placed me in their police car and, sirens wailing, rushed me to Baton Rouge General Hospital.

After leaving me to be examined by Dr. Charles Bombet, the emergency room doctor, Laper returned to the apartment building and interviewed residents, looking for anyone who might have seen who'd left me there. No one had seen anything.

Dr. Bombet determined that I was three or four weeks old and had been born in a hospital, based on the fact that I had been circumcised. He informed Captain Weiner that I was in good condition but should be hospitalized overnight for observation.

Judge Sartain assured Weiner that he would personally contact Catherine Braun, at the Welfare Department, the following morning regarding my placement in the state's Infant Center.

Laper returned to the police station just down the street and examined the blanket, towel, and pacifier that had been found with me. On the towel he noticed an imprint—815 LA or 818 LA; he couldn't be sure which it was. He found the name NATIONAL stamped on the border, and the manufacturer's name, CANNON, was attached on the back side of the towel. The items were then wrapped and tagged to be sent to the Louisiana State Police Crime Lab for examination.

The next day, the Baton Rouge *Morning Advocate* ran the story on the front page. In the article, Captain Weiner pleaded with the parents to come forward. "We don't know if the child is on special formula or has some condition that may effect [*sic*] his health. We realize the person who abandoned the child probably thought he or she had no other recourse, but there are ways of helping these people without their having to abandon their children."

Baton Rouge was abuzz about Baby John Doe. Nothing like this had ever happened before.

Mary Bonnette, sitting alone in her apartment, was no longer as excited about the parade as she had been the day before. She had not slept much during the night. She had been worried about me. The thirty-seven-year-old did not have any children of her own, and she had already begun to think of me as hers in a way. After all, she had been the one who found me. She had to know how I was doing, so she picked up the phone.

"How's my baby?" she asked Judge Sartain, her first cup of coffee still in her hand.

"Your baby's in fine hands," the judge replied. "He's going to have a good home, and everything's going to be fine."

A few minutes after she hung up, her phone rang.

"Are you the lady who found the baby?" a male voice said.

"Why, yes, I am," Mary said. "Who is this?"

The man did not answer. "The mother of the baby is destitute. She could not take care of him," was his only response.

"Are you his father?"

"Yes," the man said.

"Where are you calling from?"

Again, no answer.

"Look, the mother wants the child back. She will be at the police station sometime this morning to get the baby," the man said.

The operator's voice interrupted, instructing the man to insert more money.

The line went dead.

It was just after 8:00 a.m. when Mary called the police. She related the conversation to an Officer Reily. "I think he was calling long-distance, because the operator said his time was up," she said. "He wouldn't tell me who he was, but he did say he was the father."

Officer Reily jotted down some notes. He and Officer Reine, of the Records Division, headed to Baton Rouge General Hospital to look for birth certificates for all white males born between February 1 and March 4. Nothing matched the footprints of Baby John Doe. Records from Our Lady of the Lake Hospital did not match, either.

Captain Weiner instructed Officer Gouner to track down the laundry tag on the towel that had been found with the baby. Gouner's first stop was Kean's laundry. Wilber Amiss Kean, the owner, inspected the towel and informed him, "That's from the National Linen company, out of New Orleans."

Gouner went back to the station to share the information with Weiner, who called Major Edward Reuther, supervisor of the juvenile division in New Orleans. Weiner explained that an abandoned child had been found in his city.

"We found a towel with the baby. It has markings from National Linen. Can you help us track down where the towel was delivered?" he said.

"We'll help any way we can," the major said.

Other officers in Baton Rouge were busy chasing down leads that kept coming in about suspicious characters, unwed mothers, and pregnant women who might have had babies and left them at the apartment. The media was having a field day with the story, and the publicity was hampering the investigation.

By March 20 police had tracked down most of the leads, with no results. My parents were nowhere to be found. Sergeant Ballard of the Baton Rouge Police Department called the linen company and asked if the numbers and markings on the towel were traceable. The answer was no.

My mother did not show up at the police station to collect me.

For the next month, a state-appointed foster family took care of me while police in Baton Rouge continued their search for my parents, but they learned nothing new about the identity of Baby John Doe.

18

When my father returned to New Orleans without me, Judy begged him to tell her where I was.

"What have you done, Van? Where is my son?" she cried.

"He's fine, Judy. I left him at an apartment building where someone will find him. He'll be okay. He'll go to a good family who can afford to take care of him. Now, stop crying. This is ridiculous."

Judy cried even harder.

When he realized he couldn't console her, Van promised he would get me back.

Judy didn't believe him—she knew he hated me—and began plotting her escape.

She had met a man at the Ship Ahoy named Jerry, who flirted with her and made promises about giving her a better life. Anything was better than the life she had, and before long, Judy began flirting back.

On the morning of April 18, my mother waited for Van to leave the apartment, then she packed her meager belongings and took a taxi to 642 Dauphine Street, where Jerry lived. His apartment was small—a living room, kitchen, and bath, with a loft upstairs—but it was nicer than the places she had lived with Van. Jerry welcomed her with open arms.

Van was furious when he returned home and discovered that Judy and all of her things had disappeared. He went to the Ship Ahoy and questioned the owner, whom he had befriended when he got Judy the job there. The owner informed him that Judy had been flirting with a customer named Jerry. "Tell me where he lives," Van demanded.

"I don't know where he lives, but I'll find out for you," the owner said.

A few hours later, he gave Van the address.

Bent on revenge, Van picked up the phone and called the police.

"I'd like to make a complaint," Van told Desk Sergeant Charles Barrett, of the New Orleans Police Department, after giving his name. "I ran away from San Francisco with Judith Chandler in August last year," he said. "We came to New Orleans in January. She left me this morning, just called a cab and left. She's a wanted fugitive. Check it out. You'll see. She's living on Dauphine Street. She took all my money and my clothes. I want her arrested."

Barrett handed the complaint to patrolmen Roland Fournier and Charles Jonau, who checked with cab companies and discovered that a Judy Chandler had taken a United Cab company taxi from 1215 Josephine to 642 Dauphine.

"Pick her up," Barrett instructed the officers when Van's information had been verified.

Fournier and Jonau staked out the location, parking midway between Orleans Avenue and St. Peter Street. Facing southwest, they could not miss their suspect if she walked up Toulouse and turned onto Dauphine.

It was after midnight when they spotted Judy, walking arm in arm with a man. Before they could get inside, the officers stopped them and placed them both in handcuffs.

Jerry, a married businessman from Seattle, who had talked the teenager into sex with the promise of helping her retrieve her baby, was questioned and released. Judy was arrested for vagrancy and taken to juvenile hall, this time twenty-two hundred miles from her home.

She seemed unafraid while she was being booked into custody. She bantered with the officers, acting as though nothing were amiss. Fournier, watching her every move, would later describe her as cunning. Being arrested did not seem to bother her at all.

Aware that Van had turned her in, Judy started spilling her guts.

"I'm fifteen," she said proudly. "I don't know why you're arresting me. You should be arresting the man who called you. He took my baby and abandoned him in Baton Rouge."

Fournier and Jonau were listening.

"What baby?"

Jonau left the room to call Captain Weiner in Baton Rouge and confirm that they had an abandoned child. When he came back, he nodded affirmation to Fournier, who continued questioning Judy, who told them everything.

"We ran away from San Francisco last year," she explained, according to police reports. "We've lived in lots of cities, and I didn't want to come here. Van insisted that I should have the baby here.

We got here December 30. I had a baby February 12 of this year at Baptist Hospital. I named him after Van, but he was cruel to the baby, locked him in the footlocker with the lid down. I came home from work every night and the baby was barely breathing. Finally he took him to Baton Rouge and left him on the stairs of an apartment building on the main street. And he bounced checks across the country," Judy added for good measure.

The officers decided to hold her at the Youth Study Center while they checked out her story.

Fournier placed a call to San Francisco and learned that Van was wanted for child stealing, rape, and conspiracy. Upon verification that he was indeed a fugitive, a warrant was issued for his arrest. Fournier and Jonau went to Van's address on Josephine Street with the warrant in hand. His landlady informed them that their suspect had moved out "to parts unknown," assuring them that she would call them if she heard from him.

The next day, Captain Weiner traveled to New Orleans with another officer to meet my mother. He wondered what kind of person could just abandon a child like that. The captain was somewhat surprised when he learned that Judy was just a teenager. When he showed her pictures of me, Judy tearfully identified me as her own. Weiner interrogated her as he would any criminal until he was satisfied that the story he heard was the truth. He then transported her to Baton Rouge to attend a hearing about what should be done with me.

Judy was on her way out of New Orleans that afternoon when her former landlady telephoned the police. She said that Van had called. "He told me he was at St. Louis Cathedral," the landlady said.

Jonau and Fournier headed to Pirate's Alley, an appropriate area in which to find their subject. Legend says that the one-block-long alley, which runs from Chartres Street to Royal Street, was once a safe haven for pirates, although its very location, with the historic St.

Louis Cathedral to the right and the Cabildo, the site of the Louisiana Purchase transfer, in 1803, to the left, contradicted the tale. The Faulkner House, where William Faulkner wrote his first novel, is located near Royal Street in Pirate's Alley and attracts thousands of tourists each year. During the day, the alley is welcoming, filled with artists and street performers, but in the wee hours of the morning, when sin runs rampant in the Quarter, Pirate's Alley takes on an eerie cast. Its salvation, perhaps, is the huge cathedral that overlooks the alley, reminding the sinful below that God is in this place.

Van might have been looking for a safe haven when he chose to visit the cathedral, some absolution for his sins before he was forced to pay his penance. Or perhaps he wanted to view the cathedral's organ and the artwork of Italian painter Francisco Zapari, who mimicked Michelangelo by painting the arched ceilings of the church in the bright colors of the Renaissance before adding his own Baroque signature.

Van walked to the front of the church and exited through a side door into an alley. The rectory was directly in front of him, and he went inside.

When Fournier and Jonau arrived at the rectory, they learned from the receptionist that Van was still there. He did not resist when they took him into custody.

Van admitted to being cruel to me, locking me in his footlocker, and abandoning me because he and Judy had decided they didn't want me. "We didn't have the money to feed it," he told the officers, who noted that this father had referred to his son as "it." They took him to the First District station and booked him as a fugitive.

The next day, April 20, the headline in the *San Francisco Chronicle* read, "Love on the Run: Ice Cream Romance's Bitter End," and Paul Avery detailed the capture of the runaway couple. Another headline announced, "Ice Cream Romance Ends on Bourbon St." All across the country, newspapers repeated the tale of the lovebirds who had become fugitives to be together, only to be torn apart by the product of their love.

In Baton Rouge, Judy sat alone in a small, cold room near a window that faced the Mississippi River. Her heart was racing, her nerves twitching. She folded her hands together, trying to focus on the handcuffs that now bound her wrists, but she could not see clearly because of the tears that blurred her vision.

After hours of interrogation, Judy had finally given the police her mother's telephone number. The director of social services had called Verda and informed her that Judy had given birth to a son and that the child had later been abandoned.

"Your daughter has been arrested," the director informed Verda.

Calling on her own experience with her rapist's child, Verda decided that Judy could be returned to her custody only after she agreed to voluntarily relinquish custody of me to the state of Louisiana. Verda knew that was the right thing to do. Judy was too young to be burdened with a permanent reminder of the man who had kidnapped and raped her. My mother signed the papers giving me up for adoption. She had no other choice. She would be allowed to see me for a few minutes before she was transported back to San Francisco.

Judy could not control the stream of tears that ran down her face as she waited for someone to bring me to her. Just when she thought she could no longer bear the silence in the room, Margie Stewart, an attractive young social worker, opened the door. Awakened by the movement, I let out a startling squeal. Margie, who would soon become my adoptive aunt, placed me in my mother's arms.

Another social worker and a uniformed officer had followed Margie into the room. "Ma'am, we'll give you ten minutes," the social worker told her in a solemn voice. Judy barely registered the words as she lifted me up and kissed my forehead. Searching my face, she noticed for the first time that I had huge dimples. She kissed me on my nose, my cheeks, my hands. I grabbed a handful of her hair but didn't pull it. I just held it in my tiny grip.

"Mommy loves you," Judy repeated over and over. "Mommy loves you so much."

The steel door opened, signaling that Judy's time with me had come to an end. My mother let out a scream, which made me scream. She pulled me tightly to her chest, as if to protect me from what was about to happen.

"Ma'am, we have to be going now," Margie said.

"No," Judy moaned.

Margie reached out to take me, but Judy held me tightly.

"No! You can't take my baby! I'm not leaving him. I'll be a good mother. He needs me. See, he's crying. He needs his mommy."

The officer held her by her shoulders while Margie pried me from her arms.

"Mommy loves you," Judy cried. "I'm sorry, baby. I'll come back for you."

With one final tug, Margie managed to wrench me away. In my hand, I held a few strands of my mother's hair.

Judy stopped fighting and listened intently to my cries as they took me away, until she could hear me no more.

She laid her head on the table, sobbing.

19

Judy and Van were extradited to California. Judy was sentenced to six months to two years in the youth correctional facility in Camarillo, and Van was sent back to a cell in the Hall of Justice.

Earl received the news from Gertrude.

"They caught Van in New Orleans," she told Earl over the phone. "They sent him back here. He's in jail. I don't think you can get him out of this one."

"I'm on my way," Earl said.

He booked the next flight to San Francisco and made the familiar trck to the police station on Bryant Street.

"I'm here to see my son, Earl Van Best Jr.," he announced to an officer sitting behind a glass partition.

"Sign in," the officer instructed.

The officer looked at his identification and told Earl to wait.

"You can go through there," he said a few minutes later, directing the chaplain into a small room.

"Is my son all right?" Earl asked, taking a seat.

"Sir, your son is pure evil," the officer said.

Earl didn't reply. He couldn't. But he would share the frightening comment with his family later.

While he waited, Earl prayed for God's guidance.

The door finally opened, and Van was ushered in by another officer.

Earl tried to get Van to explain why he had abandoned me, but Van was uncooperative. He didn't want to listen to his father preaching about the consequences of sin. Earl assured Van that he would try to get the baby back, but Van was not interested.

Disgusted, Earl walked out of the room.

The following day, Earl flew home, collected Ellie, and boarded another flight, this one bound for New Orleans International Airport.

"I can't let the baby be raised in an orphanage," he explained to his wife en route. "I hope you understand. He's my grandson and probably scared to death. You know they don't take proper care of babies in those places."

"Well, I don't know about that, but I do understand. It'll be okay. We'll find him, honey," Ellie said. "We'll bring him home with us." She understood more than Earl thought. She knew that I would be Earl's atonement for his sin, for his failure with my father.

After they landed, my grandfather hired a car to take them to Baton Rouge. They went first to the police station and then to the state child welfare agency.

"I'm trying to find a baby," he told the receptionist. "The newspapers called him Baby John Doe. His mother is Judy Chandler, and his father is Earl Van Best Jr. I am his grandfather. I would like to adopt the child."

"I'm so sorry, sir," the receptionist said. "Baby John Doe has already been adopted."

"Who adopted him?" Earl asked.

"That's confidential. I cannot reveal that information," the receptionist said.

My grandfather was too late.

A few days later, Earl traveled to Battery Park, in New York City, an invited guest of the president of the United States, to honor him for the work he had done as a commander in the U.S. Naval Reserve and as national chaplain of the Veterans of Foreign Wars. He led the invocation before John F. Kennedy dedicated the East Coast Memorial to the Missing at Sea. In his opening remarks, Kennedy referred directly to my grandfather, addressing him as "Reverend."

What should have been the proudest moment of Earl's life was tainted by the stain Van had placed on his name.

20

On May 17, 1963, Leona Stewart received a call from the state child welfare agency.

"We have a three-month-old boy for you," the social worker announced. "Can you meet me in the parking lot at Piccadilly Cafeteria, on Government Street?"

Leona hobbled outside to tell Loyd the good news. Her husband looked up from the lawn mower, noting that Leona was moving faster than usual.

"We have a son!" she exclaimed. "They have a baby for us. We have to go. They're waiting."

Loyd left the mower where it was and helped Leona walk back into the house. He did not say a word. He couldn't. His heart was in his throat. All of the doubt, the heartache he had experienced, came welling up in this one moment.

All of the anger toward himself.

And God.

Leona Ortis and Loyd Stewart had both been born in the small Louisiana town of Krotz Springs just after the Great Depression. Although Loyd grew up in nearby Baton Rouge, much of his family still lived in the fishing village and farming community, and he visited them often. Krotz Springs had a very small population, and Loyd and Leona were from opposite sides of the tracks.

Leona's father owned a fish market and a country general store, and she worked behind the counter after school and on weekends. The beautiful brunette soon captured the eye of the dapper Loyd, who would trot up to the store on his old horse to call on her, or, as Loyd used to say, "to spark her." Although Loyd's family didn't have money, Leona didn't care. Every afternoon, she waited impatiently for the young Cajun gentleman to arrive, riding proudly on horseback to woo her. The couple began dating in high school and married when they were twenty years old. Loyd soon got a job in the mailroom at Ethyl Corporation, in Baton Rouge, while Leona worked at Webre Steel as a secretary and bookkeeper.

They settled into their new lives easily, their love for each other strong, and soon they began thinking about starting a family. What seemed like a good idea turned into steely determination as month after month, and then year after year, Leona waited to become pregnant.

"I don't understand," Leona said to Loyd as another year went by without her becoming pregnant. "Dr. Miller says I can have a child, but he won't tell me when."

Loyd began to worry that it was his fault, and the frustration they both felt began to take its toll. Even Leona, who believed God would answer her prayers, became less optimistic as the years wore on.

She finally approached Loyd with the idea of adoption, but to him that represented failure, and he resisted the idea.

"Let's just keep trying," he insisted.

Nine years into their marriage, they gave up and made the decision to adopt.

Loyd held Leona's hand as they entered the child welfare agency for their first interview with a social worker. "Don't say nothing. The room's bugged," he joked, trying to settle Leona's nerves. Loyd always joked. It was his way of dealing with any stressful situation.

It wasn't long before the state of Louisiana awarded them custody of a beautiful newborn baby girl. Leona named her Sheryl Lynn, after her boss, Lynn Webre.

"Look at her, Loyd. Isn't she beautiful?" Leona whispered, holding her new baby in her arms.

"She is," Loyd agreed, in love already.

Ten months later, the unthinkable happened.

On January 7, 1961, Loyd and Leona drove down Highway 190 toward Opelousas, Louisiana, for the wedding of L. J. Ortis, Leona's younger brother, to Mary Ann Fontenot. Leona's sisters

Evelyna Ortis Parker and Loretta Ortis Courville sat in the backseat, talking about the wedding. Loretta loved weddings. She had been the last of the Ortis girls to wed, and her marriage to Lawrence Courville was still in the honeymoon stage. Leona gleaned only bits and pieces of their conversation as she played with her adopted daughter, who was sitting on the seat next to her.

Theirs was the second-to-last car in a procession of family members driving to the wedding.

Loyd drove quietly, listening to the chatter of the ladies, careful not to follow too closely behind his brother-in-law, in the car ahead of him. Loyd had always been a cautious man. His father, Boone, had raised him that way.

"Patty cake, patty cake, baker's man," Leona sang to Sheryl, watching as the baby's smile revealed two tiny teeth that had just broken through her gumline. "Roll 'em and a roll 'em and a throw 'em in the pan," she continued, enjoying Sheryl's squeals of delight. Dressed in a light green dress with a white collar, the baby wore a gold bracelet around her small wrist, a present from Uncle Snook and Aunt Dorothy ten months earlier. Before leaving Baton Rouge that day, Uncle Snook had been sneaking Sheryl small pieces of chocolate until Leona caught him.

"Stop that," she'd admonished him. "My baby is not going to this wedding with chocolate all over her dress."

Loyd was smiling to himself, remembering his wife's reaction to that incident, when out of nowhere, a white 1960 Chrysler thundered into his lane, striking his 1959 Chevrolet head-on. The force of the impact propelled Leona into and then under the dashboard.

Loyd tried to protect his daughter from being thrown forward with his right arm, but his own body was already slamming into the steering wheel. His face hit the windshield, breaking his nose.

The baby did not stand a chance. Her forward motion had

been stopped too abruptly by the dashboard, and her neck was broken from the impact. Little Sheryl died instantly.

Snook swerved to avoid hitting the rear of Loyd's vehicle and watched in horror as Loyd's car flew through the air and landed in a ditch. When he wrenched open the door, he was stunned by what he saw.

Sheryl was lifeless, although there was not a drop of blood on her tiny body. Leona's mangled legs were pinned under the dashboard, and Loyd was bleeding profusely. Evelyna and Loretta, safer in the backseat, had not sustained serious injuries.

Uncle Snook and Aunt Dorothy rushed Sheryl to the nearest hospital, praying all the way for a miracle. Loyd, tears mixing with the blood on his face, held his wife's hand as he waited impatiently for paramedics to remove Leona from the wreckage.

For the next few days, Leona remained in a coma. When she finally regained consciousness, she asked for Sheryl.

"I'm so sorry, honey," her mother said. "Your baby died in the crash."

"And Loyd? Where's Loyd?" Leona screamed, struggling to sit up.

"Loyd's fine. He's in the hospital, but he'll recover," her mother said. "Now, be still. They don't want you to move."

Leona lay back in the bed, unable to control the sobs that shook her body. She had waited so long for a baby, and now the little girl who had brought so much love and light into her life was gone.

Leona's hip, knee, and pelvis had been shattered in the accident. When orthopedic surgeon Moss Bannerman examined her, what he found frightened him. He informed her family that although she might not survive the ambulance ride from Opelousas to Baton Rouge, she needed to be transferred to Baton Rouge General Hospital right away. Bereaved over the loss of his daughter, Loyd signed the consent form to have Leona moved, fearful that he would lose his wife, too.

Loyd and Leona were both still hospitalized when family members gathered to bury their baby. For both of them, the pain of not being able to attend Sheryl's funeral was unbearable.

As she lay in her hospital bed day after day, Leona wondered why God had taken her baby away. "God must have decided I'm not fit to be a mother," she told Loyd.

"Nonsense. You can't think like that. You were a wonderful mother," Loyd reassured her, although he wasn't feeling any better. Inside, he was feeling guilty because he had resisted the idea of adoption at first. He wondered if he was being punished, but he kept his thoughts to himself as he held his wife's hand.

Understanding how this tragic loss would affect his son and daughter-in-law, Boone Stewart visited the child welfare office where his other daughter-in-law, Margie Stewart, worked. He appealed to her and to anyone else who would listen, telling them that they needed to place Loyd and Leona back on the prospective adoptive parents list, even though they were still in the hospital.

Over the next few weeks, Leona was pieced back together by the orthopedic surgeon. Dr. Bannerman instructed Loyd, who had been released from the hospital, to build a makeshift traction bed out of plywood and two-by-fours set on an angle and tilted sideways so that he could hang the counterweights of traction at different angles. The doctor needed to stretch Leona's broken body to equal lengths if she were ever to walk again.

Boone went to Goudeau-Huey Hardware & Paint Company, on Plank Road, and bought the wood and twelve-penny nails needed to build the bed. "We're moving Leona into our house," he informed Loyd. "We've got more room there, and we can help get her through this."

Loyd went to his parents' home to help build the bed, but he gasped when he saw his father driving nails through the two-by-fours and right into the beautiful hardwood floors in the living room.

"Daddy, what on earth are you doing? You're going to ruin your floor," he said.

Boone looked up at his son. "It's only wood, son. It's only wood."

When she was released from the hospital, Leona began her recovery in her father-in-law's living room. Every day, Boone and Loyd twisted and turned and adjusted her as she lay in that bed, unable to walk. Every day, Leona's screams of pain could be heard throughout the house. There were times Loyd and Boone thought they were killing her, but they followed the doctor's orders meticulously. And each day after they got her settled down, they went outside to cry. They could not let her see how much her pain was hurting them. But their efforts paid off.

Leona was just beginning to walk nine months later when, on August 21, 1961, she received a phone call. "Loyd, come here," she yelled when she hung up the phone. "We've got a baby. We've got a baby girl," she cried into his shoulder as he hugged her tightly.

Together they welcomed another child, whom they named Cindy Kaye, into their new home in Baton Rouge, both feeling very blessed that they had been given a second chance. Loyd and Leona showered Cindy with love, allowing their beautiful new baby to fill the void Sheryl's death had left, but no amount of love could heal the emotional wounds they had sustained from her loss.

Almost two years later, Leona received another call.

When his wife told him the news, Loyd rushed into the shower to get cleaned up. His heart was pounding as he scrubbed the sweat from his body. He had lived with the weight of Sheryl's death for so long. He had berated himself, wondering whether, if he'd paid more attention, maybe driven a little slower, his daughter would still be alive. He had challenged God repeatedly, asking Him why He had allowed this to happen. The whole town of Krotz Springs had attended the funeral at the First Baptist Church. Everyone but he and Leona had been able to say good-bye to their little girl, who looked so much like the Gerber baby. He had not understood how God could do something like that to them.

And then, when he had gone to Opelousas General Hospital and seen his unconscious wife with tubes and wires and bandages covering her bloodied body, again he blamed God.

However, he had listened when God spoke through the opening of Leona's eyes, through the movement of her hand when it had gently squeezed his, and then when she walked for the first time after the accident. He'd heard when God blessed them with Cindy, and now He was speaking to Loyd again.

Giving him another gift.

A son.

Leona had called Loyd's parents, and the two couples drove to the restaurant together. Boone pulled up next to a white van with a round decal denoting that it was a state-owned vehicle.

Loyd opened the back door and took Cindy from Leona's arms so she could use both hands to maneuver her way from the car. After handing Cindy to her grandmother, Loyd reached into the car, putting his left arm under Leona's legs, moving them outside onto the pavement. He squatted down, put his right arm around her waist, and gently pulled her onto her feet. Once she felt stable, they walked toward the van.

A lady holding a blanketed bundle emerged from the vehicle. Loyd saw me first, then Boone, and finally Leona.

"Look at those blue eyes," Loyd said. "And that strawberry blond hair."

"And he's smiling. Look at his dimples, Loyd," Leona said.

"He's precious," admired Evelyn.

Boone couldn't even speak. He just stared at me, trying to swallow the lump in his throat.

"We don't have much information about him except that one of his parents loved music," offered the social worker as she handed me to Leona. "We called him Philip while he was in foster care, but I'm sure y'all will want to give him a special new name. He's kind of colicky, and we've got him on goat's milk. Seems to agree with him better than anything else. Must've been plenty music around his home before, because sometimes when he won't stop crying, if we hum or sing to him, he calms right down. We'll check in with you in a day or two. If you have any questions or need anything, you know how to reach us. Congratulations."

There was no mention of Baby John Doe, no mention of my parents or the train ride. There was no mention of the stairwell. Loyd's sister-in-law, Margie, who had been instrumental in placing me with Loyd and Leona, didn't tell them that she had pulled me from my teenage mother's arms. She couldn't; it was a closed adoption, and Louisiana law forbade her from saying a word about my background. Loyd and Leona had no way of knowing what I had already experienced in only three months of life. All they knew was that God had given them another gift, and they were going to cherish me.

My new family walked into Piccadilly Cafeteria for dinner and a celebration. Leona kissed me on my forehead and pulled me close to her heart.

My new parents named me Gary Loyd Stewart.

Back in San Francisco, my real name was not mentioned again. That had been forbidden by Judy's mother. It was time for her to move on, to forget her past.

Three years later, on October 3, 1966, Leona miraculously would give birth to a baby girl, Christy Lee Stewart, after medical experts said her crushed womb would never support the birth of a child. Doctor Miller had once told her she could have children, but Leona and Loyd had long since given up on that dream. God had blessed them yet again.

21

In San Francisco, Van's troubles were mounting, but Earl went to bat for him. Convinced that his son must have some kind of mental disorder, Earl decided that Van did not belong in prison and that perhaps a mental health care facility might be the better consequence for his actions—a place where his son could get the help he needed. He suggested that Van write to South Carolina senator Strom Thurmond and ask the senator to act on his behalf. Thurmond agreed to speak with Superior Court Judge Norman Elkington, because Van was the son of a military commander. The judge would later state that he "wasn't swayed at all by Thurmond's letter asking that he look carefully into the case," according to the *San Francisco Chronicle*.

"Thurmond, former judge and a former governor, was ignorant of a number of aspects of the case, including the fact that California's statutory age is 18, not 16," the article stated. "These statutory cases are usually just young love," Thurmond's aide, Ed Kenney, tried to explain.

Others also stood up for Van—Reverend Hubert Doran, who testified before the court that Van's character was quite good, and Van's high school teacher Norval Fast, who stated that Van had never seemed like a common criminal.

William Lohmus, still upset with Van for not helping him at his own court hearing, refused to testify for his old friend. William eventually pleaded guilty to a misdemeanor for driving Van and Judy to the airport the first time they ran away and was sentenced to probation—a stigma that would follow him throughout his career.

In a plea bargain orchestrated by Van's attorney and Earl, my father was sentenced to one year of confinement for the rape of a female under eighteen years of age, which was reduced to time served and four years' probation.

Two charges of fraud by wire had been lodged against Van in U.S. District Court in New Orleans at the same time he was facing rape charges in San Francisco. The U.S. Marshal's office soon began following the paper trail of bad checks and forged documents he had left across the country while on the run. Marshals discovered that Van had misrepresented his identity when he had bought and subsequently sold documents to finance his adventure with Judy. In San Francisco, he was charged with document fraud and fraud by wire. Van was sentenced to three years in San Quentin State Prison. Soon, Lompoc, California, would file another charge of fraud by wire against him.

The judge honored Earl Sr.'s request and first sent Van to Atascadero State Hospital for ninety days to cure him of his obsession with Judy.

Located between San Francisco and Los Angeles, Atascadero is a maximum security facility for sexually deviant, criminally insane males. Opened in 1954, this psychiatric hospital features a security perimeter to protect the outside world from the patients, whose mental disabilities might pose a threat of danger. The thought of being perceived as "crazy" did not sit well with Van, who preferred to think of himself as intellectually superior.

At Atascadero, doctors designed an intensive regimen of electroshock therapy and drugs to exorcise Van's pathological need for Judy. Although his senses became a little duller with each passing day, Van resisted therapy, preferring to cling to his thoughts of the beautiful blonde who had ultimately betrayed him.

Behind the halfhearted smile he gave his doctors, rage, menacing in its intensity, boiled inside him. William would later say, "If Van wasn't crazy when he went to Atascadero, electrodes frying his brain for so long guaranteed that he was crazy when he came out."

While Van was "being cured of his obsession," San Pedro, California, filed another charge of fraud by wire against him.

Upon his release from Atascadero, he was sent to San Quentin State Prison.

The oldest prison in California, San Quentin is surrounded on three sides by San Francisco Bay. Built by inmates in the early 1850s, it's the only prison in California that has an execution chamber, and all prisoners sentenced to death in the state live on Condemned Row. For those like Van, small, narrow cells with uncomfortable beds made of metal and a toilet against the wall became home. Murderers, robbers, and rapists peered out at passing guards from behind the vertical bars that kept them locked away from proper society. Prisoners, taken outside for periodic exercise, could view the hills of San Francisco from the yard—freedom, almost close enough to touch, yet so far from reach. For Van, the view was excruciating. He knew Judy was out there, somewhere in those hills, living her life without him.

For the next year and a half, he bided his time, planning how he would win her back and protecting himself as best he could. Labeled a pedophile, Van could not have had an easy time in prison, as many inmates view child rapists as suitable prey for their aggression.

He was paroled on July 12, 1965, two days before his thirty-first birthday.

It had been a little more than two years since he last saw Judy, and finally he was a free man.

22

In 1964, while Van served time in San Quentin, Rotea Gilford, a tall, thin African American man, one of the few black men who served on the San Francisco Police Department, sat at his desk in the Hall of Justice, not quite believing what he had just heard. He had just earned a promotion. Never before in the history of the department had a black man been promoted to inspector in the robbery division.

The civil rights movement was in full swing and had finally resulted in the passage of the federal Civil Rights Act. Even with the act being signed into law, African Americans had to struggle to get a small foothold on the ladder of success. Rotea knew when he was first hired at the department that his climb would be a difficult one, but he dreamed of becoming a homicide investigator, of being a part of the team that tried to solve the numerous murders that plagued the city by the bay.

Rotea had moved with his family from Texas to the Fillmore District of San Francisco in the 1930s. Back then, the Fillmore was the logical place to move to if you were black. Filled with immigrants from all over the world, here a black child could fit in with the other kids. That was a little more difficult in other areas of the city, but the Fillmore was not like other neighborhoods. From its inception, it had a different pulse, a distinctive beat that could be heard every night in the jazz clubs and theaters that sprang up along its streets.

Rotea grew up on those streets in the 1940s and '50s. He knew where he could go and where he couldn't. His parents had told him stories about how they had not been allowed to go into the clubs and restaurants in their own neighborhood because they were people of color. In reaction, African Americans began opening their own clubs, the music that streamed from open doors so powerful that they began to attract attention. Residents from other districts around the city began to make their way to the Fillmore, drawn there by black artists such as Billie Holiday, Louis Armstrong, and Ella Fitzgerald, who demanded respect through their talent.

And while the Fillmore District was nothing like living in the South for African Americans at the time, Rotea grew up with a strong sense of what was right and wrong. And discrimination against African Americans because of their color was simply wrong in his opinion. From an early age, he set out to effect change in the mind-set of white San Franciscans. He determined that he would be the best he could be at whatever he did. Because he was tall and fit, sports became the natural way for him to express his equality. At Polytechnic High School, Rotea became a star, before moving on to San Francisco State's football team. Excelling on and off the field, Rotea received interest from the Chicago Cardinals, but a shoulder injury crushed any hope he had of succeeding in the National Football League.

He was forced to change his focus. In college, Rotea became friends with a young civil rights activist named Willie Brown. Also from Texas, Willie had experienced discrimination, even mob violence, firsthand, and he had moved to San Francisco when he was seventeen, determined to make a difference. Willie worked hard as a janitor to pay his way through college, and Rotea respected that. He also liked that Willie had an instinctive knack for knowing how to get things done.

After college, Rotea applied for jobs that had previously been held only by whites. He worked as a toll taker on the Bay Bridge, a Muni bus driver, and a cable car conductor, but those types of civil service jobs were only the first steps. His true calling was to become a police officer. After serving with the Alameda County Sheriff's Office for two years, Rotea excitedly made the move to the SFPD in 1960.

In his early days, he was known to people on his beat as "Mr. Smiley." Rotea worked his home court, the Fillmore District, where he was already known and trusted. In what had once been known as the "Harlem of the West," Rotea spent much of his time settling disputes in the Westside Courts housing projects and trying to help the children who lived there realize that a much bigger world existed outside of their sometimes impoverished existence.

A tireless storyteller, Rotea often exaggerated his exploits in the Fillmore for his fellow officers, who rarely believed him but always wanted to hear his stories. As the years went on, Rotea expanded and enlarged the stories until they became bigger than life.

By 1964 Rotea had broken ground in the SFPD by earning the title of inspector. Willie Brown was also making huge strides. He had just been elected to the California Assembly. Determined men both, Rotea and Willie would go on to earn further respect and break more new ground throughout their careers.

But only Rotea's life would one day become inextricably intertwined with a serial killer's.

23

Much had changed in San Francisco by the time Van was released from prison in 1965. The Beatles had sparked a British Invasion the previous year, altering the face of music, and the beatniks in North Beach had moved into the Haight, followed by another counterculture movement that was flowing in from around the country: young people rebelling en masse against the conservative ideas of their parents and an escalating war in Vietnam. In

1965, United States combat troops tripled in number as America fought against the spread of communism. Unlike many of their parents, whose patriotism ran deep after surviving World War I, the Great Depression, World War II, and the Korean War, this generation wanted peace, not war. They arrived by the thousands, chanting antiwar slogans in the middle of a drug-fueled lovefest. The older residents of the Haight watched helplessly as the beautiful old Victorians that had been spared from the fire of 1906 were divided into low-rent apartments that housed as many of these hippies as could be crammed into the space.

As he walked through the Haight, Van would have noticed that these young people who had invaded his old stomping grounds looked scraggly. Many of the girls had long, straight hair and wore flowing dresses, and the men were dressed in tattered jeans and multicolor T-shirts. All of them appeared to be stoned as they sang songs and talked about being brothers and loving everyone. At first, Van viewed the hippies with disdain. At least the beatniks had dressed well and tried to appear educated.

"What the hell is going on around here?" he asked Anton LaVey one afternoon. Van had arrived at LaVey's California Street residence unannounced shortly after his release from prison. LaVey, who did not usually see visitors without an appointment, made an exception in this case. "And what have you done with this place?"

LaVey laughed. The house was undergoing a transformation similar to what LaVey was experiencing. As his philosophic explorations had expanded further into the dark side, the decor in the house had become more and more ritualistic. Skulls, writhing demons, and skeletons had been placed strategically in various rooms for maximum effect. But it was the organ in the main ritual chamber that drew Van's attention.

Van stayed for only a few minutes, long enough to hear LaVey's take on what was happening in the Haight and to learn that LaVey was writing a book, a bible of sorts. He couldn't wait to tell William, but his old friend seemed disinterested when my father called. William had not yet gotten over Van's refusal to testify for him.

Disgruntled by the brush-off, Van headed to the Avenue Theatre, hoping to find a job. LaVey had described the stage house and pipe organ there, and he wanted to see it. From the moment my father entered the theater, he was hooked.

Built in 1927, the theater's marquee—AVENUE—announced to everyone that this was the place to be on San Bruno Avenue. A glass-enclosed ticket booth faced the street, where people stood in line to gain entrance to the darkened theater. On Tuesday and Wednesday nights, silent movies were featured, accompanied by a Wurlitzer playing in the background. Organist Robert Vaughn, known around San Francisco for the sweet sounds he could pull from the instrument, often accompanied the silent movies. While most people came to watch the films, Van attended to hear Vaughn play, hoping to one day get his turn on that beautiful instrument.

Van would eventually befriend Rick Marshall, the manager of the theater, a strange fellow who wore cheap clothes that were always too small. Like Van, Marshall was an avid reader and loved antiques, old films, and plays. Marshall enjoyed reciting Keats and Shakespeare. He also loved the theater's ten-ton Wurlitzer, and after he heard Van play the massive organ, he sometimes let my father sit in when Vaughn was not available.

While music might have come back into Van's life soon after he was released from prison, Judy had not, and Van was determined to rectify that situation. But Judy was not the same girl he had once known. Her impetuousness had caused her too much heartache, and she had learned her lessons. After nine months spent in a youth correctional facility, she had finally been returned to Verda's custody. On February 3, 1964, at the age of sixteen, she enrolled in high school in San Francisco, and some sense of normalcy returned to her life. Verda and her husband divorced the following year, and Judy moved with her mother to Daly City, a suburb of San Francisco.

It was there that Van found her.

Having tracked down her mother's number in a telephone listing, he called from a pay phone at a nearby shopping center.

"Hi, it's me," Van said when Judy answered the phone.

At the sound of his voice, my mother froze.

"Please come talk to me," Van said. "I miss you. I'm sorry for what happened. I'll get the baby back. I promise. I love you, Judy. Please. I'm right across the street."

Judy collected her wits and took a deep breath. "I would not even cross a street to see you," she said. "I never want to hear your voice again. And if I ever see you again, it would be too soon!"

"Judy, please. I love you."

Judy hung up the phone, and for the first time in her life, she felt her own strength. A sense of power flowed through her. A fearlessness.

She was finally free.

Van was heartbroken. Livid. But there was nothing he could do. He returned to his bedroom on Noe Street to brood.

When he could stare at those walls no longer, my father immersed himself in his music and in the readily available psychotropic drugs being passed from person to person in Haight-Ashbury, escaping for a time from his pain.

By the middle of the decade, music in the San Francisco area was evolving as groups like the Warlocks (later the Grateful Dead) and Jefferson Airplane, whose signature psychedelic sound would embody the hippie movement, moved into Haight-Ashbury and honed their skills in local clubs, the same clubs where my father had honed his a decade before. Van listened with interest as the doo-wop sound of the fifties turned grittier, dirtier, and more instrument-oriented. Loud guitars replaced harmonies, and lyrics about sex and drugs gave teenagers permission. On the flip side, folk groups like the Mamas and the Papas and the Youngbloods would gain the same audience through lyrics about love and peace. Even John Lennon and Yoko Ono would visit the Haight, finding inspiration in the revolution against the establishment that was occurring there.

Older, and a conservative dresser, Van did not fit in with the kids in the Haight, but he was accepted in the music scene because of his talent. He soon resumed his business dealing in antiquities, in spite of having been convicted of fraud, and on his return trips he jammed with local musicians, including LaVey.

On April 30, 1966, Anton LaVey officially declared that the Age of Satan had started. Over the years, his audience had grown, and his Magic Circle had increased to include celebrities such as underground filmmaker Kenneth Anger. His followers from the Lost Weekend tavern formed much of the membership of LaVey's new Church of Satan. The group now met in his house on California Street, which had been painted black and featured a main ritual chamber where church meetings were held. Ever the showman, LaVey regularly performed black magic for his enthralled congregation. In this room, LaVey's teaching far surpassed the rebellion taking place against the government in the Haight.

On the streets, the rebellion was against traditional thinking. Against society's rules.

In LaVey's church, the rebellion was against God.

LaVey had transformed himself into an imposing figure, with his shaved head, clerical collar, black clothing, and the horns he sometimes wore for added effect. Van was impressed. LaVey had taken the philosophies they had been discussing for years and turned them into a sideshow that attracted people from all walks of life and outraged Christians across the country. My grandfather would have been horrified if he had known Van sometimes sat in that living room, listening with the others as LaVey's booming voice rang out from behind the altar.

But there was much my grandfather didn't know.

— PART TWO —

SIGNS OF THE ZODIAC

24

When Van met Edith Elsa Maria Kos, she reminded him of Judy, but she was older, twenty-six. Edith had grown up in Graz, a city in the state of Styria, Austria, without a father, and she had little experience with men. She had dedicated her life to helping others through her job as a social worker. Perhaps she saw something in my father that was broken and hoped she could fix it. Maybe she simply couldn't resist when he turned on the charm. Or maybe it was because he could speak her language. Whatever the reason, Van quickly won her over, hoping that she could erase his memories of Judy.

On June 6, 1966—6/6/66—Van, paying homage to LaVey by choosing that date, married Edith in Year One of the Age of Satan.

As had happened in his two previous marriages, a few months after the wedding, my father's charm began to wear thin. He had moved with his bride to 797 Bush Street, on the corner of Mason, in Lower Nob Hill. At first he had been fascinated with Edith, mostly because she was from Austria. She was beautiful, but not sweet and innocent like Judy had been. She was older, more mature, not as pliable. His new wife was often away from home, rescuing this person or that, and Van was left to his own devices.

And by now he had suspicions that Edith was pregnant. He certainly did not want to go through that again.

Most of the time, he kept his feelings under wraps. Edith had no idea yet what kind of man she had married, although she knew he could be cruel at times.

She just didn't know how cruel.

No one did.

But someone was about to find out.

Given what I have discovered and what I will present in due course, there is only one place that Van could have been on the day before Halloween in 1966, just five months into his marriage to Edith. The evidence I have collected indicates that Van left home that morning to make his usual drive from San Francisco to Mexico to hunt for rare documents. As he drove along California's coast toward Tijuana, he decided to stop in Riverside, a little more than four hundred miles into his journey. He had loaded his car with books, hoping he would have some luck selling them at libraries along the way, as was his habit. He turned down Magnolia Avenue, toward Riverside City College, and drove through the campus until he reached the library.

My father had just gotten out of his car, his arms overflowing with books, when he saw her.

He stopped and stared, his heart pounding.

The girl looked just like Judy. She had the same wide eyes, same arched eyebrows, same beautiful cheekbones. Her hair flipped up on the ends. His eyes followed her intently until she walked into the library.

Then it must have started—the rage building inside of him. All the rejection he had experienced throughout his life from his mother, from Judy, washed over him. He put his books back in his car and looked around to make sure no one was watching before walking quickly toward the Volkswagen. He opened the hood and pulled on the distributor coil and condenser until he had loosened them completely. After disconnecting another wire to ensure that the car would not start, Van went into the library to spy on the girl.

Cheri Jo Bates, an eighteen-year-old sophomore at Riverside City College, browsed through the aisles of books in the archives and then sat down to read for a while, unaware that someone was watching her and waiting impatiently for her to walk outside. Cheri Jo had been a cheerleader in high school and enjoyed popularity with her peers that most teenage girls never achieve. Hoping to become an airline stewardess when she finished her degree, the young girl worked hard to achieve her goals. She lived with her father, Joseph, a machinist who dedicated himself to caring for his pretty daughter while her mother was away in a rest home.

Van sat down at a desk, keeping a close eye on his prey. He opened the top of the foldable desk and began etching a warning on the underside:

> Sick of living/unwilling to die
> cut.
> clean.
> if red /
> clean.
> blood spurting,
> dripping,
> spilling;
> all over her new
> dress.
> oh well
> it was red
> anyway.
> life draining into an
> uncertain death.
> she won't

die.

this time

someone ll find her.

just wait till

next time.

Van then signed the poem with the lowercase letters *r* and *h*—
the first initials of two of his aliases, Richard Lee and Harry Lee.

When he finished, he waited for Cheri Jo to walk outside. He
followed her and watched as she got into her car, dug in her purse
for her key, and put it in the ignition.

The car wouldn't start. She kept trying until the battery ran
down.

It was time.

Van emerged from the shadows and asked her if she needed
help.

He looked nice enough, like a well-dressed businessman.
Cheri Jo decided she could trust him.

Van opened the hood and moved some wires, then told her to
try to start it again.

He talked with her as he worked on the car, his charming
manner easing any misgivings she might have experienced.

A little after ten, he tired of playing the game.

"My car is parked down the street," Van said. "I'd be happy to
give you a lift."

Fooled by his charming manner, Cheri Jo agreed.

As they walked toward the spot Van had indicated, darkness
hid them from view. When they reached an isolated area between
two houses, Van turned to Cheri Jo and said, "It's about time."

"Time for what?" Cheri Jo asked, not yet aware that she was
in danger.

"Time for you to die," Van said.

Cheri Jo did not have time to respond before my deranged father began stabbing her, burying his three-and-a-half-inch blade over and over into her body.

Retribution for betrayal the girl knew nothing about.

Cheri Jo refused to die easily. She scratched at Van's face, drawing blood. She tried to stop the hand that was hurting her, holding his wrist so hard that when he drew back to stab her again, she tore his Timex off his arm.

Nothing worked. He was too strong, and he was determined to keep stabbing until she was dead.

Finally, after forty-two wounds covered her body and her blood saturated the ground, Van was satisfied. She wasn't breathing. He took a final look at her bloody face before he turned and walked away.

For the moment, he had exorcised his demon.

Neighbors in the 3600 block of Terracina Drive heard the screams, the first at a little after 10:15 p.m. and two more at 10:30 p.m.

Cheri Jo had fought hard for her life.

Van calmly got into his car and drove on to Mexico, unconcerned about the clues he had left behind—his watch, the heel print of his shoe, and greasy palm prints on the driver's-side door of Cheri Jo's car.

None of that would matter. Police were stumped. This was not a typical homicide. There did not seem to be a motive. The girl had not been robbed. The key to her car was still in the ignition, her library books on the seat. She was fully clothed and had not been sexually assaulted.

It had to be personal. Forty-two stab wounds was overkill.

The palm prints yielded no matches, and police could not connect any of the clues Van left at the crime scene with a suspect.

The poem Van had left on the desk would not be found until

December. It would long be debated whether it was written by the killer or by a student who might have been contemplating suicide.

On his way back from Mexico, Van picked up some Riverside newspapers and read about the investigation. Realizing that police were not close to solving the murder, he arrogantly decided to help them out.

On November 29, the Riverside Police Department and the Riverside *Press-Enterprise* each received a confession letter, typed on teletype paper, the kind often used by railroad clerks—and the same paper that Van's stepfather, Harlan, a Southern Pacific Railroad clerk, often brought home from work. The letter read:

```
THE CONFESSION


                    BY_____.
SHE WAS YOUNG AND BEAUTIFUL BUT NOW SHE
IS BATTERED AND DEAD. SHE IS NOT THE FIRST
AND SHE WILL NOT BE THE LAST I LAY AWAKE
NIGHTS THINKING ABOUT MY NEXT VICTIM.
MAYBE SHE WILL BE THE BEAUTIFUL BLOND THAT
BABYSITS NEAR THE LITTLE STORE AND WALKS
DOWN THE DARK ALLEY EACH EVENING ABOUT
SEVEN. OR MAYBE SHE WILL BE THE SHAPELY
BRUNETT THAT SAID NO WHEN I ASKED HER FOR A
DATE IN HIGH SCHOOL. BUT MAYBE IT WILL NOT
BE EITHER. BUT I SHALL CUT OFF HER FEMALE
PARTS AND DEPOSIT THEM FOR THE WHOLE CITY
TO SEE. SO DON'T MAKE IT TO EASY FOR ME.
KEEP YOUR SISTERS, DAUGHTERS, AND WIVES
OFF THE STREETS AND ALLEYS. MISS BATES WAS
STUPID. SHE WENT TO THE SLAUGHTER LIKE A
```

LAMB. SHE DID NOT PUT UP A STRUGGLE. BUT I
DID. IT WAS A BALL. I FIRST CUT THE MIDDLE
WIRE FROM THE DISTRIBUTOR. THEN I WAITED
FOR HER IN THE LIBRARY AND FOLLOWED HER
OUT AFTER ABOUT TWO MINUTES. THE BATTERY
MUST HAVE BEEN ABOUT DEAD BY THEN. I THEN
OFFERED TO HELP. SHE WAS THEN VERY WILLING
TO TALK TO ME. I TOLD HER THAT MY CAR WAS
DOWN THE STREET AND THAT I WOULD GIVE HER
A LIFT HOME. WHEN WE WERE AWAY FROM THE
LIBRARY WALKING, I SAID IT WAS ABOUT TIME.
SHE ASKED ME, "ABOUT TIME FOR WHAT?" I SAID
IT WAS ABOUT TIME FOR HER TO DIE. I GRABBED
HER AROUND THE NECK WITH MY HAND OVER HER
MOUTH AND MY OTHER HAND WITH A SMALL KNIFE
AT HER THROAT. SHE WENT VERY WILLINGLY. HER
BREAST FELT WARM AND VERY FIRM UNDER MY
HANDS, BUT ONLY ONE THING WAS ON MY MIND.
MAKING HER PAY FOR ALL THE BRUSH OFFS THAT
SHE HAD GIVEN ME DURING THE YEARS PRIOR.
SHE DIED HARD. SHE SQUIRMED AND SHOOK AS I
CHOCKED HER, AND HER LIPS TWICHED. SHE LET
OUT A SCREAM ONCE AND I KICKED HER IN THE
HEAD TO SHUT HER UP. I PLUNGED THE KNIFE
INTO HER AND IT BROKE. I THEN FINISHED THE
JOB BY CUTTING HER THROAT. I AM NOT SICK. I
AM INSANE. BUT THAT WILL NOT STOP THE GAME.
THIS LETTER SHOULD BE PUBLISHED FOR ALL TO
READ IT. IT JUST MIGHT SAVE THAT GIRL IN
THE ALLEY. BUT THAT'S UP TO YOU. IT WILL
BE ON YOUR CONSCIENCE. NOT MINE. YES, I DID
MAKE THAT CALL TO YOU ALSO. IT WAS JUST A

WARNING. BEWARE . . . I AM STALKING YOUR
GIRLS NOW.

    CC. CHIEF OF POLICE
    ENTERPRISE

Using the techniques he had learned in his forensics classes, Van wiped the letter and envelope clean before putting it in the mail.

The following year, on April 30, the first anniversary of the Age of Satan, Van, upset that coverage of the murder had dwindled, decided to stir things up. He sent two letters—one to the Riverside *Press-Enterprise* and another to the Riverside Police Department. The unpunctuated letters stated, "Bates had to die There will be more." He signed both letters with an inverted *E* and a sideways *V*, a thinly disguised symbol for "Earl Van," although this cryptogram would later be construed as a *Z*.

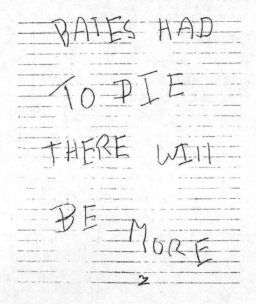

In a third letter, this one sent to Cheri Jo's father, Van cruelly wrote, "She had to die There will be more." This letter he left unsigned.

The envelopes, postmarked in Riverside, all had double postage attached.

Before long, although police would follow useless leads for years, Cheri Jo's case, file number 382481, went cold.

25

As Van made his way through the crowds of young people gathered on Page Street, one block over from Haight, he could hear a group of hippies singing along with Grace Slick on the radio. Jefferson Airplane, born in the bars of Haight-Ashbury, had captured the hippie zeitgeist in an anthem about drug use, titled "White Rabbit," that was rapidly climbing the American music charts during the Summer of Love.

Van got it.

Everyone got it.

It had started with the Monterey Pop Festival on June 16, 1967, a three-day concert organized by Lou Adler and John Phillips and held at the Monterey County Fairgrounds. More than fifty thousand people attended the event (some historians place the number at ninety thousand), which featured artists like the Who and the Mamas and the Papas. But it was the other artists, the unknowns, who made the biggest splash—Jimi Hendrix, Janis Joplin, Jefferson Airplane, and Otis Redding, who was backed by Booker T. and the M.G.'s. Many of the festival attendees migrated into the Haight afterward and, digging the vibe, stayed.

While the hippie movement might have been intriguing

to Van in its more subtle nuances—the hedonistic pursuit of pleasure, the music it generated, and the antiwar sentiments it proclaimed—the idea of everyone loving everyone was laughable to him.

Finally reaching his destination, Van walked through a doorway and entered a warehouse, his eyes slowly adjusting to the dimly lit room. The sweet smell of marijuana greeted him at the door. He took a deep breath, then looked around and noticed Robert Kenneth (Bobby) Beausoleil, surrounded as he always was by pretty young girls. A sometimes member of LaVey's congregation, Beausoleil was just another lost soul searching for truth on the streets of San Francisco, but he was a talented musician.

And very good-looking.

He had earned the nickname Cupid through his ability to attract the ladies, among them Susan Atkins and Mary Brunner, who sat on the floor watching him as he strapped on his guitar.

Beausoleil knew Van's reputation as an organist, and he desperately wanted to be accepted by respected musicians in the Bay Area, so he had invited Van to jam with his band. Beausoleil was working his way into the music scene through people like LaVey and filmmaker Kenneth Anger, who were good friends. Anger had recently cast him in the role of the devil for his upcoming film *Lucifer Rising* and had introduced him to members of the Grateful Dead and Big Brother and the Holding Company, which featured up-and-coming singer Janis Joplin. Van sometimes hung out with LaVey at Anger's ornate home, known to locals as the Russian Embassy. He liked to jam with the bands. He liked the drugs, and he liked the young girls who always hung around.

"This guy plays a mean Hammond organ," Beausoleil announced to his bandmates.

For the next hour, Van proved him right.

He felt a kinship with Beausoleil. Like so many others who

admired LaVey, Beausoleil chose to walk on the dark side, hoping the darkness would hide the emptiness inside them.

"Drop by anytime," Beausoleil told Van as he made his way to the door.

Over the next few months, my father stopped in every now and then to play with the band. At the time, he needed something, anything, to keep him away from home.

Edith was pregnant and making demands that he was unwilling to meet. She wasn't like Annette and Judy had been. He couldn't control her. She was more like Gertrude: domineering. She expected him to support the family with a regular paycheck and to be home when he wasn't working. Before they married, she had insisted that he find suitable work so that he didn't have to travel to Mexico so much. Van had joined the teamsters' union and had gotten hired as a cabdriver, an easy position for an ex-convict to obtain. Being a cabdriver was demeaning to a man of his intelligence, and driving around picking up fares could only have exacerbated his resentment. He preferred to be in Mexico City, sitting at the bar in the Hotel Corinto, drinking and impressing patrons with his literary knowledge. Not catering to a woman whose swollen belly repulsed him.

But, as he had with Gertrude, Van complied, all the while seething inside.

As the summer wore on, more and more of America's youth flooded into the city, drawn there by songs like Scott McKenzie's "San Francisco (Be Sure to Wear Flowers in Your Hair)" and exaggerated stories of the freedom to be found in communal living and mind-altering drugs. These young people, enamored of the notion of sex, drugs, and rock and roll, did not sense the undercurrent that was rippling through the California music scene—a darkness that was descending over the state, an evil that was being grown in music venues throughout the Haight.

When the terror came, they would be long gone.

Rotea Gilford was worried. He didn't like what was happening to his city. Its charming appeal had gotten lost in the trash that littered the streets, in the overcrowded parks that had become sleeping quarters for teenagers not fortunate enough to crowd into an apartment. The glassy eyes that stared at him as he walked through the Haight did not bode well. The police force was not staffed or equipped to handle the influx of people, and he and his fellow officers in the robbery division worked longer and longer shifts to investigate the growing number of thefts, which corresponded to the rise in drug use.

Rotea had a real problem with what these young people were doing to themselves and to the city he loved. He was a family man, a father who spent time with his children and the kids in his neighborhood. He coached them in baseball, football, and basketball. He mentored them, showing them through his own successes that they could rise above their individual situations to make a difference in the world. What he saw in the Haight was disturbing—America's children scorning the values of their parents—and the inspector did everything he could to steer them in the right direction.

Even as he arrested them.

By the fall, many of the summer inhabitants of the Haight had returned home to attend college and spread their message of peace in their own towns and cities. On October 6, Haight Street filled with the die-hards who had stayed behind to march behind an empty gray coffin in a ceremonial parade that signified the death of the hippie. Those who had come to San Francisco to experience peace and love had become disillusioned with their own hype.

Soon even they were gone, leaving behind a changed world.

26

Killing Cheri Jo Bates had done nothing to relieve Van's obsession with Judy. If anything, his feelings of hatred toward her had escalated through his use of drugs and alcohol. And Edith's pregnancy wasn't helping matters. She soon gave birth to a boy named Oliver. My father ignored his new son. If the baby needed to be fed or changed, Edith took care of it. When Oliver started crying, Van left. Edith couldn't understand why her husband wanted nothing to do with the child, but she was unaware that Van already had a son whom he had thrown away. My father knew better than to mistreat their child in front of this wife, so he stayed away as much as possible.

Again Van felt no attachment, no love, for the child he had created. This time, however, he didn't really care if his wife gave the child attention. Edith wasn't Judy.

Edith soon became used to his being gone at all hours of the night and for days at a time. He always told her he was working—either collecting fares or running down to Mexico to look for ancient documents. She believed him and did not suspect there was anything seriously wrong in her marriage.

Van was moody, yes, and he sometimes flew into rages, but she tried to understand.

Near the end of 1968, Van's frustration must have reached a boiling point. He was tired of being married, tired of his screaming child, tired of wondering where Judy was and what she was doing.

As Edith began decorating for Christmas, Van began making Christmas plans of his own.

On December 20, sixteen-year-old Betty Lou Jensen, an honor student at Hogan High School, in Vallejo, California, about an hour outside San Francisco, excitedly prepared for her first date with David Arthur Faraday. The two had met just the week before, and it had been love at first sight for both of them.

Seventeen-year-old David had lived in Vallejo for three and a half years and was a senior at Vallejo High, where he was on the wrestling team and participated in school government. He was also active in the Presbyterian church his family faithfully attended.

Betty Lou told her parents that she wanted to go with David to the Christmas concert at Hogan High. Her parents agreed to meet him before their date.

That evening, Betty Lou excitedly reached into her closet and tried on a variety of dresses, searching for just the right one to impress her new beau. She finally decided on a purple dress with a white collar and cuffs and strappy black shoes and then carefully arranged her dark hair on top of her head.

David was just as excited. He asked his mother, Jean, if he could borrow some money, and she gave him a dollar and some change. Before he left, at 7:30 p.m., to pick up his date, David put a bottle of breath drops in the pocket of his brown corduroy pants.

He kissed his mother good-bye.

David arrived at Betty Lou's around eight. Her parents seemed pleased with the polite, good-looking young man who wanted to date their daughter. "Make sure you bring her home by eleven," Betty Lou's mother said.

"I will," David promised.

They did not go to the concert. There was no concert being held that night at the school. Instead they visited Betty Lou's best friend, Sharon, stayed at her house until 9:00 p.m., and then drove southeast along Lake Herman Road toward Benicia.

Lake Herman Road was well known by local teenagers as a great place to make out. The entrance to the Benicia water-pumping station was perfect—isolated and surrounded by rolling hills. A locked gate prevented kids from entering the pumping station, but a small area to the side of the road, at the entrance, invited them to park there. Teenagers could see lights from approaching cars from a distance and would usually wait until they passed to resume their inexperienced groping.

David and Betty Lou weren't paying attention to the passing cars. It was dark, foggy, and cold outside—about forty degrees—a perfect night to snuggle, to experience the excitement of a first kiss. Betty Lou sat in the front seat of David's 1960 brown Rambler station wagon, her pretty head resting on his shoulder while they talked. Absorbed in each other, they didn't pay attention when a vehicle pulled over and parked parallel to their car.

Perhaps my father had been watching Betty Lou. Her mother would later report to police that the gate to their home had been found open on several occasions when it should have been closed. The young girl resembled Judy—the way she had looked when Van had forced her to dye her hair black to avoid recognition while they were on the run. Betty Lou, cuddled up next to David, had no way of knowing that my father perceived that as a betrayal.

Van had carefully prepared for this night. Realizing that he would not be able to sight his gun if his prey took off running, he had taped a small penlight to the barrel of his .22-caliber semi-automatic pistol.

David and Betty Lou were oblivious to the man standing just feet away, until bullets started ripping through the car—through the back passenger window, through the roof, and then suddenly their attacker was on the driver's side, aiming his gun through the window. He shot David, whose exit had been slowed by Betty Lou's escape, just behind his left ear at point-blank range. David's body slammed sideways and he fell out of the passenger side of the car.

In his left hand, he clenched the class ring he had planned to give Betty Lou that night.

Betty Lou ran for her life but could not escape the five bullets that ripped into her back. She had managed to run about twenty-eight feet when the last bullet felled her.

She died there, on the side of a dark road, at the hands of a man who had once loved a girl who looked like her.

Van stood over her for a moment, staring at her face, then turned and walked back to his car.

His mission accomplished, my father drove away.

Around 11:15 p.m., Stella Borges, who lived on a nearby ranch, passed the pumping station and saw someone lying on the ground near the road. She slowed down and spotted another person on the ground, near a station wagon. She sped away toward Benicia, flagging two police officers a few minutes later.

Captain Dan Pitta and Officer William Warner hurried to the scene and immediately determined that the female was dead. They followed the trail of her blood back to the car, where they discovered David, still alive but fading fast.

Pitta called for paramedics while Warner drew a chalk outline around David's body.

David died at 12:05 a.m. at Vallejo General Hospital.

A gray wool blanket was placed over Betty Lou's lifeless body.

Investigators would find ten spent shell casings, later determined to be Winchester Western Super-X copper-coated long-rifle ammunition.

They also discovered footprints, but the indentions were so light that they could not determine what type of shoe had left the print.

Solano County sheriff deputies were baffled. There had been

no robbery—Betty Lou's purse with all its contents intact was in the backseat, along with her stylish white fur coat. There had been no sexual assault, which investigators often suspect when the victim is a pretty girl. David had been shot only once; Betty Lou had been shot five times, her wounds in a tight circle on her back. Whoever had shot her had been an expert marksman. The murders did not make sense.

There were no real clues aside from reports by a few witnesses who had been driving down Lake Herman Road and reported seeing a white Impala parked near the station wagon. No one had witnessed the crime.

Again, the case would remain unsolved.

27

Back in Louisiana, I had no way of knowing that I now had a little brother named Oliver.

I knew I was adopted, though. Leona had read me a book about being adopted when I was three years old, but I didn't really understand what it meant then. She had told me that out of all the boys in the world, she had chosen me to be her son because I was special.

What she meant didn't sink in until one afternoon when I was playing with my friends Jeff and Tommy.

"Your real mama didn't love you," Jeff informed me, having overheard his parents say that I was adopted. In the South, gossiping about neighbors is a pleasant way to spend a humid afternoon.

"Yeah, your mama gave you away," Tommy added.

"That's not true," I cried.

"Is too," they replied in unison.

"Is not," I shot back, before running away from them as fast as I could. When I got home, I ran into my room, thinking about what they had said, wondering if it was true.

At dinner, Leona could tell something was wrong as I picked at my food with my head down.

"What's the matter, honey?" she said.

"Jeff and Todd told me that my real mommy didn't love me, so she gave me away. Mama, why did my real mommy give me away?"

Loyd softly kicked Leona under the table, warning her to handle this with care.

Leona chose her words carefully, realizing the impact they could have. "Oh, honey, that's just not true. Your mommy loved you so, so much that she gave you to us because she knew she couldn't be a good mommy for you and take care of you the way we can. God wanted you here for me and your daddy to be your family, so you would have a wonderful home and a mommy and daddy to take care of you the way your mommy wished she could."

Loyd and Leona held their breath as they waited for my reaction.

I sat there for a moment, thinking about what she had said, and then I smiled a big, happy smile. "I'm glad God told my mommy to give me to you and Daddy. I know she loved me, too."

I never questioned why my mother hadn't wanted me again. But after that, I always felt as though my aunts and uncles stared at me more than necessary, as if they were trying to figure out who I was and why my mother had given me away. They never said anything and always treated me well, but my red hair and freckles made them wonder. Did that red hair come from my real mother or from my real father? It seemed I would never know the answer to that question, but I felt so loved in the Stewart home that it hardly seemed to matter.

Even after Loyd and Leona's biological child, Christy, was born, there was never any differentiation between us. My parents loved all of us equally and went out of their way to make sure that Cindy and I knew we were as important as Christy.

But all the love in the world wasn't enough to stop me from experiencing anxiety that I couldn't comprehend. It began one Saturday when I was six. Loyd and Leona had taken us to visit our Courville cousins in Krotz Springs. My cousin Ken and I spent the day climbing trees and placing pennies on the railroad tracks on top of the ring levee that surrounded the town. When Ken invited me to spend the night, I hurried to ask my parents. Loyd and Leona agreed that I could and promised they would return to collect me the next day after church. After kissing my mom and dad good-bye, I watched my parents drive away.

Suddenly, an unexpected lump formed in my throat, and my heart began to race. I was terrified. I knew I had made a mistake and prayed the car would stop, that my parents would turn around and get me. They didn't.

I was still standing there watching for their car when Ken came out to find me. "Come on. Let's go play," he said.

Reluctantly, I followed my cousin into the house. Crawling through the hoop tent that Ken had in his bedroom and playing with toy soldiers distracted me for a while, but later, when Aunt Loretta said "Lights out" and Uncle Bub shut off the light, panic set in again.

I couldn't breathe. My heart was pounding. I couldn't sleep.

All I could do was lie in that pitch-black room and pray that my mother and father would come back to get me.

I knew nothing, consciously, about the baby who had been left in the stairwell, nothing about the man who had so callously walked away from me, yet my fear of abandonment was palpable from a very early age.

28

Edith had no such fear.

By 1969 she had given birth to another son, named Urban, and she was pregnant again. As she happily prepared for the arrival of her third child, Edith didn't know that her husband was sinking further and further into darkness and already looking for his next victim. There was much she didn't know about her husband, including the fact that he was a friend of the high priest of the Church of Satan.

LaVey had recently published *The Satanic Bible* and was enjoying the controversy the book had caused.

Rick Marshall, the manager of the Avenue Theatre, thought it was funny. He had been struggling for years to keep the theater afloat and had been quoted the year before in the *San Francisco Chronicle* as saying, "I feel the smartest thing I could do would be to pull an Anton LaVey. He couldn't make it as a bar organist, so he looked at himself in the mirror one day and said, 'I'm a character,' then he hired a press agent and became Satan."

And now Satan had written a bible. Van couldn't wait to read it. In the prologue, he skimmed through the Nine Satanic Statements:

Satan represents indulgence, instead of abstinence!
Satan represents vital existence, instead of spiritual pipe dreams!
Satan represents undefiled wisdom, instead of hypocritical self-deceit!

Satan represents kindness to those who deserve it, instead of love wasted on ingrates!

Satan represents vengeance, instead of turning the other cheek!

Satan represents responsibility to the responsible, instead of concern for psychic vampires!

Satan represents man as just another animal, sometimes better, more often worse than those that walk on all-fours, who, because of his "divine spiritual and intellectual development," has become the most vicious animal of all!

Satan represents all of the so-called sins, as they all lead to physical, mental, or emotional gratification!

Satan has been the best friend the church has ever had, as he has kept it in business all these years!

Van and LaVey had been discussing these principles for years, in one form or another, principles that were diametrically opposed to the Ten Commandments with which Van had been raised. Whether he embraced these statements out of philosophical belief or rebellion against his father is unknown.

"Maybe I should send a copy to my father," Van once said to William.

Earl would have been appalled. My grandfather didn't have a clue how far downward his son had spiraled. And it was about to get worse.

Van might have spotted her at the Avenue Theatre: a pretty blonde who might have smiled at him when she walked in. He would have immediately noticed her resemblance to Judy—her innocent eyes, her wide smile. And the wedding ring on her finger.

Darlene Ferrin was a friendly girl, a party girl who loved men. She had met her first husband, James Phillips, in the Haight and married him in Reno on New Year's Day 1966. The marriage did not last long, and Darlene remarried, to Arthur Dean Ferrin, in 1967, soon after her divorce.

In the beginning, Darlene would have thought what other girls thought when they met Van: that he was charming, intelligent, and interesting.

Soon after they met, she began to find unusual gifts from Mexico on the doorstep of her home, at 1300 Virginia Street in Vallejo. Although she was married, Darlene was flattered by the attention she was receiving from this older man. As with Gertrude so many years before, marriage vows had never kept this free-spirited girl in check. Darlene liked the attention of men. It was as simple as that.

To Van, she was Gertrude and Judy all wrapped up in one pretty package.

Soon he began showing up at her home without an invitation, and Darlene became wary of him, even mentioning her concern to her sisters Pam and Linda.

She was right to be concerned.

On July 4, 1969, Van followed Darlene from her home to Caesar's Palace Italian Restaurant and waited while she visited with her husband, Dean, who worked there as a cook. When Darlene left with her sister Christina and drove to Terry's Restaurant, where she worked as a waitress, Van must have been there, too.

Following.

Watching.

Later that night, Darlene dropped Christina off and drove to pick up her friend Michael Mageau. Darlene and Michael headed down Springs Road to grab a bite to eat. It was a little after 11:30 p.m.

"I need to talk to you about something," Darlene said when they reached Mr. Ed's restaurant, according to police reports.

"Why don't we go to Blue Rock Springs Park?" Michael suggested.

"Good idea," Darlene said, turning the car around. They listened to the radio as Darlene drove four miles from downtown Vallejo on Columbus Parkway toward the park. Neither was aware that Van must have been following from a safe distance.

When she reached their destination, she turned into a deserted parking lot and drove to the last parking space on the right, near a walkway lined with tall eucalyptus trees. Although the highway was only a few yards away, trees and bushes blocked them from sight.

Darlene turned the car off, leaving the radio on.

It was just before midnight when a car, maybe a Corvair, pulled in a few feet from them.

When Darlene seemed to recognize the driver, Michael asked, "Who is it?"

"Oh, never mind," Darlene responded when the car suddenly left.

A few other cars pulled in, and a group of teenagers got out and set off some fireworks.

When they left a few minutes later, the car came back.

Van, holding a flashlight, got out and approached the passenger side of the car, where Michael was sitting. He shined the light into Michael's eyes.

Van raised his nine-millimeter semi-automatic pistol and began firing.

Michael was hit first in the neck. Trying to jump into the backseat, he was shot again, in the knee this time. With Michael incapacitated, Van, moving quickly to the driver's side of the car, turned his attention to Darlene.

Bang. Bang. Bang.

Three shots into her arms and her left side.

Satisfied, Van turned to walk away. But then he heard a scream. It was Michael, voicing his pain.

Van turned around and walked back. He shot Michael two more times before turning his gun on Darlene and firing twice.

Michael tried to open the door, but the handle was broken. Reaching out of the window, he opened the door from the outside and fell to the tarred ground. Writhing in pain, he watched as Van sped away toward Vallejo.

A few minutes later, another car pulled in. Bleeding profusely, Michael yelled for help. Inside the car, Darlene could only moan.

A young girl came over and told Michael to lie still while her friends called the police.

Police, lights flashing and sirens blaring, flew to the scene. By the time help arrived, Darlene was struggling for each breath. Before she succumbed to unconsciousness, she tried to speak. The responding officer could only make out what he heard as "I" or "my," before the young woman passed out. Darlene was pronounced dead when paramedics got her to the hospital.

Michael required emergency surgery to remove four bullets, but he survived. He would later describe the killer for police: late twenties to early thirties, brown hair, round face, stocky build. He would also indicate that he thought they had been followed to the park.

Forty minutes after the shootings, Van stopped at a service station on Tuolumne Street and Springs Road, four blocks from the sheriff's office, and called the Vallejo Police Department from a pay phone.

When the operator answered, he said in a steady voice, "I want to report a double murder. If you go one mile east on Columbus Parkway to the public park, you will find kids in a brown car. They were shot with a nine-millimeter Luger. I also killed those kids last year. Good-bye."

The operator, Nancy Slover, would later describe his voice as "rather soft but forceful." She stated, "The only real change in the voice was when he said 'good-bye.'" Then his voice "deepened and became taunting."

Van had been wrong about the double murder. Michael was still alive.

Darlene's husband, Dean, and her former husband, James, were soon cleared as suspects. Again police had no motive for the attack, although in one police report it was noted that a possible motive was jealousy or revenge. They also noted the proximity and similarity to the murders that had occurred on Lake Herman Road in December of the year before.

In Darlene's address book they found the name Vaughn, the organist at the Avenue Theatre, and police deduced that she had some connection to the theater but couldn't put the pieces together. No one could remember the name of the man who had been at her house, although Darlene's sister Pam would later state that it was a short name, like Lee.

Or Stan.

According to police reports, Darlene's sister Linda also reported that Darlene had a friend named Lee who brought her gifts from Mexico. One of Van's aliases, listed in his criminal file with the FBI, was Richard Lee. Another alias, listed in Baton Rouge police reports, was Harry Lee.

During that horrible night, Darlene's husband, worried that his wife had not arrived home with the fireworks he had asked her to pick up, waited and waited. Darlene did not show up.

Dean was left to raise their daughter, Deena, alone.

29

As was now his habit, Van read the newspapers religiously, studying each article about his murders in the Vallejo *Times-*

Herald, the *San Francisco Chronicle*, and the *San Francisco Examiner*. He realized that police had no clue as to his identity. His arrogance increasing with each murder, Van decided to help them out.

Using the simple techniques he had learned from his father as a child and honed throughout his life, he began to craft a cryptogram. First he wrote his message, deliberately forgoing punctuation and misspelling words:

```
I like killing people because it is so much
fun it is more fun than killing wild game
in the forrest because man is the most
dangeroue animal of all to kill something
gives me the most thrilling experience it
is even better than getting your rocks off
with a girl the best part of it is thae when
I die I will be reborn in paradice and all
the [people] I have killed will become my
slaves I will not give you my name because
you will try to sloi down or stop my
collectiog of slaves for my afterlife
```

He included a series of letters at the end that had no meaning: "ebeorietemethhpiti."

He had also included a variation on LaVey's satanic principle that man "has become the most vicious animal of all."

Van then began to encode his message, embedding his name and initials through the cipher.

When he was satisfied that the code was unsolvable and that he had left enough clues to his identity, he cut the finished cipher into three sections. Then he wrote a letter to include with the cipher:

Dear Editor

I am the killer of the 2 teenagers last
Christmass at Lake Herman and the Girl last
4th of July. To Prove this I shall state
some facts which only I + the police know.
Christmass
  1 Brand name of ammo Super X
  2 10 shots fired
  3 Boy was on back feet to car
  4 Girl was lyeing on right side feet to
west
4th of July
  1 Girl was wearing patterned pants
  2 Boy was also shot in knee
  3 Brand name of ammo was Western
Here is a cyipher or that is part of one.
The other 2 parts of this cipher have been
mailed to the S.F. Examiner + the S.F.
Chronicle.

I want you to print this cipher on your
frunt page by Fry Afternoon Aug 1-69, If you
do not do this I will go on a kill rampage
Fry night that will last the whole week end.
I will cruse around and pick off all stray
people or coupples that are alone then move
on to kill some more untill I have killed
over a dozen people.

The letter was signed with a symbol—a circle with a cross in
the middle:

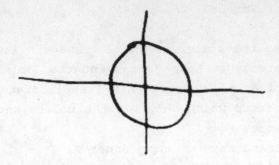

Van addressed an envelope to the Vallejo *Times-Herald*, including a note on the front that said, "Please rush to editor," and stuffed the letter and cipher inside. He wrote a second letter—similar to the first, with only a few slight changes—to the *San Francisco Examiner*. He included the second part of the cipher with this letter.

Van sent the third part of the cipher with a letter to the *San Francisco Chronicle*. In this letter he added, "In this cipher is my identity," letting police and the public know that if the cipher was decoded, they would have their killer. This cipher would become known as the 408 cipher, because it had 408 letters and symbols.

He attached double postage to each letter and put them all in the mail on July 31, 1969, the seventh anniversary of his arrest for child stealing.

All three ciphers were published in the newspapers as Van had instructed.

In a news article, Jack E. Stiltz, Vallejo's chief of police, asked the killer for more information.

It was time for Van to formally introduce the world to the name he had chosen for himself—Zodiac, from the Greek word *zoion*, meaning "animal," or, in Van's mind, "dangerous animal."

Enjoying the attention he was receiving, he sent the *San Francisco Examiner* a letter postmarked August 4, 1969:

This is the Zodiac speaking. In answer to your asking for more details about the good times I have had in Vallejo, I shall be very happy to supply even more material. By the way, are the police having a good time with the code? If not, tell them to cheer up; when they do crack it, they will have me.

On the 4th of July:

I did not open the car door. The window was rolled down all ready. The boy was origionaly sitting in the frunt seat when I began fireing. When I fired the first shot at his head, he leaped backwards at the same time, thus spoiling my aim.

He ended up on the back seat then the floor in back thashing out very violently with his legs; that's how I shot him in the knee. I did not leave the cene [scene] of the killing with squealing tires + raceing engine as described in the Vallejo paper. I drove away quite slowly so as not to draw attention to my car.

The man who told police that my car was brown was a negro about 40-45 rather shabbly dressed. I was in this phone booth having some fun with the Vallejo cop when he was walking by. When I hung the phone up the damn X@ thing began to ring & that drew his attention to me + my car.

Last Christmass

In that epasode the police were wondering how I could shoot + hit my victims in the dark. They did not openly state this, but implied this by saying it was a well lit night + I could see silowets on the horizon. Bullshit that area is srounded by high hills + trees. What I did was tape a small pencel flash light to the barrel of my gun.

If you notice, in the center of the beam of light if you aim it at a wall or ceiling you will see a black or darck spot in the center of the circle of light about 3 to 6 in. across. When taped to a gun barrel, the bullet will strike in the center of the black dot in the light. All I had to do was spray them as if it was a water hose; there was no need to use the gun sights. I was not happy to see that I did not get front page coverage.

On August 8, the three-part cipher was solved by a Salinas high school teacher, Donald Harden, and his wife, Bettye, who had seen it in the newspapers. Their results were verified by the FBI. The couple would later explain that they assumed the word "kill" would be in the message, so they began by looking for letters or symbols repeated twice in a row that could represent "ll." They also determined that the author of the cipher would be egotistical and would begin the message with "I." After finding the word "kill" and then the words "killing" and "thrilling," they were able to break the code.

Investigators now realized they were looking for a serial killer and diligently searched the ciphers for the name of the person responsible for the murders. They noted the use of the word "shall" instead of "will" and the spelling of "Christmass" and determined their suspect may be British. They also recognized the reference to the Nine Satanic Statements. That didn't help. Even though the cipher had been decoded, they couldn't take the next step of deciphering the killer's name, because they didn't know what name to look for.

For my father, the game had intensified. When he learned that his cipher had been decoded, he knew there was a possibility he would be caught soon. He waited for police to arrest him, but no one came.

And although San Francisco and the surrounding areas were buzzing about the cipher-writing killer, another series of high-profile murders would soon steal Van's thunder and bring even more terror to the Golden State.

30

On July 27, 1969, four days before Van sent his ciphers to newspapers, Bobby Beausoleil, the young musician my father had jammed with at the warehouse in the Haight, murdered Gary Hinman, a music teacher who lived in Topanga Canyon. Beausoleil had long since left Anton LaVey's flock, and he, along with Susan Atkins and Mary Brunner, had moved to Spahn Ranch, in Los Angeles County, to join the Manson Family, a cult that had come together around 1967 under the leadership of Charles Manson. Still trying to fit in with his elders, Beausoleil set out to impress Manson—first by bringing sexy women into the fold and later by proving his worth through violence.

Over a two-day period, Beausoleil and the girls held Hinman captive while trying to extort money from the gentle teacher, who had allowed Manson Family members to crash at his house from time to time. When they were unable to fulfill their mission, Manson arrived and slashed Hinman's face and left ear with a sword. The girls attempted to sew Hinman's ear with dental floss while Beausoleil tried to persuade him to give them his money. On the twenty-seventh, realizing their efforts were futile, Bobby stabbed Hinman twice in the chest, killing him.

Atkins and Brunner then wrote the words POLITICAL PIGGY on the wall in Hinman's blood. A paw print was drawn near the words, their effort to frame the Black Panthers for the murder.

Beausoleil would later claim that he committed the crime because he had a desperate need to be accepted, to be considered a man in the eyes of those he admired.

Beausoleil was arrested on August 6, two days before Van's ciphers were decoded. The killing of Gary Hinman did not receive the publicity in San Francisco that Van's letters did, but what happened in the early-morning hours of August 9 would stun the nation and take the focus away from the Zodiac. The Manson Family was about to commit some of the most notorious and heinous murders in American history.

Charles Manson had ordered Charles "Tex" Watson, Patricia Krenwinkel, Susan Atkins, and Linda Kasabian to kill everyone in a beautiful home located at 10050 Cielo Drive, in the Santa Monica Mountains, which had formerly been rented by Terry Melcher, Doris Day's son. Previously home to Hollywood stars such as Henry Fonda, Cary Grant, and Melcher's girlfriend, Candice Bergen, it was now the residence of Roman Polanski and his wife, Sharon Tate.

On the night of August 8, Sharon, eight and a half months pregnant, was at home preparing for the arrival of her new baby. Her friends Jay Sebring, screenwriter Wojciech Frykowski, and Frykowski's girlfriend, Abigail Folger, were also at the house.

Steven Parent, an innocent eighteen-year-old, was the first

victim. He had been visiting a new friend, William Garretson, who was the caretaker of the property. The unfortunate young man was in the wrong place at the wrong time when he rolled down his window to push the button that would open the electronic gate. Watson, reportedly high on acid and methamphetamine, walked up to Parent's car and stabbed him once in the hand as Parent tried to defend himself against the knife that had suddenly come out of nowhere. Watson shot him four times before continuing on to the house.

After entering the home through a window, Watson, Atkins, and Krenwinkel gathered the occupants into the living room. Tate and Sebring were tied together with a rope around their necks, and Frykowski's hands were bound with a towel. While protesting the treatment of his pregnant friend, Sebring was shot by Watson.

Frykowski, a martial arts expert, freed himself from his bonds and began fighting his captors—first Atkins, who stabbed him, and then Watson, who pistol-whipped him, stabbed him, and shot him twice as he was trying to escape. The autopsy report would later identify fifty-one stab wounds on his body.

Folger escaped the house and made it to the pool area before Krenwinkel caught her. She would die there from the twenty-eight stab wounds her attackers inflicted upon her.

Sharon Tate pleaded for the life of her unborn child, but the deranged killers would not hear her pleas and stabbed her sixteen times before writing messages on the walls of her home in her blood.

Even the most seasoned detectives were horrified by what they found when they got to the scene of the murders.

Manson decided to have his family members kill again the following night. Together with Watson, Atkins, Krenwinkel, Kasabian, Leslie Van Houten, and Steve Grogan, Manson headed to 3301 Waverly Drive, in Los Angeles, the home of Leno and Rosemary LaBianca. Manson and Watson were the first ones to enter the house. They found Leno sleeping on the couch. Rosemary was in her bedroom. After bringing Rosemary into the living room, they tied the couple up with leather cords. Manson stole Leno's wallet, then went back to the car and instructed Krenwinkel and Van Houten to go into the house. After Manson drove off with Grogan, Atkins, and Kasabian, Watson covered the frightened couple's heads with pillowcases and gagged them with lamp cords. Krenwinkel and Van Houten led Rosemary down the hall and into her bedroom, where Krenwinkel began stabbing her with a knife she had found in the kitchen. In the living room, Watson stabbed Leno in the throat with a bayonet.

Rosemary fought with Krenwinkel and Van Houten until Watson came into the room and stabbed her with his bayonet, ending her life. She sustained forty-one stab wounds, some of them inflicted postmortem by Van Houten. Watson then returned to Leno, stabbing him repeatedly until he was certain he was dead.

The word WAR had been carved into Leno's stomach, and RISE and DEATH TO PIGS had been finger-painted in blood on the walls. HEALTER [*sic*] SKELTER had been written in blood on the refrigerator.

The LaBiancas would be found by family members nineteen hours after their deaths.

Because stolen vehicles had been spotted on their property, Charles Manson and twenty-five members of his family were arrested on August 16 at the ranch where they lived together. Police had no idea when they arrested the suspected auto-theft ring that they had in custody some of the killers who were terrorizing Los Angeles.

Although there were so many similarities between the cases, police did not link the Hinman, Tate, and LaBianca murders for several months. It wasn't until Atkins told her cell mates that she had participated in the murders that the pieces began to fall into place.

Manson, Atkins, Krenwinkel, and Van Houten were found guilty and sentenced to death, but their sentences would later be commuted to life imprisonment when California outlawed capital punishment. Manson would also be found guilty of two more murders: those of Donald Shea, who lived on Spahn Ranch, and Gary Hinman. Grogan was also found guilty of the Shea murder and was sentenced to death. After his sentence was commuted to life imprisonment, he would become the only member of the family involved in its murders to be paroled. Grogan was released from prison in 1985.

Beausoleil was sentenced to death at the age of twenty-two, but his sentence also would be commuted to life in prison. Brunner was granted immunity for her unwilling testimony against Beausoleil, testimony she later recanted. Kasabian was granted immunity because she had not participated in the actual murders. Prosecutors needed her testimony to help convict the others.

Although Manson's followers revered him as their spiritual leader, most people in America thought he was the devil incarnate.

Unfortunately, Charles Manson was not the only devil residing in California as the decade of love, peace, war protests, and a culture-changing civil rights movement came to an end.

31

September 27, 1969, was a perfect fall day in San Francisco. The sun shone brightly over the Golden Gate Bridge, and the air was crisp and cool. Twenty-year-old Bryan Hartnell had stopped by the cafeteria at Pacific Union College to grab a bite to eat and was surprised when he saw Cecelia Shepard, his ex-girlfriend. He had heard that she was transferring to the University of California at Riverside because of the excellent music program there.

Bryan was a nice young man, studious, and Cecelia liked him tremendously, even though they no longer dated. Bryan felt the same way about her. Cecelia was gentle, a kind soul who loved to sing and play the piano.

"I came here with Dalora to spend the weekend," she told him, referring to her friend, "but I have to go back tomorrow."

"Can we spend some time together this afternoon?" Bryan asked hopefully.

They decided to take a drive to Lake Berryessa, some two hours away in Napa County. The man-made lake, with 165 miles of shoreline, attracted people from all over the region. Its grassy hills provided a haven for wildlife and picnickers, while warm water temperatures invited swimmers and boaters. The hills and forests offered privacy and, when no one else was around, a hushed romanticism.

My father had been to the area several times for the Lake Berryessa Bowl—concerts held every weekend from May to September in a huge amphitheater about a quarter-mile from the lake, featuring acts like Alice Cooper, Sly and the Family Stone, Iron Butterfly, and the Sons of Champlin, a Bay Area band that Beausoleil had played with on occasion. Although music had originally drawn Van to the area, it was the beautiful young girls who tanned by the lake that brought him back again and again.

Cecelia Shepard was beautiful, with blond hair that flipped up at the ends and a friendly smile that reflected her sunny personality.

Like Judy.

It is possible that Van saw her at the college and followed her there, or maybe he was already at the lake when he saw Cecelia, and she made his heart race. Either way, he was prepared.

Cecelia and Bryan chose a spot by a large tree near the western shore of the lake, at Twin Oak Ridge. Bryan spread a blanket on the ground, and they lay down to admire the cloudless blue sky. A light breeze blew across their bodies as they laughed and talked about what had happened in their lives since they had last seen each other.

My father, hidden behind a nearby tree, watched jealously, his fury mounting with each giggle that floated toward him on the breeze.

He had to get closer, and slithered as quietly as he could to another tree.

According to police reports, Bryan heard the crunch of leaves. "Did you hear that?" he asked Cecelia, looking around for the source of the noise. "Do you see anything?"

"Look, over there. There's a man behind that tree," Cecelia said, pointing, becoming a little nervous at the idea of a man spying on them.

"What is he doing?" Bryan asked, unable to see him from his place on the blanket.

"I can't tell," Cecelia said, watching as the man ducked behind another tree.

Bryan jumped up when Cecelia suddenly cried, "Oh, my God. He has a gun!"

In his previous murders, Van had enjoyed the element of surprise. This time, his prey saw him coming.

Petrified, the friends froze as Van, wearing a black hooded mask that covered his head and shoulders, trained his gun on them.

He informed them that he needed their car keys and money to get to Mexico. He said that he had escaped from Deer Lodge State Prison, in Montana, where he had killed a guard. His words had the desired effect.

Bryan moved closer to Cecelia, trying to keep Van talking while he figured out a way to get away from the masked man. He noticed a white symbol on the front of the part of the executioner's hood that covered Van's stomach. It looked like a circle with a symmetrical cross inside. Sunglasses were clipped over the cut-out eyes of the mask, and Bryan glimpsed brown hair through the holes in the mask.

The other thing he noticed worried him even more than the symbol: a long-bladed knife tucked into a sheath on his belt and a piece of what looked like rope hanging from his pocket.

"Is that gun loaded?" he asked.

Van removed the magazine and showed Bryan a bullet, taunting his victims.

He then threw a piece of clothesline at Cecelia and ordered her to bind Bryan's hands behind his back. Cecelia, her hands shaking, complied with the demand. She took the wallet out of Bryan's pocket and threw it at Van, hoping that if he got money he would not hurt them.

Her ploy didn't work. Their money was the last thing Van wanted.

Van bound Cecelia's wrists, seeming to Bryan to become nervous when he touched her. Van retied Bryan's to make sure he couldn't free himself. Then he tied them both together at the ankles.

"Lay on your stomachs," he demanded, pulling out his knife. "I'm going to have to stab you."

"Stab me first," Bryan begged. "I can't stand to see her stabbed first."

Without another word, Van plunged the knife into Bryan's back, over and over, until he was sure his victim was incapacitated. Although the pain was intense, Bryan played dead, praying his attacker would stop.

It worked.

Van turned his attention to the girl, but it wasn't Cecelia he saw.

It was Judy, and he began viciously stabbing her in the back, frenzied now, not methodical, as he had been with Bryan, the large blade ripping through her again and again.

Cecelia, trying to shield herself, turned over, and Van stabbed her several more times in her stomach, in the chest.

And then lower.

His rage finally sated, Van turned and walked away, leaving them for dead.

He did not take anything; the car keys, the wallet—nothing.

He simply took out a black marker and drew his symbol on the door of Bryan's white Volkswagen. Underneath it he wrote:

Vallejo
12-20-68
7-4-69
Sept 27-69-6:30
by knife

When he was sure his attacker was gone, Bryan tried to crawl to the road. He and Cecelia screamed for help. A man named Ronald Fong heard their cries and called Archie and Elizabeth White, owners of a boat repair shop at the Rancho Monticello Resort, nearby.

"I just saw a man and woman lying on the beach south of the resort, covered in blood. They said they had been stabbed and robbed," Ronald told Archie.

Elizabeth called park headquarters and agreed to meet the park ranger, Sergeant William White, at the beach. Together with Ronald, they boarded a ski boat and hurried to help Bryan and Cecelia. By this time, an hour had passed since the pair had been brutalized.

When they arrived at the scene, they found Cecelia crouched on her elbows and knees, rocking back and forth as if the constant motion could ward off the pain. The sweater dress she was wearing was soaked in blood. Elizabeth tried to calm her down, to make her more comfortable, but nothing worked.

"He was a man with a hood. His face was covered. He was wearing black pants. It hurts. It hurts," Cecelia cried.

"Did he rape you?" Elizabeth asked.

"No. And he didn't take anything," Cecelia said, the conversation helping her to regain her composure a bit.

"He was wearing glasses with dark clip-on glasses over his hood. He had a black pistol," Cecelia said before the pain became too much to bear.

It wasn't long before ranger Dennis Land found Bryan close to the nearby road. He carefully put the injured young man in his pickup truck and radioed for police and an ambulance. He drove to the beach where the others had gathered.

Sergeant White tried to talk with them about what had happened. Bryan was more coherent than Cecelia and told him how they had been tied up and stabbed. Noticing a lot of blood near

Cecelia's groin area, the ranger stopped asking questions, because she seemed to be going into shock.

The sound of sirens indicated that help was nearby, and the rangers waved the paramedics in.

Cecelia and Bryan were taken to Queen of the Valley Hospital and placed in intensive care. The next morning, Cecelia underwent emergency surgery and lived one more day before succumbing to the numerous stab wounds she had endured.

Bryan survived, and he described the killer for police: twenty to thirty years old, pleated, old-fashioned pants, sloppy dresser, black ceremonial hood that came down to his waist, symbol on front of the hood, stomach hanging over trousers, not too intelligent but not illiterate, voice even-toned with a slight drawl that was not southern.

Van would have been disappointed to hear that description, because he took pride in the way he dressed and in the way he spoke. But he had disguised himself well for this event.

Just over an hour after his attack, Van pulled into a car wash located at 1231 Main Street in Napa. He plugged coins into the pay phone and dialed the operator, who put him through to the Napa Police Department.

"I want to report a murder—no, a double murder," he told the switchboard operator calmly. "They are two miles north of park headquarters. They were in a white Volkswagen Karmann Ghia."

"Where are you calling from?" the operator said.

"I'm the one that did it," Van replied before letting the receiver slip from his hand to dangle there as he walked away. He had learned his lesson the last time and would not risk drawing attention again by hanging up so the operator could call back.

And again he was wrong. Only Cecelia would die, but for Van, that was all that really mattered anyway.

32

My father was beginning to unravel. As often happens with serial killers, the stress in his life, coupled with his thirst for revenge and his narcissistic tendencies, was starting to get the better of him.

By October 1969 Edith's swollen belly was a constant reminder that there would soon be another screaming child in his home, and Van could not take the demands of being a husband and father much longer. While Edith began busily preparing for the birth of her baby, Van began plotting ways to rid himself of his children.

His need to kill was escalating.

It had been more than two years between the murder of Cheri Jo Bates and the Jensen/Faraday attack, almost seven months between Jensen/Faraday and Ferrin/Mageau, and only two months and three weeks between Ferrin/Mageau and Shepard/Hartnell.

On October 11, just two weeks after he'd attacked Cecelia and Bryan and three days after Judy's twenty-second birthday, Van hailed a cab two blocks from his apartment in the five-story building on Bush Street.

Paul Stine, the driver of Yellow Cab number 912, was working nights to support his wife, Claudia, and to help with the cost of his grad-school tuition. At twenty-nine, Paul was on track to graduate from San Francisco State College with a doctorate in English in December. The years he had worked nights and sacrificed to pay for school would soon pay off. His dream of becoming a college professor was finally within reach.

Paul had clocked in at 8:45 p.m. and had taken his first fare from Pier 64 to the air terminal. At 9:45 p.m., he was on his way to pick up his next dispatch at 500 Ninth Avenue when he saw a man dressed in dark trousers and a parka flagging him down. It is possible that Paul knew Van, which would explain why the cabbie stopped to pick him up on the way to get another fare and allowed him to sit in the front seat. But the moment Paul pulled over on the corner of Mason and Geary Streets, his destiny was sealed.

Van asked Paul to drop him off near the Presidio, a military installation that overlooked the city and its surrounding areas. Near the end of the nineteenth century, reforestation of the installation had begun in an effort to beautify the post, which had been opened to civilians. Its national cemetery, the largest on the West Coast, boasted many decorated officers, and its collection of military artifacts attracted visitors from around the country, including Van. He knew the area well.

Near the corner of Cherry and Washington Streets, in Presidio Heights, an affluent enclave that borders the Presidio, Van pulled out the nine-millimeter semi-automatic he was hiding beneath his jacket and told Paul to stop the car. The cabbie did as his passenger demanded, pulling over close to a stop sign.

Van put the gun up to the right side of Paul's face and shot him at point-blank range right above the ear.

Paul slumped over the steering wheel.

Van pulled him across his lap. Three teenagers in a home across the street at 3899 Washington Street watched through a second-story window as Van went through Paul's pockets and took out his wallet. One of the teens called police while the other two observed Van leaning over his victim, wiping the dashboard and interior of the car with a handkerchief.

The teenagers couldn't see that Van was also tearing a bloodstained section of Paul's striped shirt from his body.

They stared in horror as he got out and wiped his fingerprints off on the outsides of the passenger and driver's-side doors.

Without even looking around to see if anyone was watching, Van casually began walking north on Cherry Street toward the

Presidio. He turned east on Jackson Street and then north on Maple.

Ambulance number 82 responded, but there was nothing paramedics could do.

Paul Stine was dead.

Officers on the scene spoke with the teenagers, whose responses were somewhat jumbled because they were in shock. They did, however, give police a description of their suspect: white male, early forties, reddish-blond hair, crew cut, glasses, heavyset, dark brown trousers, dark parka, dark shoes.

"Suspect should have many bloodstains on his person and clothing," the dispatcher repeated over the airwaves. "Suspect may also be in possession of the keys to the Yellow Cab. Probably has wallet belonging to the victim. Suspect is armed with a gun. Last seen walking north on Cherry Street from Washington Street."

In a crucial miscommunication, the dispatcher also said, "Negro male."

Patrolman Donald Fouke and his partner, Officer Eric Zelms, were searching for the black suspect when they saw a white man walking east on Jackson Street. The man turned north onto Maple and headed toward Julius Kahn Playground, in the Presidio. Fouke would later state that the subject did not appear to be in any hurry. They reported that they did not stop him.

It was a few minutes before the correction crackled through police radios. "We now have further information: a Caucasian."

In those few minutes, Van had disappeared.

My father couldn't wait to gloat. In a letter to the *San Francisco Chronicle* postmarked October 13, he wrote:

```
This is the Zodiac speaking. I am the
murderer of the taxi driver over by
Washington St + Maple St last night, to
```

prove this here is a blood stained piece of
his shirt. I am the same man who did in the
people in the north bay area.

The S.F. Police could have caught me
last might if they had searched the park
properly instead of holding road races with
their motor cicles seeing who could make
the most noise. The car drivers should have
just parked their cars + sat there quietly
waiting for me to come out of cover.

School children make nice targets, I think
I shall wipe out a school bus some morning.
just shoot out the front tire + then pick
off the kiddies as they come bouncing out.

The threat caused panic among the parents of schoolchildren
in San Francisco, but police did not pick up on the subtle clue my
father had embedded in the message, which only he could have
understood. Van had met my mother when she came bouncing
off a bus eight years earlier.

Enclosed with the letter was a piece of Stine's bloodied shirt
that Van had ripped from the dead man's body.

Paul's brother, Joe Stine, was infuriated by the murder of his
brother and the arrogance of his killer. When interviewed by the
Chronicle, he stated, in an October 23, 1969, article, that "Zodiac
has to be sick, a maniac. I hope that by offering myself as a target,
I can bring him out. I work at Richfield service station at 706
Sutter Street in Modesto near Rouse Street. I start work at 7:00
a.m. I go to lunch at Walk-In Chicken in a shopping center two
blocks away, riding a bicycle along Sutter Street and leaving the
station at noon each day.

"I go back to the service station and work until five. Let him come and get me. I'm in excellent shape. I'm tough enough to handle Zodiac if I can get my hands on him. I don't carry any weapons. I don't feel I need any."

SFPD Chief of Police Thomas J. Cahill also was alarmed by the murder of Paul Stine. The Zodiac had moved into his territory. He assigned detectives Dave Toschi and Bill Armstrong to the case, instructing them to stop at nothing to find the killer. Cahill took the Zodiac's threats toward the children of San Francisco seriously. He knew he was dealing with a crazed killer who was capable of anything.

Toschi, who loved to court the media, could not have been happier. Here was the assignment of a lifetime—to catch the Zodiac.

It would not be easy.

The *Chronicle* received another correspondence from Zodiac on November 8. On a forget-me-not card, Van had drawn a pen on a hangman's noose dripping what appeared to be either ink or blood. "Sorry I haven't written, but I just washed my pen," he wrote.

```
This is the Zodiac speaking I though you
would need a good laugh before you get the
bad news you won't get the news for a while
yet
   PS could you print this new cipher on your
frunt page? I get awfully lonely when I am
ignored, so lonely I could do my Thing!!!!!!
```

Running down the right side of the page, next to the main text, were the words "and i can't do a thing with it!"

It was signed with the circle and crosshairs and what appeared to be a tally of his victims: "Des July Aug Sept Oct = 7."

Included with the card was another cipher. Upset that his first cipher had been decoded, my father took a different approach to constructing this puzzle. Using the kanji style of writing he had learned as a child in Japan, he began on the right side of the page, arranging letters and symbols in vertical columns. Instead of a coded message, he included his full name, written backwards. This cipher, comprising seventeen columns with twenty characters each, would become known as the 340 cipher. Investigators and amateur sleuths would spend the next four decades trying to find its hidden message.

Van watched the newspapers and waited to see if someone would discover his name.

No one did.

My father indicated in this letter that he had killed seven people, but there were only four known murder victims and two surviving victims that had been linked to him at that point.

On November 9, *The Chronicle* received yet another letter:

> This is the Zodiac speaking up to the
> end of Oct I have killed 7 people. I have
> grown rather angry with the police for their
> telling lies about me. So I shall change
> the way the collecting of slaves. I shall no
> longer announce to anyone. when I committ
> my murders, they shall look like routine
> robberies, killings of anger, + a few fake
> accidents, etc.
>
> The police shall never catch me, because I
> have been too clever for them.
>
> 1 I look like the description passed out
> only when I do my thing, the rest of the
> time I look entirle different. I shall not

tell you what my descise consists of when I
kill

2 As of yet I have left no fingerprints
behind me contrary to what the police say
in my killings I wear transparent fingertip
guards. All it is is 2 coats of airplane
cement coated on my fingertips—quite
unnoticible + very efective.

3 my killing tools have been boughten
through the mail order outfits before the
ban went into efect. Except one & it was
bought out of the state.

So as you can see the police don't have
much to work on. If you wonder why I was
wipeing the cab down I was leaving fake
clews for the police to run all over town
with, as one might say, I gave the cops som
bussy work to do to keep them happy. I enjoy
needling the blue pigs. Hey blue pig I was
in the park—you were useing fire trucks to
mask the sound of your cruzeing prowl cars.
The dogs never came with in 2 blocks of me
+ they were to the west + there was only 2
groups of parking about 10 min apart then
the motor cicles went by about 150 ft away
going from south to north west

p.s. 2 cops pulled a goof abot 3 min after
I left the cab. I was walking down the hill
to the park when this cop car pulled up +
one of them called me over + asked if I
saw anyone acting suspicious or strange in
the last 5 to 10 min + I said yes there was

this man who was runnig by waveing a gun &
the cops peeled rubber + went around the
corner as I directed them + I disappeared
into the park a block + a half away never
to be seen again. "must print in paper."
Hey pig doesnt it rile you up to have your
noze rubed in your booboos?

Van went on to describe his "death machine"—the bomb he
planned to place on the side of a road to blow up a school bus—
and the materials he had used to build it. He was having fun now.
Taunting police and terrifying the public made him feel powerful. He was leaving all kinds of clues for them, but they weren't
getting it.

My father sent one more letter that year—to San Francisco
attorney Melvin Belli, postmarked December 20, 1969, the one-
year anniversary of the murder of Betty Lou Jensen and David
Faraday. He included another piece of Paul Stine's shirt with this
correspondence. On the back of the envelope he wrote, "Mery
Xmass + New Year."

Dear Melvin

This is the Zodiac speaking I wish you a
happy Christmass. The one thing I ask of you
is this, please help me. I cannot reach out
because of this thing in me won't let me.
I am finding it extreamly dificult to keep
in check I am afraid I will loose control
again and take my nineth + posibly tenth
victom. Please help me I am drownding. At
the moment the children are safe from the

bomb because it is so massive to dig in &
the trigger mech requires so much work to
get it adjusted just right. But if I hold
back too long from no nine I will loose
complet [crossed out] all controol of my
self + set the bomb up. Please help me I can
not remain in control for much longer.

Law enforcement officials throughout California worried that
the Zodiac would indeed lose control. Multiple jurisdictions had
witnessed his handiwork firsthand; clearly he was capable of anything.

33

By the end of 1969, the Fillmore, once a thriving community,
had deteriorated into a ghetto filled with unemployed workers
who had been laid off from the shipyards that had attracted them
to San Francisco and a better way of life. LSD had been replaced
with the more lethal heroin, and addicts plagued the Fillmore,
pilfering from residents and business owners to feed their growing habits. The hippie movement—and the proliferation of drugs
it brought—had left destruction in its wake. The city of San Francisco began implementing a plan of urban renewal, changing the
facade of the neighborhood as rows of quaint Victorian homes
were smashed by bulldozers and gentrification wiped away the
past.

Slowly, the music that had attracted so many to the Fillmore
began to disappear as club owners moved to other, more profitable
parts of the city. A few die-hards remained on Divisadero Street,

just outside the Fillmore—the Both/And Club, featuring the Ike and Tina Turner Revue on occasion, and the Half Note, where a young George Duke first heard Al Jarreau mimic percussion with his voice. Other legends, such as Dizzy Gillespie, Miles Davis, and Sarah Vaughan, frequented the Half Note, where Duke and Jarreau had become regular performers.

Over the years, the Half Note also became a favorite watering hole for police officers, who gathered there after their shifts to discuss their cases, and reporters, who lingered at the bar eavesdropping on their conversations, hoping for a scoop. Barkeep Lionel Hornsby was more knowledgeable than most about the latest developments in the Zodiac case and passed along what he heard from police to patrons and reporters. The conversation was good for business.

Rotea Gilford liked to stop by the Half Note on his way home from work. There, he often visited with fellow black officers who were similarly discouraged by the discrimination they felt they experienced in the SFPD. Rotea felt as though it was his duty to pump them up and organize the fight for equality.

But in November 1969, the talk was not about discrimination. It was about the serial killer who had the audacity to taunt them in such a public manner.

As Rotea sipped on his drink, he listened to the conversations around him, wishing he were working the case. Like many other SFPD officers, he had puzzled over the ciphers, hoping to be the one to discover my father's identity. He knew nothing about homophonic substitution, a method of creating ciphers that uses more than one symbol or letter for a single high-frequency letter of the alphabet, which experts would later theorize the Zodiac had used for the 408 cipher. He simply scanned the ciphers, hoping that a word, a name, would jump out at him. Though he had worked his way up through the ranks, Rotea had not made it into homicide; still, that didn't stop him from learning everything he could about the case. He worried about this killer, worried who and where he would strike next. The Zodiac had brought his war to the SFPD, and Rotea wanted to help Toschi and Armstrong take him down.

But he couldn't. In the history of the department, a black officer had never been promoted to homicide. Toschi and Armstrong had the case.

Rotea knew they had pulled the case files from Vallejo and Napa County and were going over them, diligently looking for clues. They had interviewed the three teenagers who had witnessed Paul Stine's murder. Fouke and Zelms had worked with a police artist to create a composite sketch. They had provided a description of what Zodiac was wearing that night: a dark blue jacket and baggy, pleated brown wool pants, although they had not noticed the blood on the jacket. Fingerprints, some bloody, had been collected from the doors of the taxi, but they had not matched any suspect so far. They learned from Vallejo police that Darlene Ferrin had written Robert Vaughn's name in her address book; they brought the organist in and questioned him. They recognized the killer's reference to the Nine Satanic Statements in the message in the cipher and went to California Street to question LaVey. They began to think Zodiac had some connection to the Avenue Theatre, because two of their suspects played the organ there, but they had no other evidence linking the men, and they had no choice but to let them go.

And they had the letters filled with clues, but even though they tracked down every lead that came in, Toschi and Armstrong had come up with nothing.

Rotea looked up from his musings and smiled when he saw Earl Sanders walk into the bar.

"Sit down," he said, motioning to the stool next to him.

Sanders had spent his teenage years in the Fillmore watching Officer Smiley (Rotea's nickname on the street) walking his beat and keeping unruly kids in line. It had been Sanders's admiration for Rotea that had influenced him to join the police academy after he graduated from Golden Gate University. And when Sanders graduated from the academy with the highest grades in his class, Rotea had been honored at the ceremony as well, with a 1st Grade Meritorious Service commendation. Ten years younger, Sanders often turned to Rotea for advice, and Rotea was happy to mentor the young officer. Together they set out to change the racial climate on the force, becoming good friends in the process.

"How's it going?" Sanders asked, taking a seat and ordering a drink.

Rotea shrugged. "Not bad, School," addressing his friend by the nickname he had given him because he was always studying something. Rotea enjoyed teasing him about it.

Sanders could tell something was wrong. "How's Patricia?" he asked.

"Good. You know, same old shit," Rotea said, picking up his drink and downing it.

Sanders patted him on the back. He knew what that meant. Rotea and his wife were always fighting over something—long work hours, drinking, cute blondes.

Rotea had met Patricia, a tall, slender, vivacious black woman from New Orleans, while attending City College of San Francisco. They had married in 1951 and had three children: Michael, Steven, and Judy. Patricia went to work as an accountant, and Rotea set out to conquer the world of crime. That required dedication, and although Rotea spent as much time as he could with his family, the demands of his job required more of her husband than Patricia liked to share. The fights had been escalating lately, and Sanders knew that Rotea was very unhappy. He could tell by the way he looked at the young ladies who frequented the bar. Usually, Sanders was long gone before Rotea finally made his way home to Patricia.

San Francisco Chronicle reporter Paul Avery, sitting at the end of the bar, was one of the reporters who observed all the goings-on, hoping to overhear some new information. Avery had written an article in mid-October, quoting Chief of Inspectors Marvin Lee as saying that the Zodiac was a "clumsy criminal, a liar, and possibly a latent homosexual," and the police had warned Avery to be careful.

What no one realized was that the Zodiac and Avery had a long history, one that Avery barely remembered but my father had never forgotten.

34

Shortly after Paul Stine's murder, a very pregnant Edith returned to Austria with her two sons, and in 1970 she gave birth to a baby girl she named Guenevere. I will never know the complete truth about what happened between my father and Edith.

Did she see the blood on Van's clothes when he returned home after killing Stine?

Did she threaten to turn him in to the police?

Did she run for her life?

Edith raised her children to believe that my father had taken them to Austria and abandoned them there. That, too, is plausible, considering my father's history.

What is clear is that something serious must have happened that forced Edith to raise three children alone and without any financial help or emotional support from my father. Although Van made several trips to Austria in the years following their separation, he never bothered to visit his wife and children. Guenevere, Oliver, and Urban grew up without him, just as I did—the pain of being abandoned haunting them throughout their lives.

Van now had the freedom to prowl for victims whenever he wished. That was part of the fun—the knowledge that he held the life of every person he saw in his hands. It must have been a heady feeling for the narcissistic killer, and people on the California coast had good reason to be terrified.

On March 22, 1970, Van was driving along Highway 132, which runs through Modesto, in the Central Valley, on his way back from Mexico, when he spotted a woman in a maroon-and-white station wagon. Kathleen Johns, a pretty, blond-haired mother, was on her way from San Bernardino to visit her family, almost seven hours away in Petaluma. She began to get nervous when she noticed that the car that had been following her since she passed Modesto was still behind her. It was late, around midnight, when Kathleen decided to slow down so the car could pass.

Van flashed his lights and honked his horn, trying to get her to stop.

Kathleen had her ten-month-old daughter, Jennifer, in the car and was not about to stop. She kept driving slowly, waiting until he finally passed her near Interstate 5. Thinking the driver might have been trying to tell her something was wrong with her car, she stopped to check.

My father stopped a short distance ahead, then backed up.

"Your rear tire looks a little wobbly," he said when he

approached her car. "That's why I was trying to flag you down. I'll fix it for you."

The nervousness Kathleen had felt while driving dissipated. Van was well dressed, harmless-looking. A good Samaritan.

She watched while he returned to his car and retrieved a tool, then walked back and knelt down by the tire. He pretended to tighten the lug nuts.

"Thanks," Kathleen said, feeling grateful to the helpful stranger. Her mother had warned her that driving alone at night was dangerous, especially with a child in the car, and the incident had been worrisome.

Relieved, she got back into her car and started the ignition. As she attempted to drive away, the car lurched to a stop. She got back out to see what had happened.

The left rear wheel had fallen off.

Watching in his rearview mirror for what he knew would happen, Van made a quick U-turn.

"Come on. Get in my car. I'll bring you to a service station," he told Kathleen, pulling his car alongside hers.

Stuck in the middle of nowhere, Kathleen did not see any other option. She picked up her baby and got into Van's car.

Van had not noticed the baby.

Undeterred, he drove west on Highway 132 until he saw a Richfield gas station on the corner of Chrisman Road. He pulled in, but it was closed.

He got back onto the highway and began driving down country roads and then through the small town of Tracy. They passed service station after service station.

"Why didn't you stop?" Kathleen asked each time.

"It wasn't the right one," Van replied.

Kathleen was getting nervous again, even though the man seemed friendly enough. She pulled her baby closer.

"Where do you work?" she asked, trying to initiate conversation to quiet her fear.

"I usually work for two months at a time, then just drive around, mostly at night," he said, his answer doing nothing to alleviate the tension that was building in the car.

"Do you always go around helping people on the road?"

"When I get through with them, they won't need my help," Van informed her.

Kathleen could feel fear tightening her stomach. She sat there quietly as they drove for more than an hour, waiting for an opportunity to make her escape. She hoped he would stop the car.

He didn't.

She distracted herself by memorizing everything about him that she could: his face, what he was wearing. The backseat and dashboard of the car were covered with books and papers, as if the man worked out of his car. She noticed that his shoes were extraordinarily shiny, spit-shined like a military officer's.

Finally, Kathleen noticed a stop sign ahead and began praying her captor would stop.

He did.

She jumped from the car with the baby in her arms and began running as fast as she could across a nearby field. Looking back, she saw that Van was still in the car. He had turned off the lights and was sitting there watching her, contemplating his next move.

Kathleen climbed up an embankment before turning around to discover that he was driving away. Fearful that he would come back, she ran toward a nearby road and flagged down a passing car, whose occupants drove her to the police station in Patterson, a suburb of Modesto about twenty-seven miles from Tracy. It was 2:30 in the morning.

Van had waited for her to leave. He drove back to her car and carefully wiped his fingerprints from the hubcap he had touched. Enraged that his victim had escaped, he set the car ablaze before he drove away.

Sergeant Charles McNatt took Kathleen's statement. As he listened to her story, suddenly the young woman began screaming.

"What's wrong?" the startled officer asked.

Kathleen pointed to a police sketch that had two pictures hanging side by side on the wall. "That's him. That's the man who picked us up," she cried.

"Which one of those men was your abductor?" McNatt said.

"That one," Kathleen replied, pointing to the one that had been amended by Detective Fouke, who had seen Zodiac in the Presidio Heights neighborhood moments after he had killed Paul Stine.

"Have you ever seen this picture before?" the officer asked.

"No."

"That's a sketch of the Zodiac," McNatt told her.

Kathleen became hysterical, and McNatt spent the next moments trying to calm the distraught woman before calling the Stanislaus County Sheriff's Department and asking that a deputy be sent to the area where Kathleen had left her car.

Deputy Jim Lovett found the car on Maze Boulevard about two miles east of Interstate 5. It had been completely burned.

Police were not quite sure how to handle the incident. They did not know if it was actually a kidnapping. Kathleen had told them that the man did not threaten her or her child. She had been scared, yes, but she had not been physically forced at any time to stay in the vehicle.

Later, Kathleen would change her story and tell people that the man had looked at her and said, "You know you're going to die. You know I'm going to kill you. I'm going to throw the baby out."

I don't know if that is true, but if it is, that was certainly something that Van had done before.

The *San Francisco Chronicle* received another letter from the Zodiac on April 20, 1970. It read:

```
This is the Zodiac speaking
By the way have you cracked the last
cipher I sent you?
My name is _____
```

Van was telling police that the 340 cipher contained only his name. Investigators who tried to crack the 340 cipher were destined to fail because the symbols weren't standing in for letters. There was no message—just "Earl Van Best Junior," written backwards in plain sight.

My father then included a new cipher with thirteen characters, including letters and symbols—the exact number of letters in "Earl Van Best Jr."

According to the Zodiac, the number of his victims was now at ten, but police had not yet connected any other murders to him.

Paul Avery also did not connect the fact that this letter was postmarked exactly seven years from the date he had published his article "Love on the Run: Ice Cream Romance's Bitter End" in the *Chronicle*.

35

Her mirror told her what she already knew—she looked good. Judy had spent the past hour carefully applying her makeup and choosing the perfect outfit for her date. Although she had her fair share of admirers, she was much more selective now.

Cautious.

She had learned the hard way where her impetuous nature could lead her. She ran a brush through her hair one last time and went into the living room to wait for her date.

Since her return to San Francisco, Judy had turned her life around. She had graduated from high school and taken a job caring for a woman with degenerative bone disease. Although it had been difficult, she had finally forgiven her mother for forcing her to give me up for adoption.

That had not been easy.

Verda had banned the mention of my name, and Judy had been left to deal with what had happened on her own. In silence.

It was like she had never had a son.

As Judy grew into adulthood, the life she had shared with Van influenced her emotional reactions to almost everything. She had a fear inside of her that she couldn't quite shake. A lack of trust.

But on this night, she determined to let her guard down. She happily contemplated the evening as she waited for her date to arrive.

She waited.

And waited.

He didn't call. He didn't show up.

When her sister, Carolyn (or Lyn), dropped by, Judy was busy nursing a bruised ego.

"Don't worry about him," Lyn said. "Come out with me instead."

"I don't feel like it," Judy said. She didn't want to go out and pretend she was having a good time when her feelings were so hurt.

"Come on," Lyn said. "We'll have fun."

Finally Judy relented, and the girls headed off to a nearby club.

"Oh, look who's at the bar," Lyn said, making her way over to a tall, good-looking black man she had met through her job at a legal firm.

"This is Rotea Gilford," she said, pulling Judy closer. "He's a cop. Rotea, this is my sister, Judy."

"Hi," Rotea said, unable to say much else for a moment. Lyn's sister was beautiful.

Stunning.

"You have lost some weight," Lyn observed when Rotea stood up to offer his seat.

"Fifty-two pounds," Rotea said proudly. "High blood sugar. I had to."

"How did you do it?" Lyn asked.

"High protein, low carbohydrates," Rotea responded, but he didn't want to discuss his weight with her. He wanted to talk to the attractive blond woman standing next to Lyn.

"Would you like to dance?" he asked Judy when the band began playing the first notes of a slow song.

She nodded, and Rotea took her hand and led her onto the small dance floor, liking the way the tall girl fit snugly against him.

Judy forgot all about being stood up as Rotea twirled her around the dance floor. She liked this big, strong man. She felt safe in his arms.

They spent the rest of the evening flirting and laughing, learning all they could about each other.

Rotea was forty-six. Judy was twenty-two. He was black. She was white.

None of that mattered.

By the end of the night, Rotea was smitten.

He had no way of knowing that the face that had instantly

captured his heart was the very same face that had fueled a serial killer's rampage.

36

Van wrote five more letters in 1970, using his threats to generate terror while mocking police efforts to catch him. On April 28, eight years to the day since he had kidnapped Judy from the Youth Guidance Center, he mailed what would become known as the Dragon Card to the *Chronicle* and again threatened to set off a bomb.

On the cover he had placed a Santa Claus character riding a dragon and another character riding a donkey. Written on the card were the words "Sorry to hear your ass is a dragon."

```
    I hope you enjoy your selves when I have
my Blast.
            ⊕
    P.S. on back
    If you don't want me to have this blast
you must do two things. 1. Tell everyone
about the bus bomb with all the details. 2.
I would like to see some nice Zodiac butons
wandering about town. Every one else has
these buttons like, ☮, black power, Melvin
eats bluber, etc. Well it would cheer me
up considerably if I saw a lot of people
wearing my buton. Please no nasty ones like
Melvin's
    Thank you ⊕
```

For some reason, Van had targeted attorney Melvin Belli again.

On June 26, he sent another letter to the *Chronicle*, this time expressing his displeasure that no one was wearing his Zodiac buttons. He also claimed to have killed a man with a .38.

Van signed the letter,

 — 12 SFPD - 0

At the bottom, he included a thirty-two-character cipher that, coupled with a map he included, was supposed to tell police where his bomb was set. This cipher has never been decoded.

On July 24, Van claimed responsibility for Kathleen Johns's abduction in a letter sent to the *Chronicle* that would become known as "Zodiac's Little List":

> This is the Zodiac speaking.
>
> I am rather unhappy because you people will not wear some nice buttons. So I now have a little list, starting with the woeman + her baby that I gave a rather intersting ride for a coupple howers one evening a few months back that ended in my burning her car where I found them.
>
>

Van included his "little list," which gave the police even more to mull over. Through a variation of verses lifted from a song—"As Someday It May Happen," from *The Mikado*—Van listed all of the types of people who could become potential victims. Police were able to deduce from that letter that the Zodiac was a Gilbert and Sullivan fan, that he listened to opera, and that his misspellings and grammatical errors were possibly an act. This killer was learned. Cultured.

Van had included references to preachers, organists, writers, children, and lawyers on the list of people who would not be missed if they disappeared.

Two days later, another letter arrived, this one explaining in graphic detail Van's fantasies about what he wanted to do to his slaves. It revealed just how sick and out of control he was becoming:

    This is the Zodiac speaking

    Being that you will not wear some nice ⊕
    buttons; how about wearing some nasty ⊕
    buttons. Or any type of ⊕ buttons that
    you can think up. If you do not wear any
    type of ⊕ buttons, I shall (on top of
    everything else) torture all 13 of my slaves
    that I have wateing for me in Paradice. Some
    I shall Tie over ant hills and watch them
    scream and twich and squirm. Others shall
    have pine splinters driven under their nails
    + then burned. Others shall be placed in
    cages + fed salt beef until they are gorged
    then I shall listen to their pleas for water
    and I shall laugh at them. Others will hang
    by their thumbs + burn in the sun then I
    will rub them down with deep heat to warm
    them up. Others I shall skin them alive
    + let them run around screaming. And all

billiard players I shall have them play in
a darkened dungon cell with crooked cues +
Twisted shoes. Yes, I shall have great fun
inflicting the most delicious of pain to my
Slaves.

He signed it:

$$SFPD = 0 \quad \bigoplus = 13$$

Each envelope, each letter, was tested for fingerprints and searched
for clues to the identity of the sender. Numerous law enforcement
agencies around California, as well as the FBI, were stumped. They
could not crack the codes my father sent, nor could they stop the
murders. Their hands were tied, and Van was rubbing it in.

At the time, police still had not connected the latest rash of
murders with the murder of Cheri Jo Bates; however, Van had
left them a clue in his latest letter. He had misspelled "twich" the
same way he had misspelled "twiched" in the confession letter he
had sent to police in Riverside.

It was a frustrating time for Toschi and Armstrong. They had
the killer's fingerprints, his handwriting. They had so many clues
to his personality. They realized he used British vernacular in his
writing. They just couldn't catch him. They even had the killer's
name, and they didn't know it.

Van was having the time of his life.

San Francisco Chronicle reporter Paul Avery was not.

He was as deeply entrenched in the Zodiac case as the police.
Avery worked long hours trying to be the first to report any
new developments. Van observed his dedication with interest,
reading every word the reporter wrote and taking offense at
much of it.

On October 27, Avery received a Halloween card from my father.

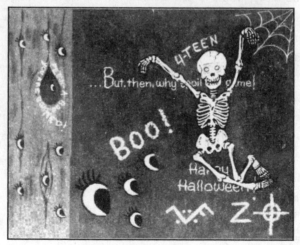

Avery did not like being singled out by Zodiac and became afraid that he would be targeted as his next victim. He immediately bought a gun for protection.

The reporter also did not realize that his "secret pal" was someone he knew—a man he had met in a jail cell in the Hall of Justice. He had made a mockery of Van's love for Judy, had insinuated that he was a child molester, and my father had not forgotten.

The methods of killing mentioned in the card prompted further investigation by police. Zodiac had not been linked to murders using rope, although there were many murder cases in the area involving women who were strangled during the years Zodiac was killing. The card made them go back and look at those cases to see if they could be linked to Zodiac, but the pieces didn't fit. His modus operandi was different.

The *Chronicle* published the Halloween card on October 31 on the front page of the paper.

Chronicle staff members soon began sporting buttons that stated, I AM NOT PAUL AVERY.

In November, an anonymous tip would lead Avery to make the connection between Zodiac and the Riverside murder of Cheri Jo Bates. Sherwood Morrill, the document examiner who had validated the Zodiac letters, soon confirmed that the handwriting in the Zodiac letters matched the letters and the desktop poem in the Riverside case.

Suddenly Avery, in addition to the police, was being bombarded with leads. He checked out every one, obsessed now with this killer who had singled him out. In a television documentary aired in 1989, titled *Zodiac: Crimes of the Century*, Avery explained, "At one point, I received a phone call from Anton LaVey, who was the founder and the high priest of the Church of Satan, which was very big in the late 1960s and early '70s. He thought one of his parishioners, one of his members, might be the Zodiac killer. And he provided me with some material. I mean, the Zodiac killer was so bad that even the Church of Satan didn't want him."

Did LaVey's association with Van prompt that phone call? Unfortunately, I will never know, because Avery never publicly revealed the name LaVey had given him. On March 13, 1971, the *Los Angeles Times* received its first correspondence from my father. It had been almost five months since he had sent anyone a letter. He wrote:

```
This is the Zodiac speaking

Like I have allways said, I am crack
proof. If the Blue Meannies are evere going
to catch me, they had best get off their fat
asses + do something. Because the longer
they fiddle + fart around, the more slaves
I will collect for my after life. I do have
to give them credit for stumbling across
my riverside activity, but they are only
finding the easy ones, there are a hell of a
lot more down there. The reason I'm writing
to the Times is this, They don't bury me on
the back pages like some of the others.
   SFPD — 0  ⊕ — 17+
```

Van's alleged victim count had climbed even higher. Again, police could not positively link him to any new murders during that time.

Then, just as suddenly as he appeared, the Zodiac stopped communicating. It would be three years before anyone heard from him again.

It is unknown why my father disappeared from the limelight during those years, but I know that he spent some time in Austria forging documents, and he also spent a lot of time in Mexico.

Weary from living in fear, California residents prayed they had heard the last of the Zodiac.

37

In 1971, Rotea finally realized his dream by becoming the first African American officially invited to join the SFPD's homicide team. He eventually chose Earl Sanders to be his partner, bringing his young friend up the ranks with him. Rotea soon learned that things were different in homicide. In the lower ranks, black officers felt like they could not depend on white officers.

In his book *The Zebra Murders: A Season of Killing, Racial Madness, and Civil Rights*, Earl Sanders recalls a time when he and Rotea were pursuing a suspect, and Rotea radioed for help. "We need some buddies as backup," he said.

"For a moment, there was silence," Sanders recalls in the book. "I'll never forget what I heard next: A man—we never found out who—came on and said, 'You two ain't got no buddies out here.'"

This was indicative of the kind of racism that Rotea and Sanders had experienced in robbery, but in homicide, detectives had to work together to be able to solve the murders that came across their desks. Rotea recognized that he was a token black, there only to make the department look good, but he was determined to prove he was just as capable as his white counterparts.

He made his point by rapidly solving the murder of a Muni bus driver. This was a major coup for the detective and earned him a place in newspaper headlines.

But that wasn't the only murder Rotea wanted to solve. Even

though it had been two years since Paul Stine was killed in his taxi, Toschi and Armstrong were still following up on the multitude of leads that continued to flow into the department regarding Zodiac. When they were too busy or had time off, Rotea ran down leads for them. That was the way it was in homicide. All of the detectives helped each other.

Rotea knew that the keys to finding the killer were in the letters and in the types of victims Zodiac had chosen. He reviewed the evidence from each case, noticing similarities and writing down crucial points. He knew from the viciousness directed toward the women that they seemed to be the main target of Zodiac's rage. He observed that they resembled one another. Rotea, like so many detectives across California, hoped, prayed, that they would soon get a lead that would break the case. He knew the answer had to be right in front of them.

It was.

Right in front of him.

All of the victims looked like his new girlfriend.

But Rotea, enamored of the beautiful young woman, missed that clue completely.

Professionally, Rotea was building respect in the department and in the community, but his personal life was in a shambles.

His oldest son, Michael, a college football lineman, had been in a terrible car crash that ended all hope of a football career. The young college star now required constant care. The accident had been devastating for the family, driving Rotea and Patricia further apart. The tension in his marriage had gotten progressively worse, until Rotea felt compelled to move into his own apartment in the Upper Haight. He spent the next year moving in and out of the home he shared with Patricia. Reconciling, breaking up, reconciling.

Rotea was not a man who liked being alone. When he was alone, he drank. Sometimes his partner came by to play dominoes, but more often than not Rotea stayed home alone when he wasn't working, drowning his sorrow in a bottle.

The one bright spot in his life was Judy. After the night they had danced together, he had asked her out for a dinner date, and she agreed to go. She liked his manners, his big, friendly smile. The respect he commanded. He liked her youth, her enthusiasm, her beauty.

They began dating, even though they knew others might not understand. Rotea explained to her the situation with Patricia, sharing his pain over their impending divorce. He talked about his son. Judy held his hand and listened empathetically.

My mother didn't mention me or my father. It was too soon for that. A police officer might not understand that she had once run away with a criminal who had abandoned their son.

My father, meanwhile, obsessed with reading newspapers to see what kind of press he was getting, couldn't help but notice the SFPD's black detective on the rise.

38

Every day that went by without a Zodiac murder allowed the city to breathe a little more easily. During this time, Rotea continued to woo Judy, asking her repeatedly to marry him after his divorce from Patricia became final.

Judy resisted. She was leery of becoming a stepmother. Her parents had not exactly provided a model for how to raise children, and her own experience with a child had been horrific.

But Rotea was relentless. A man needed a wife, and that was

that. He was just as determined as Van had been that Judy would be his.

He was equally determined to correct the way of thinking at the SFPD. Rotea became instrumental in forming a group of black police officers named Officers for Justice. In 1973, the group filed a civil suit against the department for discrimination. The good-old-boy network within the SFPD did not take kindly to the suit, and Rotea and Sanders soon found themselves working in an environment filled with hatred and bitterness. The tension boiled over one afternoon when Rotea and Sanders left the Federal Building after giving a deposition. Several hundred fellow officers were waiting on the steps when they left the building, shouting out derogatory slogans, even calling them "niggers."

Such an environment did not make Rotea's job easier, but he always maintained his composure and didn't let anything distract him from the job at hand, which at the time was to catch the perpetrators of a series of racially motivated murders that were terrorizing San Francisco.

The Zebra murders began October 20, 1973, when a young white couple, Richard and Quita Hague, were abducted while out walking and later viciously hacked with a machete by three African American men. Richard survived. Quita did not.

Over the next six months, Rotea and Sanders would spend almost every waking moment helping the lead detectives on the case, John Fotinos and Gus Coreris, track the murderers. Rotea and Sanders were invaluable to the team, because members of the black community who did not trust white officers would talk to them. Rotea used his contacts in the Fillmore to help uncover valuable clues.

On October 29, the next victim, Frances Rose, was shot several times by a man who had stopped her in her vehicle, demanding a ride as she approached the University of California campus in Berkeley. Saleem Erakat was next; on November 25, a man entered his grocery store, tied him up, and shot him execution style. On December 11, Paul Dancik was at a pay phone when he was shot three times.

On December 13, Art Agnos, who would eventually become the mayor of San Francisco, was shot twice in the back after leaving a meeting in a black neighborhood. That same night, Marietta DiGirolamo was shot three times while walking along Divisadero Street. She did not survive the attack.

Just before Christmas, on the 20th, Ilario Bertuccio died from four gunshot wounds in the Bayview District. That same evening, Theresa DeMartini was shot on Central Avenue, but she survived. On the 22nd, Neal Moynihan was killed, shot three times on Twelfth Street after leaving a bar. Only minutes later, Mildred Hosler was shot four times near her bus stop on Gough and McCoppin Streets.

On Christmas Eve, two women made a gruesome discovery on North Beach—the dead body of a man, whom police named "John Doe #196." The man had been dismembered and decapitated. His identity would forever remain a mystery, and although he sustained no bullet wounds, many investigators believed his death was connected to the Zebra murders.

In December 1973, *The Exorcist* was released in theaters to stunned audiences. Based on the 1949 exorcism of Roland Doe, the movie featured a young girl, played by Linda Blair, who is possessed by a demon that a pair of priests attempt to exorcise. For many, the satanic theme of the psychological drama was offensive, but few could resist watching, and *The Exorcist* became the top-grossing horror film of all time. Others embraced the film's focus on the power of evil, but everyone who saw it was frightened.

Everyone but Van.

On January 28, 1974, the Zebra killers went on a rampage, committing five separate shootings—Roxanne McMillan, Tana Smith, Vincent Wollin, John Bambic, and Jane Holly. McMillan was the only victim who survived.

As the families of the dead mourned their losses, in a cramped bedroom on Noe Street, Van stared at the announcement in horror.

There she was . . . beautiful and sweet. Smiling.

Staring into her eyes was the black homicide detective he had seen in San Francisco newspapers.

And the date of their nuptials.

On January 29, my father, devastated and enraged, wrote the first letter he had written in three years. He addressed it to the *San Francisco Chronicle*.

Out of the foggy mist, Zodiac reemerged to terrorize the city even further.

"I saw + think 'The Exorcist' was the best saterical comidy that I have ever seen," he wrote.

"Signed, yours truley:"

Van then predicted the figurative death of Zodiac using quotes from *The Mikado*.

```
He plunged him self into the billowy wave
and an echo arose from the sucides grave
tit willo tit willo
tit willo
PS. if I do not see this note in your
paper, I will do something nasty, which you
know I'm capable of doing
Me — 37
SFPD — 0
```

His purported victim count had more than doubled during his absence. While no murders bearing the Zodiac's signature in Austria or Mexico during those three years have come to my attention, I have to wonder if my father might have left a mark in those places. Or was he simply manufacturing victim tallies to keep police guessing?

On Valentine's Day 1974, twelve years to the day since Van's marriage to Judy had been annulled by her family, the *Chronicle* received another letter:

Dear Mr. Editor,

Did you know that the initials SLAY
(Symbionese Liberation Army) spell "sla," an
old Norse word meaning *"kill."*

a friend

The Zebra killings resumed on April 1, when Thomas Rainwater and Linda Story were shot by a man who had followed them from the Salvation Army, where they served as cadets. Linda survived her wounds, but Thomas died.

Terry White and Ward Anderson were attacked April 14 at Fillmore and Hayes Streets while awaiting a bus. They both survived.

Nelson T. Shields would be the last victim of the Zebra murders. Shields, heir to a DuPont executive, was shot and killed on April 16 as he put a rug in the back of his station wagon.

As each murder occurred, pressure to catch the killers became more intense. Mayor Joseph Alioto and Chief of Police Donald Scott initiated an unprecedented move to catch the killers, announcing that any member of the black race would be stopped and questioned if they looked like the sketch of the killer or if they had a narrow chin or a short-cropped Afro. If they were cleared, they would receive a special Zebra card that let other officers know they had already been checked out.

Rotea was appalled. As badly as he wanted to catch the killers, he could not believe that his department would stoop to such blatant racial profiling. He observed in horror that weekend as his fellow officers stopped more than five hundred black men for no reason other than that they fit the description. The Officers for Justice stepped up to voice their opposition loudly, as did other prominent members of the black community. After the NAACP and the ACLU filed a lawsuit, the SFPD's actions were ruled unconstitutional, and the department was forced to stop racially profiling blacks.

On April 23, a man named Anthony Harris, who belonged to a militant group associated with the Nation of Islam, turned himself in to police. He said he knew who was committing the random killings, and he could not let the slaughter of innocent white people continue. His testimony would help put away four other men: Larry Green, Manuel Moore, Jesse Lee Cooks, and J. C. Simon. Four more men were arrested but not indicted. After the longest trial in San Francisco history, each of the defendants was given a life sentence.

Rotea, relieved that the killers had been brought to justice, resumed his fight for racial equality within the department.

And his courtship of the beautiful blonde who took away his loneliness.

Judy had spent many evenings over the past months listening as Rotea and Sanders discussed the case. She had heard the 187 calls come in over the radio and had watched fearfully as they hurried out to investigate each new murder.

Her fear of losing him during that ordeal made her realize how much she loved the handsome detective.

On June 19, 1974, the Reverend Cecil Williams joined Rotea Gilford and Judy Chandler in holy matrimony.

And on July 8, Van wrote his final letter to the *San Francisco Chronicle*. It was directed toward *Chronicle* columnist Marc Spinelli.

```
Editor—


Put Marco back in the, hell-hole
from whence it came—he has a serious
psychological disorder—always needs to
feel superior. I suggest you refer him
to a shrink. Meanwhile, cancel the Count
Marco column. Since the Count can write
anonymously, so can I—


the Red Phantom
(red with rage)
```

Zodiac was indeed red with rage, but it wasn't because of Marc Spinelli.

Judy had married the homicide detective.

Things had just hit way too close to home.

Zodiac would never be heard from again.

39

After he sent his final letter as the Zodiac, Van left the country, worried that Rotea would somehow put the pieces together if Judy started discussing him. He traveled to Austria, feeling safe in this country that had declared permanent neutrality—there would be no extradition if Rotea discovered the truth. He spent the next few weeks searching bookstores for ancient documents that traced the history of Austria back to 996. He was unsuccessful in finding anything of real value and once again resorted to forging documents to get by.

He did not bother to get in touch with his children or Edith, to whom he was still married. As time passed, Van realized that Judy must have kept her mouth shut, because the authorities did not contact him. His paranoia about Rotea dissipated, and his confidence grew.

A few months later, Van returned to San Francisco and moved into an apartment in the William Penn Hotel, in the Upper Tenderloin. Built circa 1907, the William Penn, located at 160 Eddy Street, was one of many hotels featuring single-occupancy dwellings that sprang up after most of the buildings in the district had been swallowed by the 1906 earthquake and the fires that erupted afterwards. The neighborhood, historically famous for its accommodating attitude toward alternate lifestyles, welcomed homosexuals, drug users, and the down-and-out. Musicians were drawn there by the gigs available in the plethora of nightclubs that were nestled between restaurants, theaters, and hotels. In the fifties, jazz trumpeter Miles Davis and pianist Thelonius Monk had graced those nightclubs, along with local musicians who blatantly copied their styles.

The neighborhood, bordered by Lower Nob Hill, had been Van's old stomping grounds, and he felt safe here, in the midst of other misfits. His apartment, number 215, was small—one bedroom with a single closet and a bathroom with a short, claw-foot tub—and cheap, but it suited his needs.

Van spent his nights in the bars, drinking and watching drag queens scurry in and out, their short skirts and open blouses proudly proclaiming their true gender. Long before the Castro

District welcomed them, the Tenderloin had housed and protected them.

During the day, Van roamed the streets, blurry-eyed and hungover, often walking the three blocks from the hotel to Geary Street, where he had once lived with Judy.

Reminiscing.

Mourning his loss.

Damning his luck.

Sometimes he tried to contact his old friend William, but William wouldn't take his calls. He had long since ended his association with Van, although he could not forget him. The courts wouldn't let him. William had earned his master's degree in criminology and had become a forensic criminologist. But every time he entered a courtroom to testify as an expert witness in a case, a defense attorney brought up his arrest for helping Van kidnap Judy. William had pleaded guilty to a misdemeanor and been sentenced to probation, but the arrest had stayed on his record, haunting him throughout his career. If Van had testified to the fact that William did not know Judy was underage, the charges might have been dismissed. William felt betrayed by his friend and wanted nothing to do with him.

Van felt betrayed, too—by every woman he had ever known. And now Judy's marriage to a homicide detective had taken away the only things that gave him relief.

Murder—that gave him power.

Taunting police—that made him feel superior.

Helped him cope.

Judy had robbed him of that.

Van soon headed for the reassuring familiarity of the cobblestone streets of Mexico City. He felt comfortable in the bar at the Hotel Corinto, surrounded by Mexicans who called him Señor Best and looked at his books. They accepted him, even admired the American who had become such a fixture in their lives. When he walked down the narrow streets, shop owners waved. When he went into a bar, a Tom Collins was waiting. Antiquities dealers smiled when they saw him, recognizing there was money to be made.

But Van was no longer interested in striking it rich with antiques. He bought and sold only what he needed to survive. And he drank, but there was no escape. Judy was there, lingering in the cathedrals they had visited, in the restaurants where they had eaten, in the Hotel Corinto, where they had made love.

Over the next year, Van spent most of his time in Mexico, nursing his wounds. I don't know if my father thought about the lives he had destroyed, about the dreams he had stolen, about the children who would grow up without parents or the parents whose children had died, so unnaturally, before them. I don't know if he thought about his own children. I only know that he drank.

In 1976, my father returned to San Francisco. On the night of March 17, around 8:30, he stumbled across Reardon's Restaurant to a pay phone in the lobby.

Although he struggled to control his urges, on this night he couldn't resist. He had been out of the limelight for too long and needed the thrill of taunting the authorities.

Van inserted a few dimes and dialed the number to the San Francisco office of the Federal Bureau of Investigation.

"I have information regarding a possible plot to assassinate President Gerald R. Ford," he said to the agent who answered the phone.

"What is your name, sir?" the agent asked.

"Earl Van Best."

"What is your date of birth?"

"July 14, 1934."

"What is this information you have?" the agent inquired, trying to discern whether this was a credible threat. There had been two attempts on the president's life six months earlier—one by

Lynette "Squeaky" Fromme, a Manson Family member, who had pointed a gun at the president on the grounds of the capitol building in Sacramento, California, and one by Sara Jane Moore, a member of a leftist radical group, who had fired a shot at President Ford as he exited the St. Francis Hotel in San Francisco.

"I am an importer," Van said. "I have many intimate contacts among diplomatic circles in the San Francisco area. Two days ago, a Yugoslav national informed me of a plot to kill the president."

"What is his name?"

"I can't give you that information," Van said.

"How do you know this person?" the agent asked.

"He first contacted me in 1974 in Austria. He wanted to obtain false identity documents."

"And what is the plot you mentioned?"

"He said he was going to assassinate the president of the United States during a public appearance on March 18."

"Do you have a description of this man?" the agent said.

"He's five feet nine inches tall, brown hair and brown eyes. He has a husky build," Van replied. "I am aware of several radical plots against the president. They have been set up by a group of radical fanatics. This Yugoslav national is the leader."

At approximately 8:45 p.m., the FBI alerted the SFPD that Van's location was 100 Embarcadero Street. The Secret Service was also notified.

The agent kept Van talking while police were en route.

At 9:15 p.m., an SFPD officer took the phone from Van as another officer handcuffed him. "The suspect is in custody," the agent on the line was informed. "It looks like he's intoxicated. We are taking him to the city jail, and we'll hold him on a drunk charge."

The FBI agent informed the Secret Service that Van was in jail, but the special agent with whom he'd spoken did not show up to interrogate my father.

The SFPD released Van the following morning without consulting the FBI.

The FBI immediately began searching for him.

There was no attempt made on the president's life on March 18.

On March 19, an FBI agent went to the William Penn Hotel and spoke to Van's former landlord.

"He moved out in February of last year," the landlord said. "He lived here for about six months. I still get some of his mail, though."

The FBI agent returned on March 27 and again on April 2. "Has he been back?" he asked Van's former landlord.

"I think he might have picked up some of his mail," the landlord said.

"Please tell him to contact the FBI if he shows up."

Van never did.

Because no further attempts against the president's life had been made, the FBI eventually closed the case.

40

The Hall of Justice, which housed the SFPD, the San Francisco County Superior Court, the San Francisco Sheriff's Department, and the county jail, was erected in 1958 and designed to impress, with its marbled walls and huge, domed chandeliers. The building featured a shoeshine stand at its entrance, where lawyers, detectives, and laypeople would often gather to chat. The fourth floor, where major crimes were investigated, consisted of long corridors with doors kept tightly closed and walls of photographs depicting heroes who had left their mark on the SFPD. A metal sign, carved with the word HOMICIDE, protruded out over the wooden doorway that led to the major crimes unit. Taped to the window nearby, posters of victims and rewards offered let everyone know which cases had not yet been solved.

By the mid-seventies, the sketch of the Zodiac had been replaced with photographs of suspects who were wanted for more recent murders. But detectives like Toschi kept the Zodiac sketch handy, just in case.

So did Rotea, who often sported a furry black-and-white-striped hat. He had bought it to commemorate his participation in the investigation of the Zebra murders, and he wore it proudly. Others in the department thought it was a strange memento, but few turned down the opportunity to try it on. In Room 450, Detective Dave Toschi could occasionally be found at his desk wearing the hat, with Rotea standing nearby, ready to snatch it back.

Late in 1975, Toschi's partner, Bill Armstrong, weary of all of the death that plagued his dreams at night, left the homicide department with the biggest case of his career unsolved. Toschi wasn't about to part ways with the Zodiac; he had too much invested. While the flamboyant detective still lorded over the case in the media, Armstrong had been the backbone of the duo, and in his absence, new leads were eventually distributed among all of the detectives. There was always another killer to catch, and the focus on apprehending the Zodiac was not as all-consuming as it had been six years earlier.

Rotea finally had his shot to investigate the case more thoroughly, but another serial killer was now plaguing the homicide division. The Black Doodler, named by the media for his habit of attracting his victims by sketching their likenesses before having sex with them, had viciously stabbed and killed fourteen gay men between January 1974 and September 1975. Three other men, who had been attacked and escaped, had reported the incidents to the SFPD.

Initially, Rotea and Sanders suspected they were dealing with three separate serial killers, because the modus operandi was different in some of the cases. Five of the victims were transvestites who frequented the gay bars in the Tenderloin. Six of the victims were involved in sadomasochism and hung out at the leather bars south of Market Street. The other six victims had been on the down-low—businessmen, a lawyer, an entertainer, a diplomat, all picked up in the Castro District, wooed by promises of a fun evening.

As Rotea and the other detectives interviewed the survivors, a clear picture of the Black Doodler emerged. In 1976, they brought in a suspect and questioned him. Although willing enough to talk with detectives, the suspect refused to confess. Yet Rotea was convinced: the SFPD had the Black Doodler in its custody.

But there was a problem.

They had to let him go.

In an Associated Press article dated May 8, 1977, Rotea was reported to have explained that "for the past year, police have been questioning a young man they call 'The Doodler' about the 14 slayings and three assaults that have occurred in San Francisco's gay community.

"The suspect here, his name not released, has talked freely with police but has not admitted the slayings, Gilford said.

"He said police are 'fairly certain' they have the right man, but need the testimony of survivors who may be able to identify 'The Doodler,'" the article continued.

"Gilford said the three survivors include the entertainer, the diplomat and a man who left San Francisco and won't answer letters or phone calls at his new address.

"'My feeling is they don't want to be exposed.'"

And because the victims were not willing to come out of the closet to put a serial killer in prison, the Black Doodler was never arrested.

The case frustrated Rotea. He knew who the killer was, where he lived, but there was not enough evidence to convict him without victim identifications.

The article went on to state that Harvey Milk, "an advocate of homosexual rights, said of the victims who refuse to speak up, 'I can understand their position. I respect the pressure society has put on them.'

"Milk said many homosexuals may keep their sexual preference a secret because they fear losing their jobs. 'They have to stay in the closet,' he said."

The Black Doodler soon faded from public attention. He didn't sell newspapers like the Zodiac had. Killings of homosexuals simply weren't as mesmerizing as ciphers from the Zodiac.

Homosexual politicians—now that was another story. When Harvey Milk became the first openly gay person ever to be elected to public office in California, in late 1977, politics and homosexuality once again dominated the headlines. Backed by Mayor George Moscone, the outspoken Milk won over voters and earned his seat on the San Francisco Board of Supervisors.

Moscone, a strong proponent of gay rights, was the first mayor of the city to appoint large numbers of women, gays, and minorities to city commissions and advisory boards. With the help of Rotea's old friend in the State Assembly, Willie Brown, Moscone, as a state senator, had been instrumental in repealing California's sodomy law. In the dimly lit bars of the Castro, young businessmen had cheered and raised their glasses, saluting Moscone and Brown for the victory. But the decisions Moscone made as mayor would cost him dearly.

In the months before his mayoral election, Moscone had

recruited Jim Jones, of the Peoples Temple, to campaign for him, recognizing that Jones's huge congregation could swing the vote. Jones had moved his temple to San Francisco several years before and had been steadily working his way into San Francisco's political circles. Moscone rewarded him with the chairmanship of the San Francisco Housing Authority Commission soon after he won the election.

By September 1977, Willie Brown had also joined the Jim Jones bandwagon, delivering a speech at a banquet held at the temple headquarters on Geary Street, where he proclaimed that Jones was a combination of "Martin Luther King, Angela Davis, Albert Einstein, and Chairman Mao," according to PBS.org.

In 1978, Rotea took an early retirement from the San Francisco Police Department, making the move into politics. Moscone appointed him executive director of the Mayor's Council on Criminal Justice, even though the lawsuit for racial discrimination that Rotea had helped initiate against the city was ongoing.

And then all hell broke loose.

On November 18, 1978, Jones led some nine hundred people in a mass murder/suicide in Jonestown, Guyana, where he had moved his temple after allegations of abuse began to filter out through the media. Images of corpses—adults and children, lying side by side on the ground—filled evening news programs, and a collective shudder of horror rippled through the world. Among the dead was California congressman Leo Ryan, who was visiting Guyana to investigate the allegations.

Jones's political friends in San Francisco ran for cover, including Willie Brown, Harvey Milk, and George Moscone.

Nine days later, Dan White, a recently resigned city supervisor, walked into city hall and shot and killed Mayor Moscone and then Milk, both of whom had opposed White's requests to be reassigned to his position.

As the world mourned the tragedy in Guyana, the gay community in San Francisco mourned the loss of its two biggest proponents in city hall.

It was not a good time for anyone to enter politics in the city of San Francisco, least of all someone like Rotea, for whom integrity was so important. During his time at the SFPD, he had broken new ground for African Americans and earned fifteen commendations in eighteen years. In 1979, Judge Robert F. Peckham agreed that minorities were underrepresented in the department and ordered new standards regarding recruitment, assignments, and promotions, complete with a twenty-year review process. Rotea and the Officers for Justice had finally succeeded in their fight to end discrimination in the SFPD.

Rotea had achieved all of his goals.

Except one.

The Zodiac was still free.

41

"It's for you, dear. It's Van," Ellie said, handing the phone to her husband.

Earl picked up the phone, hoping for some good news. Lately, on the rare occasions Van called, his father could barely understand him.

"Yes, hello, son," Earl said.

"I need some money, Father."

"Why. What's going on?" Earl queried.

"I got arrested and need to pay my fines and get down to Mexico," Van said, slurring his words.

Earl sat down, preparing himself. "What did you do?"

"Just a couple of drunk-driving charges," Van mumbled.

"Van, speak up. I can't hear you."

"I said, 'drunk driving.'"

"Van, you have got to stop this," Earl said. "When are you going to pull yourself together?"

"I will, Father. I'm working on it. I just need to make one more trip and everything will be better. I promise."

Van had been arrested three times for drunk driving in 1977—on March 21 in San Bernardino, on June 24 in Riverside, and on October 24 in San Bernardino. Earl knew his son was spiraling downward, and there was nothing he could do.

By this time Earl had retired from his ministry at the Refuge Christian Church and was enjoying his retirement with his beloved wife. The country preacher had much to be proud of. He had been elected twice to serve his country as the national chaplain of the Veterans of Foreign Wars and had worked with several presidents, including John F. Kennedy, Lyndon B. Johnson, and Richard M. Nixon. For many years he had been the chaplain of the Indiana State VFW, and recently Indiana governor Otis Bowen had named him a Sagamore of the Wabash, the highest honor the governor could bestow on a citizen to recognize distinguished service. The minister had four degrees to his credit. His had been a life of service to his congregation and to his country.

His only failure had been Van.

Van spent the next five years traveling back and forth along the coast of California, living in Long Beach, while also spending long periods at the Hotel Corinto, in Mexico. Occasionally he discovered something of value on his trips, but mostly he bartered his antiquities for enough money to buy the alcohol that made his existence bearable. Merchants along the coast who had once enthusiastically looked forward to his visits, impressed with Van's knowledge and unusual finds, now hesitated before parting with their money, viewing the unkempt appearance of the once well-dressed trader. My father was no longer able to schmooze them with a charming smile and a turn of a phrase. They could smell the alcohol on his breath and see it in his eyes.

Six years after Judy married Rotea, Van rebounded for a while in 1982. Earl, relieved that his son was doing better, wrote a letter to his niece: "Van has quit drinking and writes and talks with some sense now. We talk via phone once in a while and it makes me proud to know he's living the good life."

After forty-eight years, my grandfather finally experienced a moment in which he could be proud of his son.

And then the moment was gone.

By the end of the year Van had retreated back into the bottle.

Father and son would never speak again.

Earl Van Best Sr. passed away on March 28, 1984, at the age of seventy-nine. Ellie brushed away her tears as a bugle cried out the lonesome notes of Taps. The twenty-one-gun salute, which had originated in the Navy, of which Earl had been so proud, recognized her husband as a military hero. Standing there in Arlington National Cemetery, watching as the man who had earned such respect was lowered into the ground, she looked around for Van.

He did not bother to attend.

42

In 1978, Dianne Feinstein succeeded George Moscone to become the first female mayor of San Francisco. She appointed Rotea Gilford her deputy mayor.

Judy couldn't have been prouder. She adored the man who had brought such stability to her life. Things had been a little rocky at first, but she had soon realized it wasn't Rotea's fault. She didn't know how to behave in a healthy relationship. She had been conditioned for drama, first by her father and stepfather and then by Van. She did everything she could to sabotage the relationship during the first six months of their marriage.

Rotea began to wonder what had happened to the vivacious young girl he had married. She found fault with everything he did. Then one day, about six months into the marriage, Judy had an epiphany.

"I was driving to work this morning and was thinking about what is so wrong with our marriage," she said to her husband later that evening. Judy now worked as an office manager on a construction project.

"And what did you come up with?" Rotea asked, worry evident in his tone.

"Nothing. Absolutely nothing. There's nothing wrong with our marriage. I don't know why I've been acting like this. I have a wonderful husband and a very interesting life. I will be better now. I promise."

Rotea pulled her close, relieved. He didn't know about Judy's past, but he sometimes realized she was battling demons she didn't care to share with him.

"Let's celebrate," he said. "We'll just start over."

They did, and Judy had never been happier. Three years into the marriage, she finally overcame her fear of having another child and gave birth to a boy they named Chance Michael, after Rotea's son Michael, who had recently passed away after suffering for years with injuries he had sustained in the car accident.

Judy and Rotea doted on their baby. He was a second chance for both of them.

From the day he was born, Judy was very protective of Chance. If Rotea raised his voice with the child, Judy cautioned him not to, but she needn't have worried. He had always been a loving father, and as Chance grew up, Rotea proved over and over that there were honorable men in the world.

Sometimes Judy spotted her husband sitting at their kitchen window watching Chance as he played basketball with his friends outside. Rotea would take notes, then make a list of the things Chance had done that needed improvement and the things he had done very well. When Chance came inside, they would go over the list.

She watched as her husband instilled in her son discipline, strength, responsibility. For the first time in her life, Judy knew she had made the right choice. Rotea often coached Chance and other neighborhood children and made himself available for any child who needed fatherly advice. Whenever they walked through their neighborhood in Hayes Valley, neighbors always smiled and waved, comforted by Rotea's presence among them.

Judy showered Chance with love, trying in some small way to make up for leaving me behind in Baton Rouge. Although she kept her silence, she sometimes wondered what had happened to the son she had given up for adoption. She was secure in her marriage, yet she couldn't bring herself to tell her husband, who loved children so much, that she had given away her son. Instead she threw herself into helping Rotea mentor the children in their community, and soon the couple invited twelve-year-old Terry Marshall, who had been abandoned by his grandmother, to live with them.

Rotea's mother, Viola, who lived in an apartment on the first floor of their home, helped out with the children. A wonderful baker, Viola would have dinner ready every afternoon after Judy and Rotea had retrieved the children from school.

As Rotea became more embroiled in San Francisco politics, Judy began to worry. He seemed more tired than usual. Between volunteering, coaching, and substitute teaching, he began to have trouble getting out of bed in the morning. That was not like the energetic man she had married.

Harold Butler, a young police officer with the SFPD, noticed something was amiss, too. Butler had become one of Rotea's projects, a black officer rising through the ranks in a much different environment than Rotea had experienced. The two had met through the Officers for Justice and had become fast friends, although Butler was much younger. He had heard all of the stories about Rotea and looked up to him.

"Is he all right?" Butler asked Judy one evening as they sat at the dining room table. "He looks worn out."

"He's been tired lately," Judy admitted. "I don't know what's wrong. He says it's nothing."

"He should see a doctor," Butler said.

Judy tried, but Rotea insisted that everything was okay. "It's my blood sugar," he said, his standard excuse when anything was wrong.

Rotea served his city throughout the Feinstein administration, but he withdrew from public office soon after Art Agnos became mayor, in 1988. When Willie Brown, who had served in the California State Assembly for fifteen years, became the first black mayor in San Francisco's history, in 1996, Rotea was drawn back into politics. Brown appointed him to the Recreation and Park Commission.

Every morning, promptly at 6:00 a.m., Rotea called Brown. "Good morning, Mayor," he always said, his way of acknowledging Brown's accomplishment. The two men had spent decades building a friendship that encompassed not only genuine affection for each other but also a shared fight for racial equality.

Harold Butler was excited to be a part of Rotea's inner circle. He and his wife were frequent guests at the Gilford home, and he enjoyed strategizing with his mentor about meetings Rotea was having with the mayor to discuss new projects—which was unnecessary, really, because Brown backed Rotea's ideas one hundred percent. Rotea knew how much it meant to the young officer to be a part of the politics, so he invited him over regularly. Butler often consulted Rotea about difficult cases he was working, taking advantage of the detective's experience and wisdom. He was in awe of the great man who had become such a legend on the force, but he worried about Rotea's health.

So did Judy. Throughout the last years of their marriage, she lost her husband to diabetes one limb at a time. It started with a discolored toe when Rotea was in his early sixties, and then gangrene set in. Judy had promised to care for Rotea, but sometimes she wondered how she would cope. "When he came home from the hospital, a visiting nurse came over to show me how to change the dressings," she would later write when documenting her memories of Rotea. "When she removed the bandages and I saw the gaping hole where his toe had formerly fit, I almost fainted. I got through the lesson, went upstairs and out onto the front deck, and gasped for air. How in the world was I going to do this?"

Later, after part of Rotea's left foot was amputated, Judy had to soak the remaining part in bleach every four hours, for weeks. The treatments she administered saved the rest of the foot, and Rotea was able to hobble around with a prosthetic shoe.

Then he lost the other foot.

By the time Brown appointed Rotea to the commission, his diabetes had forced him into renal failure. Every morning, Mitch Salazar, director of community-based programs and one of Rotea's success stories, came by to bring his mentor to the dialysis center. Once a street hustler and low-level drug dealer in the Mission District, the young man had turned his life around with

Rotea's help. Salazar, a high school dropout, worked his way into city politics through volunteer work, in which he helped others who had the odds stacked against them.

Rudy Smith, another childhood friend of Rotea's, had also been appointed to the commission by the mayor. He was given the go-ahead by Brown to provide Rotea with whatever assistance he needed. Loyal to a fault, Smith picked Rotea up from dialysis around noon each day, got him food from his favorite restaurants, and discussed the city's business over lunch in Rotea's kitchen.

Throughout the ordeal, Judy and Rotea became closer than ever. When the gangrene spread to his fingers, they were amputated one by one. Judy, fearful of losing the man she loved so dearly, tried to express the love she had for him in words:

> I didn't want to marry. I didn't share his vision of what or how it could be. But once I said yes, he went on to show me, really train me, just as he counseled so many others he took to his heart before and since. He taught me love of every sort, that between two people, that within our families, that for our community, state, and nation.
>
> In holding me so close, he set me free. In being my first and best teacher, he set the standard so I could surround myself with teachers and guides to help me when he no longer could.
>
> He was my radiant warrior hero and I am so very grateful.
>
> He had a willing heart.

When Judy shared her words with Rotea, he said, "I want that to be my obituary."

In expressing her love, she had captured the essence of the man who had helped so many.

On March 13, 1998, Rotea and Judy made the decision that there would be no more surgeries, no more dialysis. The next day, Rotea called the mayor and asked him to come over, informing Brown that he simply did not want to fight anymore. "I'm going to die," he said. The mayor arrived around noon.

So did Earl Sanders. Rotea's former partner had spent most of the past week at Rotea's house, encouraging his friend, helping to care for him. Harold Butler, along with the others, recognizing that the end was near, hurried to the Gilford home to comfort his friend.

Rotea sat on the edge of the bed, doing what he had always done—telling exaggerated stories about his escapades that made everyone laugh. In the midst of great sadness, no one in the room shed a tear. Rotea wasn't going to let that happen.

After his friends said their good-byes, Rotea went to sleep. Judy and Rotea's ex-wife, Patricia, sat with him, quietly observing as his breathing became more labored. Other family members soon joined them, praying aloud for the man who had touched their lives so deeply. When they were finished, Rotea took his final breath.

And then he was gone.

"It was a beautiful and peaceful passage on the wings of love in two days' time," Judy would later write.

— PART THREE -

THE TRUTH DECIPHERED

43

With Rotea gone, Judy didn't quite know what to do with herself. She had spent four years nursing him through his illness, and suddenly there was nothing left to do. By that time, Chance and Terry were grown and pursuing their own lives. Sometimes when she walked through her home, she stopped by the bedrooms of her boys and cried softly as she reminisced. The house that had once been so full of life, so noisy, was now empty, and the silence overwhelmed her. Friends and family visited and tried to keep her busy, but it wasn't the same. When they left, the silence returned to wrap around her as she stared longingly at old pictures of the man who had changed her life and the boys whose antics had filled her home with laughter. She filled her days with work and volunteering, but nothing could alter the fact that when she returned home each night, there were three empty chairs at the dinner table. For the first time in twenty-five years, Judy was alone.

With so much time to think, the memories that she had so carefully tucked away began to drift into her dreams. Years into their marriage, she had finally confessed to Rotea, revealing to her husband that she had a son he didn't know about.

"Do you want to find him?" Rotea had asked.

"I don't know if I should," she replied. "All I know is that he grew up in the South. I don't know how he would feel about learning he has a half-black brother. What if he rejects us when he finds out? They think differently there."

Rotea agreed that was a concern and said that he would support her in whatever decision she made.

Judy let it drop, fearful of what might happen if she found me, afraid of the questions I might ask.

Afraid of what Rotea might find out.

She was not yet ready to relive that terrible time in her life.

With Rotea gone, things were different. The curiosity about what had happened to me began to override her fears. About a year after Rotea died, Judy made her decision. She would try to find me, and she'd deal with the consequences later.

In a way, Rotea helped her. All those nights she had sat at the dining room table and listened to her husband and Earl Sanders discuss their cases and the investigatory techniques they used would now pay off. She eventually discovered the names of twenty-seven men who had been born in Louisiana on February 12, 1963, and she began calling and writing letters to them, hoping one of them might be her son.

It took three years, the help of an adoption search group, and a state worker in Louisiana, but my mother, relentless now in her desire to find me, finally learned my adopted name.

And thirty-nine years after my aunt Margie had pulled me from her arms, we were finally reunited.

The morning after I arrived in San Francisco, I woke my son, Zach, and headed to the Unity Christ Church on Ocean Avenue, where Judy and her boyfriend, Frank, were already waiting for us in a quaint chapel surrounded by clusters of colorful flowers. I held Zach's hand as we crossed the street and walked into the church. Judy had arranged for me to meet my grandmother, Verda, and my brother Chance there. Excited and nervous, I wasn't quite sure what I would say to these strangers who were suddenly my family.

Verda had left Sacramento early that morning, around 7:00. As she dressed, she wondered what would happen when she met me, how she could explain why she had made the decision to force Judy to relinquish her son. There had been no time to prepare for the phone call she had received in 1963 in which she learned Judy had given birth to a baby boy, and that the man who had kidnapped and raped her was the father. Verda had cried when the social worker from Louisiana described me—"Reddish blond hair, blue eyes, looks just like his mama. He's so sweet and innocent."

But she already had several children of her own, one only eight months old. She couldn't take on Judy's baby, too. She knew that's what would have happened. Judy had already shown that she could not be counted on to be responsible or listen to any kind of reason. Besides, there had been no way her husband, Vic, would have let her bring the baby into their home. She had done what was best for everyone.

But would the baby turned grown man understand? With a sick feeling in the pit of her stomach, she got in her car and drove to San Francisco.

When Zach and I walked into the church, Verda was already there, sitting alone on a pew with her hands folded across her purse, as if she had been praying. I noticed her immediately, somehow recognizing that the elderly lady was my grandmother.

I walked to the pew and stood there for a moment, not knowing what to say. I could see the uncertainty in her eyes.

"Well, I guess I ought to know you," Verda said in a high, sweet voice. She pushed herself off the bench and wrapped her arms around me.

The hug was enough. I could not hate this woman whose actions had given me parents like Loyd and Leona.

"Don't worry," I reassured her. "You have no reason for regret or guilt. Thank you for the decision you made. I love you, Grandma."

A few minutes later, Chance, his wife, Jasmine, and his daughter, Mia, found us in the church.

Everyone's eyes filled with tears as I hugged my brother for the first time. Judy's fear that my being raised in the South would be a problem had been unfounded. I could not have cared less that my brother was half-black. I had a brother, and that was all that mattered.

I spent much of 2002 getting to know my new family through phone calls and e-mails, and I was able to visit my mother four times that year. That Christmas, I went to California for a company meeting and our annual holiday party, excited because it would be my first Christmas with my mother. Frank recommended that Judy and I drive to Tahoe and Reno for a mini-vacation, to spend some time alone together.

It was in Reno, where Judy and Van had married so many years before, that the urge to know more about my father resurfaced. I had refrained from asking too many questions over the past six months, because I didn't want to do anything to upset my mother and risk damaging our new relationship. By now, I knew she didn't want to talk about my father.

But I had to know.

We spent the last day of our vacation in Tahoe, and as we drank coffee and watched the morning dawn over the snow-capped mountains, I made a confession. "I know I told you I didn't want to know about my father, but I think I want to know who he was. I want to try to find him."

Judy didn't hesitate. "Well, honey. If that's what your heart wants, then I will do everything I can to help you with your search."

"Thank you, Mom," I said, hugging her. "I just want to meet him."

I realized that it was the last thing Judy wanted to do, but she gave me her word. After I returned to Baton Rouge, she started making calls. The first number she dialed was Earl Sanders.

"Earl, I need your help," she said to San Francisco's chief of police. Years before, Mayor Moscone had vowed that one day Rotea would make history by becoming San Francisco's first black chief of police. The assassination of the mayor had prevented that from happening. Instead, Rotea's partner Earl Sanders had broken that barrier in 2002.

But there had been problems.

Sanders and two of his chief deputies had recently been indicted by a grand jury on charges of obstruction of justice. Rookie officer Alex Fagan Jr., the son of Sanders's top aide, had been involved in a bar brawl along with two other off-duty policemen. The incident, named "Fajitagate" by the media, began when the bartender refused to give the officers a doggie bag of steak fajitas as he was leaving work. A fight ensued, during which the bartender was injured. Sanders and Fagan's father ran the department side by side, and when the offending officers were not arrested, District Attorney Terence Hallinan came for blood.

Scandal in the police department was as common as the fog that blankets San Francisco Bay, so Judy had not been overly concerned when she heard about Sanders's most recent imbroglio.

"What's the matter?" Sanders said, his voice sounding weak.

"Remember I told you about my son? Well, he wants to find his father, and I don't know where to look. I'm not even sure of his full name."

"I'd be happy to help, but I'm in the hospital. I had a heart attack," Sanders said.

"Oh, my goodness, I'm so sorry," Judy cried.

"Don't worry. I'll be okay," the chief laughed. "Call Harold Butler. He should be able to help you."

"Thanks, Earl. I'll check in on you later," Judy said, hanging up the phone, worried now that the scandal was affecting her friend's health.

"Earl can't help us," she informed me. "He's in the middle of a big scandal, and he had a heart attack. He suggested we talk to Harold Butler. Harold and Rotea were buddies, and he used to come over all the time. I know he'll do anything for me."

She dialed Butler's number.

"Harold, Earl told me to call you," she said, explaining that she wanted him to help her son from a previous marriage find his father.

"I wasn't aware that you had another son," Butler said.

"No one was," Judy said. "It's a long story, but I promised my son I would help him. Can you do some digging for me? I know there's got to be a record of his father somewhere, but all I remember is that his name was Van."

Butler asked her a lot of questions, trying to glean any information he could from Judy. "Don't worry. If he has a criminal record, I'll find him," he reassured her.

It took a month, but Butler finally contacted my mother with his findings. On June 6, 2003, Judy e-mailed me. In the subject line she wrote, "Hold on to your hat, Harold came through . . ."

Butler reported that my father's name was Earl Van Best Jr., and he had been born July 14, 1934, in Wilmore, Kentucky. "He said all the info in your father's file is thirty years old. Last he was heard from here was August 15, 1967, but Harold didn't say in what regard. Honey, there are things in the file Harold won't reveal, so suffice to say we are warned. I hate it's like that, but I appreciate Harold's judgment, and after all, I was married to the guy. Why would he have chosen (or settled for) a 13-year-old girl if . . . you know what I mean," Judy wrote.

She informed me that there was no current California driver's license in my father's name, but Butler had uncovered my father's Social Security number and an old driver's license photograph. He had promised to give them to Judy. The file had Van's address listed on Haight Street, but it also included Gertrude's address on Noe Street. "Harold wants to continue to work with us on this and wants to meet you. He invited you to write him directly."

I stared at my computer, rereading the e-mail. A year after meeting my mother, I finally had some concrete information about my father. I knew his name. I knew my real last name. Best.

Excited, I booked a flight for San Francisco, eager to meet the sergeant who had promised to help me find my father.

Judy arranged for us to meet Butler and his family for dinner at Valencia Pizza & Pasta, in the Mission District. Butler arrived before us and stood up as we approached the table, his stunned, cautious gaze fixed on me. "I'm amazed at how much you look like your father," he said.

"I can't wait to see the picture of him," I said. "Thank you for finding it."

But Butler had forgotten to bring it. I had difficulty hiding the frustration and disappointment I felt as we ordered dinner. I wondered why he had not brought the picture, when that had been the point of our meeting.

"Can you tell me anything else about what you found?" I asked him.

"No," Butler replied. "Some things have to be kept confidential. It's the law."

"But it was forty years ago," I countered. "Surely it wouldn't make a difference now."

"I'm sorry, Gary. I know you probably have lots of questions, but there's nothing more I can tell you. I will send you the photograph, though."

Several times during dinner, I became uncomfortable when I

looked up to find Butler staring at me, watching my every move. I decided it was best to quit asking questions.

When we finished our meal, Butler invited us to his house for coffee. He had recently remodeled, and proudly gave me and Judy a tour. Zach had befriended his sons while we talked, and they asked him to spend the night.

"I'm sorry, but we have to get to the airport early tomorrow. Maybe next time," I promised.

As we said our good-byes, I shook Butler's hand and thanked him for helping us.

"I'll e-mail you the picture and then mail an original," he said.

I left his house feeling a little better.

When I got back to Baton Rouge, the e-mail was already in my inbox.

It seemed to take forever to download the large file, and I could feel my anxiety mounting as the seconds went by. I was about to see the face of my father for the first time since he had left me in the stairwell.

Finally, a head and shoulders appeared on the screen. I stared at the photo for a long time. It looked nothing like what my mother had described. She had said Van looked charming, that he had dimples. There were no dimples, and definitely no charm.

An emotionless face with dead eyes stared back at me.

Zach walked into the room and peered over my shoulder. "Dad, he looks like a serial killer," he said.

"No, he doesn't," I admonished, but I could see what he meant. The man in the picture did not look like a nice person. But then I started noticing similarities—the hairline, the jaw, the cleft in his chin, the shape of his eyes.

As I looked into those eyes, I felt a chill run through my body and wondered if I was doing the right thing. Butler had said there were things in the file he couldn't reveal.

What did that mean?

I mulled over that question for the next few days, returning again and again to the picture I had saved on my desktop. I wondered if I should stop trying to find him now, but that burning desire to know who I was, the one that had plagued me all my life, pushed me onward.

The sergeant had also suggested that I contact the Social Security Administration to find out if my father was still alive. I decided to start my own search there.

On July 15, 2003, at 9:00 a.m., I walked into the Social Security Administration building in Baton Rouge, eager to learn what the clerk could tell me. I pulled a number from the dispenser and sat down, counting the minutes, then the hours, until my number was finally called.

A friendly woman smiled at me from behind the counter. "How may I help you?"

"My name is Gary Loyd Stewart, and I was adopted. I have discovered the Social Security number of my biological father, and I am trying to find out if he is deceased and was hoping you could tell me if any benefits have been paid on his behalf," I said nervously.

Butler had told me that I would know if I had any siblings by learning whether death benefits had been paid.

"Can you give me the number?" the lady said.

"Yes, ma'am." I read her the number and she entered the information into her computer, then studied the monitor for a few moments. "I am not allowed to tell you if he is living or deceased. I can tell you that no benefits have been paid on his behalf, but benefits are available."

"So is my father dead or is he still alive?"

"Due to the Privacy Act, I am not at liberty to give you that information," she said. Seeing the obvious disappointment on my face, she leaned closer and whispered, "But if he had been reported deceased, I would tell you that you were eligible for death benefits right now."

I reached over the counter and gave this beautiful lady a hug.

I had my answer.

My father was alive!

44

"I think I'll call my friend at the Department of Justice," I said to Loyd and Leona. "The cop in San Francisco won't tell me anything, but I know he knows something."

"Are you sure you want to do that?" Loyd said.

"I have to try to find him. He's alive."

"But what if things don't turn out the way you want them to? What if the cop isn't telling you for a reason?" Loyd said. "You might want to slow down and think about things."

"Don't worry," I reassured him. "Judy found me, and that turned out all right, didn't it?"

"Yes, it did," Leona said. "But this seems different. This man married her when she was fourteen. I don't like it. I don't like it one little bit."

"I don't either," Loyd said.

"You two worry too much," I said, kissing both of them before I left. "I'll let you know what I find out."

Not heeding my parents' advice, I contacted my friend at the Louisiana Department of Justice.

"All I have is my father's name and Social Security number," I said, explaining the situation. "Do you think you can find anything with that?"

He promised to try and enlisted the help of some of his friends in law enforcement.

A week later, he called and said he had learned that a man with my father's name had been arrested in 1996 and was incarcerated with the California Department of Corrections.

That was the last thing I wanted to hear. I knew my father would be sixty-two years old by now. What was he doing in prison?

I e-mailed Judy. "Why didn't Butler tell me Van was arrested in 1996?" I asked her.

"I'll call him," Judy responded.

That day, I called every prison in California, to no avail. They had no record of my father's being incarcerated in 1996. I should have paid attention to that, but I was so eager for new information that I accepted his incarceration as fact.

I would pay for that mistake dearly.

"Harold said he knew about the arrest and that your father had been turned over to the FBI, but he doesn't know anything else," Judy reported a few days later.

"Why didn't he just tell me that in the beginning?" I vented.

"I don't know," Judy said, "but I'll talk to him. Look, I don't want you to think anything your father did was because of you. He hated me, remember? If he turned bad, it was because of me. I don't ever want you to think anything we find out is your fault."

I didn't understand what she was trying to say. What had my father done that had been so bad? Why had he hated my mother?

I sent an e-mail to Butler, asking again for my father's file. "I don't care what's in it. I'm entitled to know what he did," I wrote.

Back then, I really didn't care what he had done. I just wanted to meet him. Leona had raised me to have love and forgiveness in my heart. I had forgiven Judy. I was confident I could forgive my father.

Butler did not answer my e-mail. Instead he contacted my mother.

"I am not going to reveal what is in that file. It would make what he did to you look inconsequential," he told her.

"How could rape and kidnapping look inconsequential?" I asked Judy when she told me what Butler had said. "What could be worse than that? If it's that bad, I have a right to know."

"I don't know, honey. That's all he would say," Judy answered.

"I have to know what my father did," I said. "I am his son. I deserve to know."

Judy started crying. "I know. This is all so upsetting. I didn't mean for any of this to happen."

"It's not your fault, Mom. This thing is just eating at me. My father is out there somewhere, and I need to find him, or at least know why I shouldn't."

"Okay, honey. I'll call Earl Sanders and try to find out just what your father did."

A few days later, on April 6, 2004, I was out celebrating a victory with my co-workers when my phone rang. My company had just successfully completed its first major project engineered and executed by my employees in our Baton Rouge office, and we had gathered at the Lager's Ale House, on Veterans Boulevard in Metairie, a suburb of New Orleans. When I saw my mother's number on the caller ID, I left our noisy table and went into the bathroom to answer the call.

"Hi, Mom."

"Hi, honey," she said. "How are you?"

"I'm fine. I'm out celebrating our first grand-slam project. My boss is here from California, and we're doing great. How are you?"

"Well, I just left the coffee shop where I met Earl. He says he can't tell us what your father did. He says what your father did was so heinous it would destroy us. I know this is not what you wanted to hear, but he begged me to tell you just to drop this thing with your father. He was very adamant about that."

I could hear how upset she was.

"It's okay, Mom. I know you've done everything you can. So we will never know. So what? We still have each other, right?"

"Honey, I think we just need to let go now."

"I guess you're right. Besides I have the best gift of all—you. That's good enough for me," I said, trying to cheer her up.

Inside, I was conflicted. Something wasn't right here. Why did Earl Sanders care about what would destroy me? We had never met. And why would Harold Butler say that what was in that file would make what Van had done to Judy seem inconsequential? The more I thought about it, the less it made any sense at all.

Discouraged, I resolved to let it go. Maybe Loyd and Leona were right. Maybe it was best I didn't know what Van had done. For the next few months, I pushed all thought of learning more about my father out of my mind.

45

July 31, 2004

I remember that day, the feeling of horror that swept through me, like it was yesterday.

Zach and I had spent the afternoon outdoors, grilling his favorite food—baby back ribs. After dinner, we washed the dishes, and I went to shower the smell of mesquite from my body. When

I got out of the shower, I noticed that Zach was in his room playing a video game.

I walked into the living room, sat down in my chair, grabbed
the remote, and flipped through the channels to A&E. I enjoyed
watching true crime shows and saw that a special on the cold case
of the Zodiac killer was airing. I didn't know anything about this
serial killer, and at the time, I thought it would be interesting.

Not life-changing.

It happened in an instant.

The police sketch of the Zodiac flashed across the screen.

I sat there transfixed for a moment, unable to take my eyes off
the image on the television.

Sanders's words to my mother began running through my
mind. *The things in that file are so heinous that it would destroy you and
your son* . . .

"Zach, come in here," I called out. "Hurry!"

Zach rushed into the room but stopped in his tracks when he
looked up at the screen.

"Hey, Dad, it's you!" he exclaimed.

I got up from my chair, walked to my office, picked up the
picture I had printed of my father, and walked back into the living
room.

"It's not me, Zach," I said, staring from the picture to the television and back. "It's my father."

It was as if someone had taken a snapshot of Van and placed it
on the "Wanted" poster.

I sank into my chair, staring at the picture, only half listening
as the narrator on the television described Zodiac's reign of terror
all over California.

It would make what he did to you look inconsequential . . . Butler's
words reverberated through my thoughts.

It's impossible, I told myself. *There is no way my father could have done such horrific things. He kidnapped Judy. He raped a fourteen-year-old girl. Who knows what this man could have done?*

When the show was over, I went into my office and pulled up sketches of the Zodiac on the Internet, comparing the picture of my father and the two faces on the "Wanted" poster detail by detail. The similarities were stunning.

Too upset to talk, I e-mailed my mother. "I think I just discovered what is so horrible," I wrote. I told her about seeing the sketch on the show and comparing it on the Internet.

Twenty minutes later, I nervously sent an e-mail to Butler, telling him the same thing, aware of how crazy my suspicion might sound. "If I fly to San Francisco, will you meet me for coffee to discuss this?"

Butler did not respond.

Judy wrote back the next morning, explaining that she had done some research overnight. "There's so much out there about the Zodiac," she wrote. "I hope you are wrong in your assumption, but I can't give you an opinion."

For the next week, thoughts of Van plagued my mother. She remembered how cruel he could be, how much he had loved to kill animals, how she would come home to find me barely breathing after he had closed the lid on the trunk. Someone who could do that was certainly capable of murder.

On August 8, she called Butler. "Please, just tell me what's in that file, Harold. The thought that his father might be the Zodiac is upsetting Gary. I don't want him to have to live with something like this."

"Don't worry," Butler said. "The Zodiac case was solved and closed ten years ago. A guy named Arthur Leigh Allen matched the Zodiac's DNA. Tell Gary he doesn't have to worry about that."

"Harold said the case was solved," Judy reported back to me.

"That's such a relief. If I had thought your father was the Zodiac, I would have never tried to find you and subject you to something like that. Harold won't say anything else, but at least we don't have to worry about that anymore."

I wasn't so sure. All of the research I had done over the past week indicated that Zodiac had not been caught. I went back to my computer to double-check, looking for details about Arthur Leigh Allen. I was shocked by what I found. Allen had been a suspect in the Zodiac case but had been cleared two years before when it was determined that his DNA did not match a partial profile of the Zodiac's DNA that had been extracted from beneath a stamp. I noted that police were not certain the DNA they had was actually from the Zodiac—that it could have been from a postal worker who might have affixed the stamp to the envelope. But regardless, the case had not been solved.

Butler had lied to my mother.

A few minutes later, I found an article written by Tom Voigt and posted on Zodiackiller.com that reported that the Zodiac case had been closed by the San Francisco Police Department on April 6, 2004. It had been almost thirty-five years since Paul Stine had been murdered, and his cold case was to remain unsolved.

Oh, my God. That was the same day my mother had met with Earl Sanders, the same day he had begged her to make me stop trying to discover what was in my father's SFPD file.

The article mentioned that the SFPD was restructuring its homicide division and intended to direct its resources toward more recent homicides. Lieutenant John Hennessey was listed as a contact if anyone had new information to report about the case.

I printed the article and put it in my briefcase.

The next week was a difficult one for me. I tried not to think about my father and focused instead on the good things in my life—Loyd and Leona, Zach, Judy. I didn't want to think about the man who had hurt my mother. I wanted some normalcy back. The idea of murdering someone was so far beyond my realm of comprehension that just the thought that my father might have done something like that made me nauseated.

But the unsettling thought would not go away.

Finally, I decided I would keep investigating, if only to prove to myself that my suspicions were unfounded. I knew now that I could not trust Sanders or Butler, so I made another plan.

On August 17, I traveled to the Bay Area on business. When I settled into my hotel, I pulled the article out of my briefcase and dialed the contact number listed. I was directed to Lieutenant Hennessey's voice mail, which indicated he was on vacation until the 21st, the following Monday.

I called Judy on the weekend and told her what I planned to do. She had moved to Tucson, Arizona, and I hated that I could no longer visit her when I was in San Francisco.

"You're not going to drop this, are you?" she said.

"I can't. I'm sorry, Mom, but I have to know."

Judy sighed. She had not bargained for all of this when she had decided to search for her son. But she didn't understand: I had spent a lifetime wondering who I was, and now I needed to know the truth about my father.

When Monday arrived, I went to work preoccupied with how I would present my story to the lieutenant. I didn't have much hope that he would take me seriously, but I had to try.

After work, I returned to the hotel and dialed the number again. Hennessey's secretary informed me that the detective was in a meeting.

"He should be out in about thirty minutes," she said.

Thirty-two minutes later, I called back.

"Lieutenant Hennessey, homicide," the voice on the other end of the line said.

I wasn't expecting that Hennessey would answer the phone, and I was speechless for a moment. *Now what do I say?*

I cleared my throat.

"Lieutenant Hennessey. My name is Gary Stewart, and I live in Baton Rouge, Louisiana."

"How may I help you, Gary?" the lieutenant responded.

"Well, sir, I was wondering," I stammered, "has the Zodiac killer case been solved?"

The lieutenant chuckled. "No. If it was solved, I'd be retired."

"Well, sir. I have a story, a situation that developed as I was researching my family roots. You see, I was adopted as a child. My father, my birth father, had a criminal record there with the San Francisco Police Department, and one of your fellow employees, Harold Butler, helped me determine who my father was. But Harold is close friends with my birth mother, and he told her that you guys have solved the Zodiac case. My mother was married to Rotea Gilford, and when she called Earl Sanders, he told her to tell me to drop it, that the things in that file would destroy us."

I realized that I probably sounded like a bumbling idiot, but I took a deep breath and continued when the lieutenant said, "Go on."

For the next twenty minutes, I related the events of my life that had led to this point. Hennessey listened without interrupting.

When I was finished, he said, "Can you write a summary of what you just told me and mail it to me at the Hall of Justice?"

"Yes, I can do that," I said, jotting the address on the article that had listed his contact information.

"Do you have handwriting samples from your father?" he asked.

"No, sir, but I have something better."

"What's that?"

"I have DNA," I said.

"You have his DNA?" the lieutenant asked incredulously.

"No. I have mine."

Hennessey paused for a moment. "The costs of DNA analysis are prohibitive," he said. "We would more than likely not be able to justify testing your DNA, especially with the change in city management. I tell you what: I'll read over what you send me and get back to you in a few weeks."

"Can we keep this confidential between us?" I said. "I would rather you didn't discuss this with Harold Butler or my mother."

"I have no idea why Butler would have told your mother the case was solved, but I won't mention it. I did know Rotea Gilford, but I've never met your mother. For now, this will be between us."

"Thank you," I said before hanging up.

The next morning I wrote the letter to Hennessey.

And then I waited.

When two weeks had gone by and I had not heard back from him, I could wait no longer. I dialed Hennessey's number.

"Did you have a chance to read the summary?" I asked when the lieutenant picked up the phone.

"Yeah, Gare," Hennessey said, surprising me with a shortened form of my name.

I wondered if he was patronizing me.

"You have quite a story here. I'd like to sit down with you and discuss the details further. When are you going to be in the Bay Area again?"

"My next scheduled trip isn't until December 8, but this is important enough for me to get on a plane tomorrow."

"No, son. That really isn't necessary. After all, it's been thirty-five years. The Zodiac hasn't spoken in that long. I guess it can wait a little longer," Hennessey said and laughed.

"Well, sir, if I see that I have to travel out before December, I'll contact you first to see if your schedule is clear for us to get together. How's that?"

"That'll be fine, Gare. You have a great evening."

"Same to you, sir. Same to you," I said, smiling.

It sounded like he wanted to investigate this further.

46

In September 2004, Judy called to say that she had finally decided to scatter Frank's ashes. Her partner of five years had suffered a pulmonary embolism the year before, and she had seemed a little lost ever since. Frank had filled the void after Rotea passed away, and she had struggled to deal with the loss of two fine men in such a short span of time.

I had admired Frank, mostly for the kind way he treated my mother, but also because he had always done his best to be a good grandfather to Zach. Whenever I visited them, Frank had taken my son to amusement parks, Fisherman's Wharf, anywhere, so that Judy and I could have time alone to get to know each other.

Frank had half-jokingly told us that when he died, he wanted his ashes to be scattered out of the convertible with the top down as Judy drove through Golden Gate Park. Although we had often teased him about this when he was alive, after he died, my mother couldn't bring herself to commit such an irreverent act.

"I'd like to do it October 30," she said, "in Golden Gate Park. That was Frank's favorite place in the world."

I laughed. "Every place was Frank's favorite place," I said.

"I know," Judy agreed, "but I finally figured out the perfect spot. Can you meet me in San Francisco on that date?"

"Of course, Mom. I'll be there."

There was a particular bench on the edge of Stow Lake where Frank had mentored many of the people he had sponsored in Alcoholics Anonymous, and that was the spot she had chosen. One of the things that had made Frank Velasquez so special was, as he was fond of saying, that he spent the first twenty-nine years of his life chasing happiness in a bottle and the last thirty testifying as to why that addiction had been a waste of his first twenty-nine years.

It was on that bench that he took friends and family and taught them how to recover. More important, while he taught them how to battle addiction, he taught them how to pray.

When I got off the phone with Judy, I called Lieutenant Hennessey, hoping we could find some time to meet while I was in San Francisco.

"I'm available anytime after noon on the twenty-ninth," he said.

"I'll see you then," I said.

I arrived at the Oakland airport, rented a car, and headed west on Interstate 80 toward San Francisco. After paying the toll on the Bay Bridge, I called the lieutenant and left him a message, informing him that I was on my way. The traffic on Van Ness was extra heavy for a Friday afternoon, and it took nearly an hour to make the three-mile drive through the road construction around the Embarcadero. Finally, I arrived at the Francisco Bay Inn, on Lombard Street. The red cobblestone street boasts the title of the steepest and most crooked street in the world, with its eight hairpin turns, and is beautifully lined with flowers and quaint homes.

Relieved to finally be there, I splashed some water on my face, donned a sport coat and jeans, and headed to the Hall of Justice. I soon arrived at 850 Bryant Street, parked my car, and made my way up the steps of the immense building.

Rich Italian marble floors greeted me at the entrance—not what one would normally expect upon entering a police station. The once government-white walls were now painted a brownish beige, an attempt by the city to cover the dingy yellow stains caused by years of nicotine exposure from officers burning the midnight oil. *If only these walls could talk*, I thought as I removed my watch and placed my cell phone in the basket before passing through the metal detector. From photographs of blood-soaked crime scenes to the small victories of a clue that broke a case, the mourning of the faithful fallen, and internal scandals that had weakened the faith, the grand old walls had silently stood, bearing witness to it all.

I found the elevators and pressed the button for the fourth floor. When the door opened, I stepped into a long hallway. The first office to the right had a sign: HOMICIDE 450. Feeling surprisingly calm, I opened the door and walked in.

From the reception area, I could see a man in his early fifties standing behind a desk in his office, talking on the phone and rummaging through a stack of papers. The man looked up, smiled, and waved. A woman I assumed was the receptionist walked into the waiting area. "May I help you?" she asked.

"I'm here to see Lieutenant Hennessey," I replied.

She headed toward the open office, and the man behind the desk covered the receiver of the phone with his hand. "Can you give me just about five minutes? I'll be right with you."

I nodded and stepped back into the hallway.

The walls were lined with photographs of officers out in the field. I scrutinized each one, hoping to spot Rotea, but I didn't see him.

A half hour later, Hennessey finally came out and extended his hand. "I'm so sorry," he said.

I walked behind him into his office and sat down. He stared at me for a moment, scrutinizing my facial features, and I watched as his face visibly paled. He had noticed my resemblance to the sketch.

"No problem. I have all the time in the world," I reassured him. For some reason, I had not realized that Hennessey was the head of the homicide division. I had assumed that he was just another detective assigned to the Zodiac case, like Dave Toschi, about whom I had read a lot recently.

Toschi had gained such celebrity that a movie titled *Bullitt*, featuring a fictionalized version of the detective, was made in 1968. Steve McQueen played the role of Lieutenant Frank Bullitt, who sported an upside-down left shoulder holster for his primary weapon, a trademark of Toschi's. In 1971, the movie *Dirty Harry*, also loosely based upon the Zodiac case, was released; many people believe that Toschi was the inspiration for the main character played by Clint Eastwood, Inspector Harry Callahan. By the early 1970s Toschi had become so famous that he was asked to take a second look into the John F. Kennedy and Martin Luther King assassinations. He declined, insisting that it would take him away from the Zodiac case, the very thing that had put him on the map.

Often, fellow detectives wondered how the press arrived at crime scenes before they did, and always on cases Toschi worked. It didn't take long for them to figure it out. While Toschi worked the media, his partner, Bill Armstrong, worked the crime scenes. When the case went cold after Zodiac stopped writing letters in 1974, Toschi's moments in front of the camera became fewer and fewer.

On April 24, 1978, someone had mailed a letter to the *San Francisco Chronicle* bearing the name "Zodiac." The letter had too much postage, which was a trademark of Zodiac's. It read:

Dear Editor

This is the Zodiac speaking. I am back
with you. Tell herb caen I am here, I have
always been here. That city pig toschi is
good but I am smarter and better he will
get tired then leave me alone. I am waiting
for a good movie about me. who will play me.
I am now in control of all things.

Yours truly:

⊕ — guess
SFPD — 0

Sherwood Morrill, the handwriting specialist who had examined all of the Zodiac correspondence, quickly deemed the
letter a fake. On Monday, July 17, 1978, Inspector Toschi was
reassigned to robbery detail amid allegations that he had sent the
letter in a failed attempt to reignite media coverage of the Zodiac
case, although those allegations were never proved, and Toschi
vehemently denied any involvement.

I wondered how many times Toschi had sat in this very chair
going over photographs and witness statements about the killer
he would never be able to catch. While I waited for Hennessey
to get settled, I looked around his office. The walls were filled
with black-and-white photos depicting his thirty-five years on
the force.

He finally pulled out a pen and paper and said, "Okay,
Gare, I have the letter you sent me around here somewhere,
but let's just start from the beginning. What makes you think
your father was the Z-man?" His manner was not sarcastic, but
I could tell this was not the first time he had said those words.

His smile, though, was warm and friendly, and I didn't take offense.

"Well, sir, it's like this," I began, repeating what I had told him before while he jotted down a few notes.

I reminded Hennessey that my mother had been married to Rotea and had enlisted the help of Harold Butler in Internal Affairs and former chief of police Earl Sanders.

"Butler refused to share the information in my father's file with me but hinted that what was in there was so much worse than what I know. He told my mother that the Zodiac case had been solved," I said. "Sanders said the things in that file were so heinous, they would destroy me and my mother, and begged her to get me to just drop my investigation. I don't understand."

"You know, this department has been rocked over the years with scandals that have been swept under the rug for political reasons. I mean, if your kid went to school with that kid, then you have an understanding, a fraternity of sorts, to get away with anything."

"Sounds just like Baton Rouge to me, sir. South Louisiana politics are known around the world for being the shadiest of them all," I said, smiling.

"Do you suspect a cover-up here with what Harold told you?" asked the lieutenant.

"Why else would Chief Sanders and Harold Butler go to such great lengths to keep the truth from me and my mother? Are they trying to protect the reputation of the great Rotea Gilford? I don't know, but imagine if it came out that Judy Gilford, the widow of Rotea Gilford, the first San Francisco Police Department African American investigator and a well-known political figure, was once married to the Zodiac killer?"

Hennessey thought about that for a moment.

"Do you have any materials or personal effects from your

father that might have his DNA on them, such as a hairbrush?" he asked.

In 2002, police had obtained DNA they suspected might be the Zodiac's. They didn't have a full thirteen-marker profile, but they had four markers and the XY gender indicator.

"Maybe you could call the FBI and get my profile. Two years ago in Baton Rouge, police were looking for a serial killer who was targeting young women. Witnesses described a white male in a white pickup truck at some of the scenes. Police swabbed thousands of men in the area who had white pickup trucks. I was one of them. They should have my DNA."

"Have they caught this guy, the killer?"

"Yes, sir," I nodded. "His name is Derrick Todd Lee."

The lieutenant put his pen in his shirt pocket and pushed his chair back away from the desk. "That will do us no good, then. Your DNA profile will be tied up in appeals courts for the next ten to fifteen years. We will never get our hands on it. Do you have anything written by your father, a sample of his handwriting?"

"No, sir. I don't think so," I said.

Hennessey stared at me for a moment and then said, "Oh, what the hell." He picked up the phone and while dialing a number said, "Do you have a few more minutes, or do you have to be somewhere?"

"I have time."

Hennessey spoke with someone for a moment and then hung up the phone. "A forensics analyst will be here within the hour," he said.

For the next thirty minutes, the lieutenant and I got to know each other. As we talked, I got the feeling that he realized I was sincerely trying to learn about my father and was not some Zodiac groupie. But then again, he had been here before, listening to the stories of people who really believed they were somehow related to Zodiac. Subtly, he changed the conversation back to that subject.

"You know, the only solid suspect the SFPD ever named in the Zodiac case was a guy in Vallejo named Arthur Leigh Allen. He died about ten years ago, but we watched him for years. We even issued a search warrant once and confiscated some things from his home, but there was no smoking gun to be found. In fact, when he died, we had the coroner preserve a portion of his brain material for future use, and in 2002 we ran a DNA analysis to compare to the Zodiac killer."

"I read about him," I said. "I recall reading in a police report online and in some other literature that the police actually saw some coded letters that Allen said he had gotten from some crazy man at Atascadero. He said the man called himself Zodiac. I'm telling you, Lieutenant, I am certain that when you check out my father's file, you're going to find that he spent some time in Atascadero."

Hennessey looked a little surprised, but he took his pen from his shirt pocket and jotted down another note. Before he could put his pen down, the phone rang.

"Can you bring a DNA kit down here?" he said.

A few minutes later, an officer walked in, the sound of his clanking handcuffs preceding him. At five feet eleven inches, the man was slender and graying but handsome, with strong Irish features.

"First of all, he hasn't done anything wrong, so we're safe," Hennessey joked as the man nodded toward me.

"So what are we doing here?" the forensic analyst asked, his accent distinct.

"Well, you see, Gary here, um, well, he is voluntarily submitting a DNA sample," Hennessey said.

"What for, then?" the analyst persisted. This was very unusual, and he wasn't going to let it slide. "Do you have a case number for him?"

Hennessey didn't want to say that this was to be charged to case number 696314, the Zodiac case, because it was officially closed at the time. But testing my DNA would cost the department about fifteen hundred dollars, and the forensic lab needed a case number to justify the expense.

"Come with me," Hennessey told the man, leading him from the room. A few minutes later they came back.

"We have a case number," Hennessey said, obviously pleased.

"We'll just need your information here, and then you sign here stating that you voluntarily offered a sample of your bodily fluids for DNA analysis," the analyst said, pointing to the items on the form I needed to sign.

I filled in the information and signed it without reading anything, excited by the fact that Hennessey seemed to believe me sufficiently to spend the money for the expensive DNA test.

The analyst put on a pair of latex gloves and pulled a buccal swab kit out of his shirt pocket. "Now, just open your mouth," he instructed.

He swabbed the inside of my cheek twice and placed the swabs in a bag, sealed it, thanked me, and left the room.

"We will have to be patient," Hennessey said. "Our backlog of DNA samples waiting on analysis is extremely long, due to underfunding and so many new crimes."

"I understand," I said, getting up and shaking the lieutenant's hand.

"I'm going to visit Butler and try to get your father's file for review," Hennessey promised.

"Thank you so much for taking the time to listen to my story."

"If I didn't believe you and what you've told me, I would not have taken your DNA," Hennessey assured me. "We'll get to the bottom of this. I hope for your sake that your father was not the Zodiac."

"So do I, sir."

The next day I sat on a park bench with Judy and held her hand as we said our final good-byes to Frank and watched the wind carry him away.

47

When I returned home to Baton Rouge, I felt very relieved. Hennessey had seemed as though he genuinely wanted to get to the bottom of this. I had hope of finding out where my father was and what he had done. Now it was just a matter of waiting. I would know the truth and would deal with it, one way or another.

Hennessey had asked me to call him back in three weeks. On November 23, I had several meetings scheduled in Tarpon Springs, Florida. After a hectic day, I dialed Hennessey's office as I drove toward Tampa International Airport. True to his word, he had been following up on his promise to help me.

"I'm swamped right now, but I have some information for you," he said. "We have been waiting for a certain young lady here to be installed as the new head of the crime lab, and she just got the job. Remember Cydne Holt, the gal I told you would be helping us with the DNA?"

"Yes, sir. I remember."

"Well, she has the top job in forensics now, and that's good, because she will work with me. We intentionally held on to your DNA waiting for this announcement, and now we're set. She's on vacation this week for Thanksgiving, but she'll be back next week and we'll get right on the profiling then."

I knew that Dr. Holt had developed the only partial DNA profile of the Zodiac, so this was good news.

"That's great, sir. What about my father's file? Did you manage to get your hands on it?"

"You know, I'm pissed at Butler," Hennessey announced. "Harold worked for me for years. When I asked him about your father's file, he had it sitting right on his desk, but he refused to let me look at it. I mean, he wouldn't let me touch it. This is not like the Harold Butler I've known for twenty-some-odd years. I stormed out of his office."

I cringed at his words.

"I had to go through CLETS [California Law Enforcement Telecommunications System] to get your father's rap sheet. The original records were destroyed years ago, but there's some stuff in there . . . pedophilia and other things. The FBI has files on your father, too, but I don't have them in front of me."

Hennessey seemed to be carefully choosing his words.

"And just like you suspected," he continued, "your father was confined in an institution for the criminally insane for psychological evaluation and treatment. It was Atascadero, just as you said. But, Gary, there's so much circumstantial evidence stuff here, we're just going to get to the bottom of this once and for all. We're going to run your DNA sample and see what the results are. That way we'll know for sure."

Still trying to absorb what the lieutenant had said, I thanked him and told him I would be back in San Francisco in a few weeks.

"We'll get together when you get here and discuss the rest of the information and the DNA analysis," Hennessey promised.

"Lieutenant, I can't tell you how much I appreciate your help."

"It's my pleasure, Gare. I want you to be able to get your answers and deal with them and get on with your life. Anything I can do to help with that is just part of my job."

"I hope you and your family have a wonderful Thanksgiving," I said. "I'll see you in December."

I couldn't sleep that night. I tossed and turned, my mind spinning a web of questions I couldn't answer. What if the DNA came back a match? What if Earl Van Best Jr. really was the Zodiac? How did someone deal with the fact that his father was one of the most infamous serial killers in American history? What would it do to Zach, to Judy? How would I live with this knowledge? Would all of this change me? And what if my father was still out there somewhere? What would happen when I found him? How would he react? The thought was unsettling, but I resolved not to let it deter me from uncovering the truth.

Lieutenant Hennessey seemed happy to see me when I walked into Room 450 on December 9. He waved as I moved to sit down in a chair near the receptionist's desk.

"Don't sit there. Come in here," he said, rising to shake my hand. "I wanted to let you know how much I appreciated the package you sent, but you shouldn't have done that."

The week before Thanksgiving, I had sent the lieutenant a care package filled with Cajun treats from the Deep South. He and his wife were caring for his terminally ill father after work each day, and I had thought it would be a nice gesture.

"I figured you might appreciate some goodies from Louisiana."

Hennessey smiled and then got right to the point. "As I said on the phone, Cydne Holt just got the top job over at the crime lab, and she is completely swamped with work, current forensic cases. They have a three-year backlog for more recent and pressing crimes. I feel sorry for her in a way, because she's starting behind the eight ball already, so I didn't have the heart to ask her to run your DNA. Especially right now. Only being in her new job two weeks and with all the national publicity going on with the BTK Strangler case."

Hennessey got up from his chair and walked over to the answering machine on top of his bookshelf. "Listen to this," he said as he pressed the Play button.

"Yeah, I'm calling to report the identity of the BTK Strangler. His name is _____. He lives at 129 _____ Street in Wichita, Kansas. He is also the Zodiac Killer. Again, his name is _____ and he lives at 129 _____ Street in Wichita, Kansas. He is the BTK Strangler and the Zodiac Killer. He cut off his cleaning lady's head and has it in the freezer. Thank you."

Hennessey sat down, grinning. "You see why I have chosen not to approach Cydne just yet on your case? I just don't want to get a big fat no, and with all the publicity with the Scott Peterson trial in the sentencing phase and now the BTK Strangler, my gut tells me to hold off."

"That makes sense," I said, trying to hide my disappointment. "When do you think it will get done? Sometime after the holidays?"

"I think after the first of the year things will have settled down a bit, and she will have gotten more acclimated to her new role. Then would probably be the best time to approach her. Either way, we will get it done. We need to do that for you, but we also need to do it because it smells of a cover-up. It always has. But now, with all of your information—Rotea, Butler—we have to do it."

"Are you ready, Lieutenant? I mean, have you actually thought about what it's going to be like when you announce you've solved the Zodiac case?"

Hennessy rubbed his forehead. "Oh, my God. The media will be in an absolute frenzy. I don't think you can ever prepare for that. I'm not certain I'm up for it right now," he said with a laugh. "By the way, I have your father's information off of CLETS, if you would like to go over it."

My pulse accelerated. "Sure," I said.

Shuffling through the papers on his desk, the lieutenant pulled out a stack. It was my father's rap sheet. "I could not get the original SFPD file, because Butler refused to give it to me," Hennessey continued, handing me the papers. "So I went around him."

I felt a chill run through my body as I looked at the top sheet. In the upper-right corner were two photos. One was the picture Harold Butler had given me from the Department of Motor Vehicles, and the other was a profile shot, complete with the SFPD arrest number 175639, dated February 22, 1962, a year before I was born.

As I looked at the photos, I realized that the picture Butler had given me was not from the Department of Motor Vehicles.

It was my father's mug shot.

The crime: G-11284—Sec. 261.1 of the California Penal Code. "Rape, acts contributing where female is under 18 years of age."

The lieutenant allowed me to take the stack of papers from his hand and leaned forward, quietly watching me absorb the information contained in the file. Hennessey noticed the tears that began to build in my eyes.

Turning the page, I saw my father's fingerprints, along with his signature on the booking report. The address listed was 765 Haight Street. I stared at that for a moment. Butler had led me to believe that was my father's address in the mid- to late sixties, not in 1962.

The second shock was that my father had blue eyes. Based on the black-and-white photo Butler had given me, I had believed my father's eyes were brown. It hit me that I had my father's eyes.

I flipped through page after page—rape, child stealing, enticing minor from home, fugitive, fraudulent documents, fraud by wire, criminal conspiracy, fraud by wire, drunk driving, drunk driving, drunk driving.

I could clearly envision my father's life through the progression of his crimes.

Hennessey pointed out to me where it had been noted that Van had been sentenced to Atascadero State Hospital.

Almost any crime I could think of was in those pages.

Except murder.

"I made you a copy," the lieutenant said as I got up to leave. I needed to digest all of this. "You can take it with you, but please keep this between you and me. I'm not supposed to do this."

I read and reread it on the plane ride home, looking for clues, memorizing the timeline. When I got back to Baton Rouge, I compared my father's prison stays with the Zodiac murders. Van had been out of prison when each murder occurred.

I wondered what could make a man do the things my father had done. Looking at it on paper made it seem so much more real. I thought about what Judy must have gone through. It was no wonder she didn't want to remember him.

At night, as I lay awake in bed, I fought with myself. This man was my father. Loyd and Leona had raised me to believe that family was family, no matter what. Even as I was aware of the possibility that my father was the Zodiac, I could not help but feel some compassion for him. He must have been a very sick man. I wondered what had brought him to the life of crime he had known. What had possessed him to kidnap and marry a fourteen-year-old girl?

Judy had said my father gave me to a church. That had to mean that on some level he had cared about me. He had brought me to a safe place where he knew someone would find me a home. But why? Why had my father wanted to get rid of me? What had happened to make Van turn to a life of crime?

And what did Butler and Sanders know that I didn't? Hennessey had told me that Butler refused to let him see my father's criminal file. Why?

I surmised it had something to do with Rotea.

I became more determined than ever to find out.

48

In early February 2005, I received an unexpected e-mail from Linda Woods, one of the ladies in the adoption search group that had helped Judy find me. She asked if I could meet with her in New Orleans, because she had some records from my adoption that she wanted to give me.

"It's so good to meet you," she said, standing up to hug me when I entered her office a few days later. "You are one of our success stories. How's your mother?"

"She's doing well," I said.

We chatted for a few minutes, and then she handed me a manila folder that contained the file of correspondence she had received from Judy three years before.

"It's been almost three years since your mother found you, and I feel comfortable giving you this now. I don't know if you are aware, but someone gave your mother information from your sealed record and got into trouble for it. But now that all of that's over, I felt it was time for you to have some of the remaining information I had on you."

I hoped it was my birth certificate. I had been fighting with the state of Louisiana to get my adoption records unsealed so that I could have my birth certificate, but I had not been successful.

I was disappointed to discover that it wasn't in the folder.

The file did, however, include my actual adoption decree, signed by Judge Sartain, granting my adoption to Harry Loyd and

Leona Stewart. In the document, my name was legally changed from Earl Van Dorne Best to Gary Loyd Stewart.

There it was in black and white.

My full given name. Judy had told me I was named after my father, but she had not mentioned the name Dorne. I wondered why that name had been added.

I smiled as I sifted through the rest of the file.

One letter in particular caught my attention when I recognized Judy's handwriting. In the letter, she had stated that she thought her "story or her son's story would certainly have been newsworthy." She had written the letter at a Search Finders of California meeting when someone had recommended she do a search of the obituaries to find out whether her child was still alive. (Search Finders of California is a nonprofit organization that helps people search for adult family members who have been adopted and for birth parents.) Judy wrote that she thought the report of finding "an abandoned child, as Van had abandoned her baby in Baton Rouge," would have been front-page material.

I stared at the letter, rereading it to make sure I had read it right.

Abandoned?

Judy had never said anything about me being abandoned. She said I had been turned in to a church.

And newsworthy?

What had been newsworthy about my story? Children were adopted every day.

The letter, written the year before she met me, also contained my father's full name. Judy had told me she remembered my father only as "Van," although I had asked her repeatedly to try to remember his full name.

She had lied to me.

What the hell was going on?

Had my mother lied to me about everything?

It hit me then that *of course* she had known my father's full name. How else had Butler been able to track him down?

On February 6, I went to visit the two people in the world I knew I could always count on: Loyd and Leona.

"Do you think it's possible that a woman could forget having a baby?" I asked Leona. "Judy told me that once."

"I'm not sure. I know we forget the pain of childbirth, but I don't see how anyone could forget having a baby."

"That's what I thought," I said.

"But you need to try to understand what she was going through at the time," Leona quickly added. "She was a traumatized young girl, a child, really, who was living in an abusive environment. Maybe forgetting about everything was the only way she could cope with the trauma she experienced."

Loyd agreed. "You should listen to your mama. Give her the benefit of the doubt. She went through a lot."

"But she does remember things," I said, sharing with them what I had learned.

"Well, maybe she couldn't bring herself to tell you," Leona said. "It was a painful situation. Maybe she thought you would be hurt."

"I *am* hurt," I said. "It would have been better to have been told in the beginning than to find out like this."

"What are you going to do?" Loyd asked.

"I'm going to find out what really happened."

When I left, I drove to the East Baton Rouge Parish Library to see if I could find the "newsworthy" story. Relying on the only information I had—my birth date and the date of my adoption—I knew that whatever happened had to have occurred somewhere between February and May of 1963.

Back then, Baton Rouge had two newspapers: the *Morning*

Advocate and, in the evening, the *State Times*. I started looking at newspaper articles dated February 12, 1963, and worked my way forward. I expected to find an article, some black-and-white text, about a baby and a church buried somewhere in the back of either or both papers.

What I found in the *Morning Advocate* broke my heart—a picture of a baby held in the arms of a Baton Rouge police officer. The headline, on March 16, read, "Tot Abandoned Here Is Put in Hospital for Observation."

I could barely breathe as I looked at my picture plastered on the front page of the newspaper. The caption underneath the photo stated, "ABANDONED BABY BOY—Mrs. Essie Bruce of the city Juvenile division holds a blond, blue-eyed baby boy after he was found abandoned on a stairway landing in an apartment house on North Boulevard. Police are attempting to find a new home for the child and to determine the identity of his parents."

I stared at the article in disbelief. There was no mention of a church. I had been found unexpectedly by a lady named Mary Bonnette, on the stairs in her apartment building.

Stunned, I searched for more articles and found a headline on April 19 that read, "Teenager may be the mother of abandoned tot." This article indicated that a fifteen-year-old had been picked up for vagrancy in New Orleans and may be the mother of the abandoned infant.

An article on April 20 stated, "Nab Father of Child left here." It reported that Earl Van Best Jr., twenty-eight, of San Francisco, had been arrested for abandoning his two-month-old son in Baton Rouge.

I realized the newspaper had it wrong. I had not been two months old.

I had been only four weeks old when my father abandoned me.

Slowly, I got up from the microfiche machine, collected the articles I had printed, and made my way to my truck. I got in, started the engine, and steered it toward downtown Baton Rouge. I knew North Boulevard well. I had driven on that street many times.

I had not been left in a safe haven by people who had loved me but simply couldn't care for me. I had been thrown out like the trash, left there to be found or not.

An intense feeling of rejection washed over me as I looked for the address the paper had listed: 736.

Within a few minutes I was there. Just across the street stood an old Anglican church, almost hidden by the beards of Spanish moss draped on the sloping limbs of the oak trees that shaded it. I parked the truck and got out.

Looking around, I walked to the back of the building and entered a parking area with a courtyard, retracing what must have been my father's steps so many years before. I peeked inside, hoping to see the stairwell that led to Apartment 8. The newspaper had said that was where I had been left.

As I stood there, I realized that the last time I had seen my father was in that spot. With tears streaming down my face, I turned and walked back to North Boulevard and across to the First Presbyterian Church. The old building stood just as it had in 1963, when my father had passed it.

Maybe he had tried to turn me in to this church, I rationalized, hoping to ease the pain I was feeling. Maybe the church's doors had been locked. Maybe the clergy had gone home for the day.

I stood on the steps of the church, trying to convince myself that this was what my father's plan had been. Something had gone wrong, and my father had been forced to leave me in the apartment building.

Consoled somewhat, I walked back to my truck. It was too dark to see anything more.

By the time I got home, I didn't know what to feel—anger, humiliation, betrayal, hurt.

Judy had promised that she would always be honest with me, and she had lied.

About so many things.

The next few days were rough. I felt abandoned all over again. I remembered the time when Loyd and my sister Cindy had taken me to my first visit to the barbershop. Cindy had noticed a scar on my head when the barber cropped my hair too short. Loyd and Leona could remember no fall, no injury, that would have left such a scar on my scalp. A doctor had told me that my nose had once been broken, but Loyd and Leona said that had never happened either. I wondered now if it had.

I read the articles again, realizing that my father had been arrested. The next morning, I went to Baton Rouge Police headquarters and filled out the paperwork to obtain a copy of the police report about the incident.

When the clerk asked for my name, I said, "Earl Van Dorne Best." I thought that if I used that name, I would have a better chance of getting the report. For the first time ever, I signed my birth name on a piece of paper. It took about an hour, but the clerk, Regina, finally gave me the reports. The names had been blacked out, and I asked her for a copy without the omissions. "That's protected information," she said.

"But these files are about me," I persisted. "Isn't there anything you can do?"

"I'll try," she said.

On Valentine's Day, I drove to New Orleans, hoping to obtain two things: the police reports from Van's arrest there and any news articles I could find in the *Times-Picayune*. I had been informed the day before that criminal records from that far back had been placed on microfiche at the library.

I had not talked to Judy about any of this. My anger and hurt were still too close to the surface.

In the police reports, I finally learned the whole story. I read about how Judy had run away with my father to New Orleans and given birth at Southern Baptist Hospital.

"Earl could not stand to be around the baby," she had said in her police statement. "There was no food in the house and the baby needed formula, so I went to work as a bar maid. It was about the middle of March when I was working, and when I came home from work the baby would usually be in the foot-locker with the lid closed. I asked Earl why he closed the locker, and he said he was tired of hearing the baby cry."

I couldn't read any more.

I printed the report, walked outside, and vomited.

49

Taking a deep breath, I typed Judy's e-mail address into my computer. First I sent her the police report, then an article from the *Times-Picayune*, dated April 20, 1963, which stated that my father had been arrested and had admitted to abandoning his son. The article also mentioned that Judy had been arrested for vagrancy and that she was being held in jail for criminal neglect of the child.

"I just want to know why you said that you left him as soon as he returned from Baton Rouge without me. You stayed with him for over a month before you left him. I just want the truth, enough of the lies," I wrote. Before I had time to change my mind, I hit Send.

Later that night, I sent the last arrest report. "I hope you can remember better now" was all I wrote. She responded the next morning.

I am so sad that you think I'm lying to you. Why would I do that, Gary? I did not go to all the trouble to find you in order to ruin your life, Gary. Please believe that.

I was not living with him and had not been living with him. I don't absolutely know for sure that I left him the same day he came back without you (I would have sworn on a stack of Bibles that I did), but I know absolutely for sure I had not been living with him for some time when I was arrested.

Gary, I was fifteen years old. It was a shock to me that I knew you had been left in an apartment house. I have absolutely no recollection of that. It was a shock to learn that I was already working as a barmaid before he took you to Baton Rouge—that I had gone to work because he couldn't find work. Gary, I am not a liar, and I would never lie to you.

I felt terrible when I read her response. No matter what had happened, I loved Judy and was happy that she had found me.

"I'm sorry for venting and saying, 'enough of the lies,' because that's too harsh, and I apologize," I wrote back. "I need to get this off my chest, because like you, I was shocked at the difference in the stories. Mom, I did not mean to hurt you . . . it just came blurting out. I'm sorry. I love you more every day."

Judy's answer was not quite what I expected. "This is the second time since we've reunited that I regret having made my search," she wrote. "I hope you find your answers, Baby, and I know I will never have enough of them for you. I am very uncomfortable when you ask me questions continually that I can't answer. I am sick this has led to such unrest for you. I feel sorry for you and I feel sorry for your family, your Mom and Dad. It shows me for once and for all there are no winners in this adoption nightmare."

Judy later explained that what she meant to say was not that she was sorry she'd found me, but that she was sorry that finding me had caused me pain. I believed her, but our relationship suffered for a while.

In May, I traveled to San Francisco, this time to visit the public library. I wanted to see if the newspapers there had more information that I should know. I began searching the contents of every newspaper from 1961 to 1963. The articles detailing Van and Judy's illicit romance and life on the run appeared one after the other. If I had not been there reading the stories, I would never have believed them. Spread across the pages of the *San Francisco Chronicle* and the *San Francisco Examiner* were pictures of my parents. The quotes from my father about his love for my mother only reinforced for me that he was a very sick man.

Judy went with me the second day. We were trying to mend our relationship, and now that I knew everything, she seemed sincere in her desire to help me. We started with the dates of my father's arrest that were listed on his rap sheet, adding the *San Francisco News–Call Bulletin* to our search. The amount of information we accumulated was unbelievable.

"Newsworthy" hadn't been the half of it.

Judy sat beside me at the microfiche machine, exclaiming, "Oh, I remember that one," and, "Oh, yes, I do remember that now," seemingly enjoying herself as she read about her teenage years.

I began to feel an ache in the pit of my stomach. She just didn't get it. All of this had led to my abandonment. These were criminal acts. Van had been a pedophile who had raped, kidnapped, and impregnated an underage girl. She had no idea how all of this was affecting me.

I returned to Baton Rouge in low spirits, all the painful facts I had printed tucked into my briefcase.

On June 21, 2005, I received an unexpected note from Lieutenant Hennessey, sent from his home e-mail address, not his SFPD one.

Gary:

I caught the Director of the Forensics Lab at a weak moment, and got her to agree to this.

Be patient, it takes time.

He had enclosed the laboratory examination request, which listed my case number as 041238785. Under "Complaint/Victim," he had typed "Gary Stewart."

He'd also included a note for the lab on the form: "Please analyze the booked reference swabs and develop DNA profile. Compare profile with Zodiac sample."

The date the evidence was booked was listed as October 29, 2004. The date of the lab request was June 21, 2005. The SFPD had sat on my DNA for eight months.

Even with the serious time lag, I was ecstatic. I had been so focused on coping with my new discoveries about my parents that I had pushed the Zodiac question to the back of my mind. Hennessey, by turning in the lab request, had shown me that he was taking my suspicions seriously. I knew that there had been only a few DNA comparisons with the Zodiac killer made over the past four decades. This was a huge step for the head of the SFPD homicide division to take.

With renewed vigor, I began to dig further into my father's life.

50

In 2005, Loyd and Leona were celebrating an occasion many married couples never reach: their fifty-third wedding anniversary. Loyd's mother had lived with them for the past twenty years, and on this special night, my parents needed a "babysitter." I volunteered to spend the evening with my grandmother, wanting my parents to enjoy their date without having to worry. I had always been in awe of the fact that after so many years together, they were still best friends.

I had some free time that morning, so I got on my computer and went through a new search engine I had recently discovered called Dogpile. I typed in "Earl Van Best." I expected the "No results found" that I always got, but a list appeared with about twenty Best family residences in Conway, South Carolina. I called every one of them, but no one knew Earl Van Best.

Disappointed, I searched the surrounding towns. A listing for Old Zion Cemetery, in Galivants Ferry, popped up. I clicked on the link and was directed to the Horry County Historical Society's page. I scanned a list of names provided, and there it was: "Best, Earl Van Dorn 1866–1905."

That was my name! Although Van had added an *e* to the end of Dorn, I felt sure that this man was my ancestor.

Excited about my find, I left to go to my parents' home.

Leona looked beautiful, as always. And as usual, she had picked out Loyd's clothes. Her husband was notoriously color-blind, and for fifty-three years Leona had been dressing him to make sure that his shirts matched his pants and his socks were the same color. Looking as dapper as he had five decades before, Loyd held out his arm for his bride and walked her to the car. The thought that those two were still having romantic dates at their age warmed my heart and reminded me how blessed I was that they were the ones who had adopted me.

A few days later, I returned to the website and learned that the township of Galivants Ferry still had residents named Best. Then I discovered a listing for J. M. Best in the small town of Aynor, nearby.

I dialed the number, and a young lady answered the phone.

"May I speak to Mr. Best?" I said.

"I'm Alison Best, his daughter. My daddy passed away just a few months ago, but I would be glad to help you. What is it you are wanting with my daddy?" she said.

I explained who I was and why I was calling. "I'm looking for family members of my father."

"I think you have the right family," Alison said. "I'd better have you call Uncle Pressley. He'll know for sure."

I quickly dialed the number she gave me. Before I could finish my spiel, Pressley stopped me. "Hold on just a minute, now. I know you have the right family, but I'm not so good at this genealogy stuff. You need to speak with my sister, Hattie. She's the family historian."

He gave me Hattie's number.

Hattie graciously listened as I rattled off my story for the third time that day, and then she said she knew of my grandfather, Earl Van Best Sr. "I've heard he was a wonderful minister and a good man," she said. "My father and your great-grandfather were brothers. Your great-grandfather was Earl Van Dorn Best.

WANTED

NO. 90-69   <u>WANTED FOR MURDER</u>   OCTOBER 18, 1969

ORIGINAL DRAWING   AMENDED DRAWING

Supplementing our Bulletin 87-69 of October 13, 1969. Additional information has developed the above amended drawing of murder suspect known as "ZODIAC".

WMA, 35-45 Years, approximately 5'8", Heavy Build, Short Brown Hair, possibly with Red Tint, Wears Glasses. Armed with 9 MM Automatic.

Available for comparison: Slugs, Casings, Latents, Handwriting.

<u>ANY INFORMATION:</u>
Inspectors Armstrong & Toschi
Homicide Detail   THOMAS J. CAHILL
CASE NO. 696314   CHIEF OF POLICE

The Zodiac wanted poster distributed by the
San Francisco Police Department.

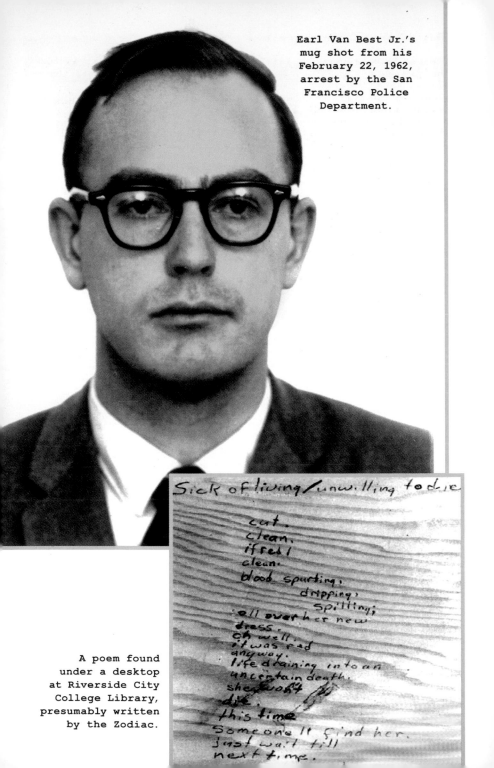

Earl Van Best Jr.'s mug shot from his February 22, 1962, arrest by the San Francisco Police Department.

A poem found under a desktop at Riverside City College Library, presumably written by the Zodiac.

Sick of living / unwilling to die

cut.
clean.
if red /
clean.
blood spurting;
         dripping;
               spilling;
all over her new
dress.
oh well
it was red
anyway.
life draining into an
uncertain death.
she won't
die.
this time
Someone'll find her.
Just wait till
next time.

This is the Zodiac speaking

I have become very upset with
the people of San Fran Bay
Area. They have **not** complied
with my wishes for them to
wear some nice ⊕ buttons.
I promiced to punish them
if they did not comply, by
anilating a full School Buss.
But now school is out for
the summer, so I punished
them in an another way.
I shot a man sitting in
a parked car with a .38.

⊕-12   SFPD-0

The Map coupled with this
code will tell you where the
bomb is set. You have untill
next Fall to dig it up. ⊕

C Δ J I ■ O X ⅃ A M ⅂ ▲ Ω O R T G
X ⊙ F D V ꝛ ▣ H C E L ⊕ P W Δ

This is the Zodiac speaking
Like I have always said
I am crack proof. If the
Blue Meannies are evere
going to catch me, they had
best get off their fat asses
& do something. Because the
longer they fiddle & fart
around, the more slaves
I will collect for my after
life. I do have to give them
credit for stombling across
my river side activity, but
they are only finding the
easy ones, there are a hell
of a lot more down there.
The reason that Im writing
to the Times is this, They
dont bury me on the back pages
like some of the others.
SFPD-0   ⊕ -17+

This is the Zodiac speaking
By the way have you cracked
the last cipher I sent you?
My name is ——

LABORATORY EXAMINATION REQUEST

CASE NUMBER (DEPARTMENT) 041 238 785	UNIT REQUESTING Homicide 5H200	DATE OF THIS REQUEST 6/21/05
COMPLAINANT / VICTIM Gary Stewart	LABORATORY NUMBER	OTHER NUMBER
DATE EVIDENCE BOOKED 10/29/04	SUSPECT	CHARGE
	EVIDENCE IN CUSTODY OF Property Control Division	NUMBER OF SPECIMENS

DESCRIPTION OF EVIDENCE AND REQUESTED EXAMINATION
(A COPY OF THE INITIAL NARRATIVE POLICE REPORT SHALL BE ATTACHED TO THIS REQUEST)

Please analyze the booked reference swabs and develop DNA profile. Compare profile with Zodiac sample.

DATE RESULTS NEEDED

REASON FOR REQUEST:

☐ M.C. TRIAL   ☐ REBOOKING

☐ ORDER OF D.A.   ☐ S.C. TRIAL

☐ Y.G.C   ☐ PRELIM. HEARING

OTHER ☐

REQUESTED BY	APPROVED BY	REFER TO
RANK / STAR #	RANK / STAR #	

SFPD 64 (06/90)*

Lieutenant John Hennessey's lab request to Dr. Cydne Holt, asking
that my DNA be compared to the Zodiac sample.

REPORT OF THE DEATH OF AN AMERICAN CITIZEN ABROAD

American Embassy, Mexico City, Mexico, August 14, 1984
(Post & date of issue)

SSA No._____

Name in full _Earl Van BEST, Jr._____ Age _49____

Date and Place of Birth _July 14, 1934, Wilmore, Kentucky_____

Evidence of U.S. Citizenship _Birth Certificate_____

Address in U.S.A. _319 Elm Ave. #34, Long Beach, Ca. 90802_____

Permanent or Temporary Address Abroad _Corinto Hotel, Vallarta # 24, Mexico_

Date of death ____May_____20_____1984__
                (Month)   (Day)   (Hour)   (Minute)   (Year)

Place of death _Vallarta # 24, Corinto Hotel, Mexico City, Mexico_
               (Number and street) or (Hospital or hotel)   (City)   (Country)

Cause of death _Asphyxiation by obstruction of major air passages by passing_
               (Including authority for statement—if physician, include full name and official title, if any)

gastric matter. Cardiomegaly and valvular aortic stenosis, according to **

Disposition of the remains _Interred at the San Lorenzo Tezonco Pantheon,_

Iztapalapa, Mexico City, Mexico.

Local law governing disinterment of remains provides that _they may be disinterred upon obtaining official permission and complying with local sanitary regulations._
Automatically subject to disinterment after six years unless the gravesite
is held in perpetuity.
Disposition of the effects_____ _In custody of U. S. Embassy, Mexico City._

Person or official responsible for custody of effects and accounting therefor _In custody of_
American Embassy, Mexico City, Mexico.

Traveling/residing abroad with relatives or friends as follows:
    NAME   ADDRESS
_alone_____ _Corinto Hotel, Vallarta # 24, Mexico_
Informed by telegram or telephone
    NAME   ADDRESS   DATE SENT
Mary Gertrude Plummer _1745 Marygold, Space # 73_   _05/21/84_

_____ _Bloomington, CA. 92316_____
Copy of this report sent to:
    NAME   ADDRESS   DATE SENT
Mary Gertrude Plummer _Bloomington, CA. 92316_   _08/14/84_

_Edith Van Best_____   _08/14/84_

_____ _____ _____

Notification or copy sent to Federal Agencies: SSA_____VA_____CSC_____Other_____
                                                                          (State Agency)
The original copy of this document and information concerning the effects are being placed in the
permanent files of the Department of State, Washington, D.C. 20520.

  Remarks: _Birth Certificate seen and returned to Mrs. Edith Van_

Best.** Dr. Aurelio Nuñez Salas, physician registration number 346788,
Niños Heroes # 102, Mexico City, Mexico. ____(Continue on reverse if necessary.)

                          Hugh Timothy Dugan   (Signature on all copies)
[SEAL]
              ____Vice Consul____ of the United States of America.

BEST (Jr.) (Last name)   EARL (First name)   VAN (Middle name)   May 20, 1984 (Date of death)

The official report
of death posted
at the American
Embassy in
Mexico City on
August 14, 1984.

My visit to my father's
unmarked grave in Mexico.
(Courtesy of Sergio Villegas Montes)

Judy Chandler and Earl Van Best Jr.'s marriage certificate, completed by my father and used for an additional handwriting comparison.

Earl Van Best Jr. and Edith Kos's marriage certificate, dated 6-6-66, which lists my father's occupation as a teamster and his address as 514 Noe Street. My father's signature on this document was used for an additional comparison with the Zodiac's handwriting.

Q9 Consulting, Inc.

December 9, 2012

Susan Mustafa
Baton Rouge, LA

Re: **Compare writing of Earl Best with letters from the Zodiac Killer**
Document Examination Case Report No. 2012-31

Dear Ms. Mustafa:

You engaged my services to ascertain whether the writing or known writing of Earl Van Best identifies him as the writer of the letters and envelopes written by the Zodiac Killer.

I, Michael N. Wakshull, declare as follows:

All of the facts stated herein are personally known to me and if required to do so, I could and would testify to the truth thereof. The conclusions of my report are:

1. I've conducted a forensic handwriting analysis on copies of the Zodiac letters, comparing them to a copy of the marriage certificate between Earl Van Best, Jr. and Judith Chandler, the writer of which you have identified as Earl Van Best, Jr.
2. I am virtually certain that the writer of the marriage certificate between Earl Van Best, Jr. and Judith Chandler is the same writer as the writer of the Zodiac letters.
3. I am virtually certain the writer of the marriage certificate between Earl Van Best and Mary Annette Player, and the envelope addressed to the Press-Enterprise are the same person.
4. I am virtually certain the writer of the marriage certificate between Earl Van Best and Edith Kos and the Joseph Bates envelope are the same person.
5. It is probable that the writer of the Earl Van Best signature on the booking sheet is the writer of the envelope addressed to the Press-Enterprise
6. The "Channel Nine" letter was not authored by the same person who wrote the other Zodiac letters
7. There are indications the writer of the "Red Phantom" letter is the same person who wrote the other Zodiac letters

I declare under the penalty of perjury under the laws of the State of California that the foregoing are my true and correct opinions.

Executed this 9th day of December, 2012 at Temecula, CA.

If you have any questions about the findings of this report, please do not hesitate to contact me.

Sincerely,
Michael N. Wakshull

Using the strongest language available to him within ASTM standards in the absence of the original documents, forensic document examiner Michael Wakshull verifies that my father wrote the Zodiac letters.

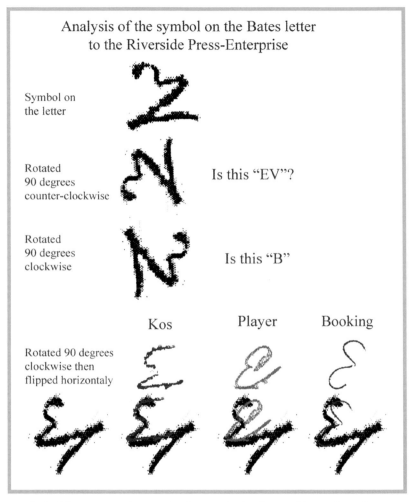

Analysis of the symbol on the Bates letter to the Riverside Press-Enterprise

Symbol on the letter

Rotated 90 degrees counter-clockwise

Is this "EV"?

Rotated 90 degrees clockwise

Is this "B"

Kos   Player   Booking

Rotated 90 degrees clockwise then flipped horizontaly

Wakshull's comparison of the symbol the Zodiac signed on the Bates letter with the *E* in my father's signatures on his marriage licenses and booking sheet.

(Copyright © Michael Wakshull)

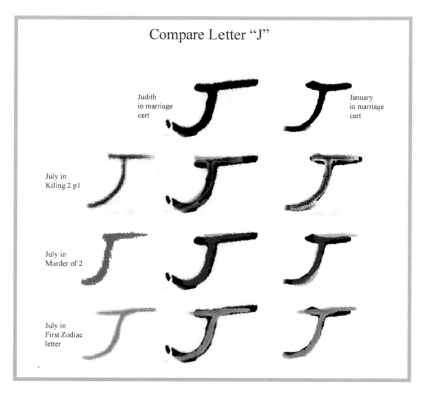

Compare Letter "J"

Judith in marriage cert

January in marriage cert

July in Kiling 2 p1

July in Murder of 2

July in First Zodiac letter

Comparison of the letter *J* on the marriage certificate to my mother against the Zodiac's handwriting.

(Copyright © Michael Wakshull)

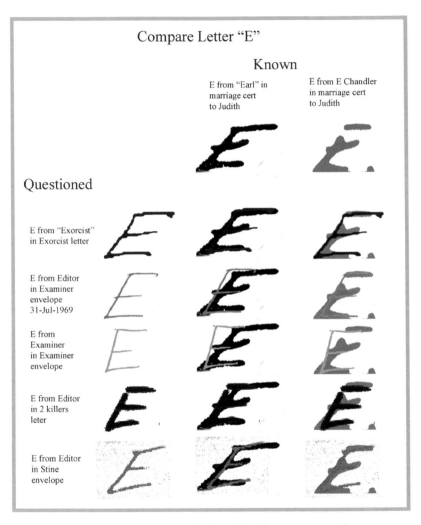

Comparison of the capital *E* in the same marriage
certificate against the Zodiac's handwriting.
(Copyright © Michael Wakshull)

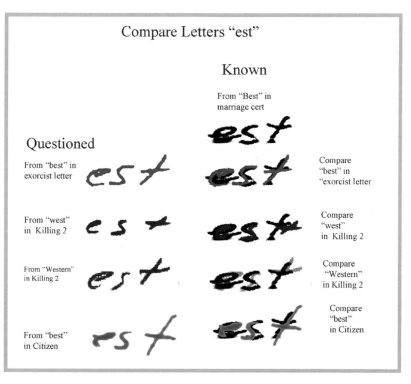

Comparison of the letters *est* in the same documents.
(Copyright © Michael Wakshull)

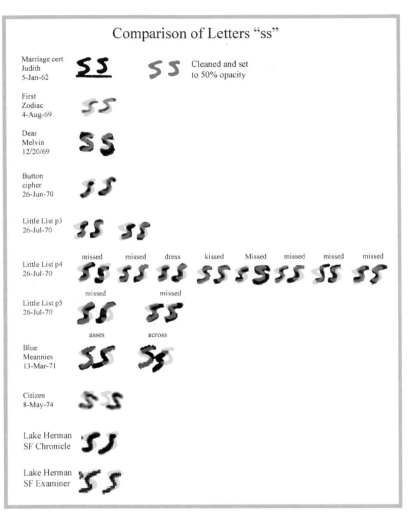

Comparison of the letters *ss*.
(Copyright © Michael Wakshull)

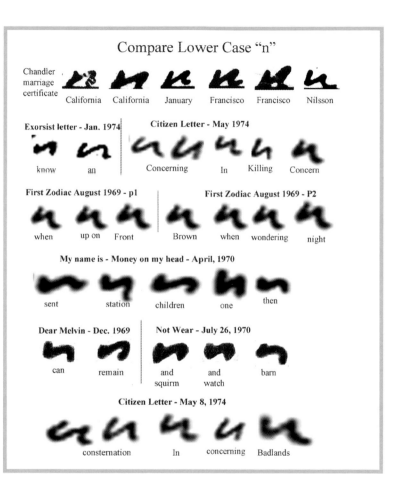

Comparison of the letter *n*.
(Copyright © Michael Wakshull)

My father's booking sheet from the San Francisco Police Department, dated February 22, 1962.

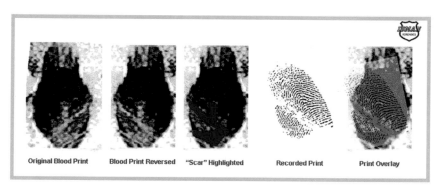

| Original Blood Print | Blood Print Reversed | "Scar" Highlighted | Recorded Print | Print Overlay |

The Zodiac print taken from Paul Stine's vehicle overlaid by Bob Garrett onto a print of my father's right index finger. Note the scar visible in both.

(Courtesy of Bob Garrett)

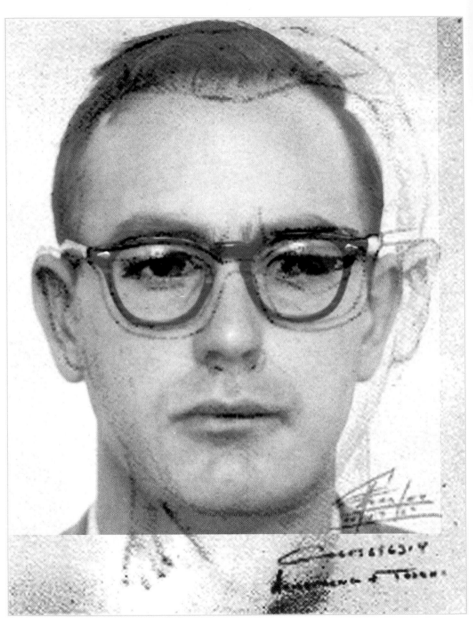

The Zodiac sketch on the wanted poster overlaid onto my
father's mug shot.

(Copyright © Michael Wakshull)

You have some relatives—direct cousins, I think—who live near the old home place by my brother, Pressley. One of them is named Bits. I believe she would be your second cousin. I remember something about your father and grandfather, but it's been so long, and it was swept under the rug. I don't remember any details."

Hoping to prompt her memory, I told her I had learned my father was a criminal.

"Was it murder?" Hattie whispered.

I was shocked. I had been talking to her for only a few minutes, and I couldn't believe that word had come up so quickly in our conversation.

"I don't know everything he did," I said. "Some of his files were destroyed."

Hattie became silent for a moment, realizing that maybe she had let something slip. Then she changed the subject, inviting me to the upcoming Best family reunion.

"I think it's wonderful that you've come out of the woodwork. It'll be fun to have you there," she said, informing me that she was the reunion planner. She said she had finally located the grave of her great-grandfather, Captain John James Best, and planned to announce it at the reunion, but this would be even better. "He was a sniper in the Civil War, one of the Pee Dee Rifles," Hattie said proudly.

I promised her I would be there, and Hattie said she would send me some information about my family.

That evening, I posted a message on the Horry County Historical Society Web page:

"My name is Gary Loyd Stewart. I was born Earl Van Dorne Best in 1963 to Earl Van Best Jr., son of Earl Van Best Sr., grandson of Earl Van Dorn Best. I was relinquished for adoption by my father and recently reunited with my birth mother. I am looking

THE TRUTH DECIPHERED | 277

for any family members that may have known my father or are distant relatives to my Best family."

I hoped my post would yield some results.

The next day, I called my second cousin, Bits Best Rosser, and introduced myself. Hattie had already informed her that I would be calling. When I told her my story, Bits said there had been rumors floating around the family about a baby, but it had been long ago and no one seemed to remember.

"Your grandfather, Uncle Earl, he was the chosen one. He was the baby of the household, and he became the prize of the Best family," Bits explained. "And he was a wonderful minister. Your daddy, well, he was, I guess I should say, 'different.' When all of us kids were at the beach house in the summer, we all wanted to go swimming and play on the beach. Van, he didn't like all that. He was interested in different things. He loved old things. I remember that old trunk that had the original land grant from the king of England and old christening gowns in it. That just fascinated your daddy. In fact, they were so old, and he opened that trunk so many times, that the air got to what was inside and it eventually disintegrated."

Bits was just warming up. "You know how kids do, and we shouldn't have, but we picked on him. Then, when he got older and we found out he was in trouble and on the run, we asked ourselves if maybe we had something to do with him turning out the way he did. Your grandmother, Gertrude, was a beautiful lady and had a beautiful voice and could play a piano like an angel. I don't know what went wrong with her, either, but she started running around on Uncle Earl, even on Sundays, when he was preaching. It just broke our heart. I know it broke your daddy's heart, too. So many times he would tell us that he would hear the bed rails squeaking and the revolving door of men in and out of his mother's bedroom. I think that may have affected him deeply. I know it broke Uncle Earl's heart."

I listened as the details of my family's past came pouring out.

"They were in Japan as missionaries when World War II broke out," Bits continued. "Uncle Earl used to write us letters and send us programs from plays and musicals and operas that he used to take Aunt Gertrude and Van to. They all loved music, and your daddy loved plays. We all thought Japan would be good for Uncle Earl and Aunt Gertrude, but we started hearing about her having affairs over there, too. When Japan bombed Pearl Harbor, Uncle Earl put Aunt Gertrude and Van on the first boat home, and he got on the last one out. He came home and joined the Navy and went to chaplain school, and they shipped him back to the Pacific. This time he went alone. This is where I think your daddy really took a turn for the worse. I know it broke his heart having his daddy gone off to war and living in San Francisco with Aunt Gertrude. The things he must have seen! It was about then that Uncle Earl came home to Galivants Ferry to tell the family he had asked Gertrude for a divorce. He knew that he would be excommunicated from the Methodist Conference if he divorced, but he couldn't live with an unfaithful wife. It broke his heart. It broke all our hearts to see our golden child going through the first divorce in the family, him being a respected minister and all. This is what must have really hurt your daddy."

Bits went on to explain how Earl Sr. had met his new wife, Eleanor Auble, and how they eventually married. "We were so happy for Uncle Earl. We just fell in love with Ellie the first time we laid eyes on her."

We talked for more than two hours. Well, Bits talked and I listened, soaking up every detail. Later that night, I received an e-mail from Joyce Long Smith, who lived in Palatka, Florida.

She was the daughter of Bits's sister Mildred. I couldn't help but smile as I read the e-mail. The Best family was coming out of the woodwork to meet Van's long-lost son. Like kids at a carnival sideshow, they all wanted to talk to the baby they had quietly discussed so many years before.

"When your grandfather found out that your father had left you in Baton Rouge, he flew back home to Indianapolis and told his wife, Ellie, that he wanted to go to Baton Rouge and adopt you and raise you as his own. Your grandfather was heartbroken when they flew to Baton Rouge only to find out that you had been placed in another home for adoption. Your grandfather never got over that," Joyce wrote.

Soon after, I received an official invitation to the Best family reunion, where Zach and I were welcomed into the family with open arms.

51

One Sunday afternoon after I got back from attending church services with Loyd and Leona, I sat down at my computer to do what had by now become second nature to me: search for more clues about my father. I remembered I had put a post on the Horry County Historical Society website and decided to check to see whether anyone had responded.

I saw a post underneath mine from someone called Anonymous William. He wrote:

"I believe that your father was arrested in San Francisco for abducting your mother. She was 14 at the time. You were born in New Orleans. I am glad you found your birth mother! There is an Earl Best living in San Francisco at this time on 46th or 47th

Avenue. He is listed. This may be you or a relative. Good luck—William."

This person had apparently known Judy and Van. I hurriedly clicked on the e-mail address and responded, asking William how he knew my father. "You are the only person that I have had any contact with that was not part of the distant relatives. Are you a Best descendant?" I wrote.

While I waited for his response, I searched the Internet for an Earl Best in San Francisco and found the listing. I nervously dialed the number, and a woman answered. After I explained that I was looking for my father, who had abandoned me, she said, "You have the wrong person," and hung up the phone.

The next day, the mysterious stranger wrote back.

William informed me that he and my father had been best friends in high school and into their adult lives. As I read his note, my heart was pounding. He said he had driven Van and Judy to the airport when they eloped.

"Should you care to hear more about his HS days and our adventures, please ask.—William."

Anonymous William turned out to be William Vsevolod Lohmus von Bellingshausen. We began to correspond weekly, if not daily, for several months. I probed him for every detail he could remember. Fortunately for me, William had a great memory, although he bluntly informed me that he had some very bad memories of my father.

"I was summoned to testify at the Grand Jury," he wrote. "I did not know what Van or your mother told the US marshals when they were apprehended. But unbeknownst to me, the Grand Jury indicted me as an accessory to child stealing. It took over one year to get me out of this mess, not to mention thousands of dollars in legal fees."

Soon we were talking on the phone regularly. At one

point, the dredging up of old memories became too much for him and he told me, "You should find a good psychiatrist, stretch out on his couch, and try and straighten out that screwed up head of yours that your father left you. Have a nice life."

I apologized immediately. I had been so eager to learn everything I could that I had not thought about how all of this might be affecting him. He had really cared about my father and had been hurt by him, too.

"I'm truly sorry for what my father did to you," I said. "Please don't hold what he did against me."

William soon began sharing more stories than I ever could have imagined. Before long, he invited me to visit the next time I was in California.

On January 25, 2005, I crossed the Golden Gate Bridge and drove into Marin County, looking for the small town of Novato, excited by the prospect of meeting my father's best friend, although I was a little uncertain whether it was a good idea, knowing what I now knew about Van.

When I pulled into William's driveway, I was struck by the beauty of the area. In the distance, tall redwoods dotted the landscape. A wooden fence enclosed the thick shrubbery, trees, and flowers that surrounded the property, almost obscuring the four-story, multitiered home from view. A gigantic hydrangea bush loaded with violet and blue flowers stood alone near the front entrance.

I walked up the stairs and rang the doorbell.

William, wearing an olive green sweater, a purple striped shirt, and blue slacks, opened the door. A beautiful silver-haired lady with a sweet smile stood next to him. William leaned his cane against the wall and reached out his left hand to shake mine. He kept his other hand carefully tucked into his pocket. I would later learn that he had suffered a stroke and a heart attack that had paralyzed his right arm.

He introduced me to his wife, Tania. "Follow me," she said as she led the way through the foyer and up a few steps. "Vsevé will be along shortly," she informed me, using her husband's nickname.

I followed her down another short corridor and turned left into the living room. "Sit down," she said, pointing to an L-shaped couch. "It takes him a little longer to get around now."

When William hobbled into the room, I realized what an effort he had made to greet me at the door. Tania visited with us for a few minutes and then told William that she would be in her studio. "She paints," William said, pointing to an impressionistic oil painting hanging on the wall, above several giant bookcases. Books about every historical artist imaginable were packed onto the shelves.

"You have your father's eyes," he said. "It's uncanny."

William seemed a little reserved at first, perhaps unsure whether he could trust the son of the man who had once caused him to be arrested, but as the day progressed and he got to know me, he relaxed.

Just being in the same room with this man who had been a friend to my father was somewhat disconcerting for me as well, but as William talked about his life as a criminologist, I could tell he was nothing like Van. And when he started sharing his stories, he seemed to enjoy bringing his memories to life.

"We weren't like the other boys in school," he said. "While they were out playing sports, we were in Van's bedroom reciting *The Mikado*. We knew every word of that opera. He also enjoyed *Tosca*."

I had read on the Internet that Zodiac quoted *The Mikado*. "Van knew *The Mikado*?" I asked William.

"Knew it?" he said, and laughed. "Your father was obsessed with it. Said your grandfather met him. I never believed him, though. Van was always full of tall tales. He once told me that he met the queen of England, too. Said he attended her coronation. That was when he went to Hinchingbrooke. He came back all messed up for a while."

William went on to relate the story about the bloody mace and Van's obsession with weaponry.

"Van had very superstitious ideas," William remembered. "His dad had bought him a car after graduation, and we were driving around, I don't remember where, but we decided to spend the night on the road. After a while, we saw a construction site with what looked to be unfinished white buildings. I should mention that we were both nearsighted and had left our glasses at home. We parked and went to sleep in the car. The next morning, we awoke to a bright, sunny day. After clearing our vision and focusing on our surroundings, we discovered that we had spent the night in a cemetery. The white buildings we saw the night before were white mausoleums and gravestones. I thought it was funny, but Van considered it an ill omen."

When I asked about my father's business ventures, William said that in the beginning, sometimes Van's trips to Mexico had been very lucrative. "Whatever Van brought back from Mexico did not last very long. In weeks, everything would be sold. I used to watch him sorting his documents, and I remember one particular paper signed by King Philip II. I know that document went for a considerable profit."

He also told me about LaVey. He said they hung out at the Lost Weekend cocktail lounge, in the Sunset District, with Van and LaVey occasionally taking turns on the pipe organ there. "LaVey and Van had much in common—music and a love of philosophy and books. Van was always fascinated with anything that had to do with 'other' ways of thinking, and he could not get enough of LaVey's unusual thought processes," William explained.

"We were at San Francisco City College studying forensics when your father met Mary Player," William remembered.

"Who is she?" I interrupted.

"His first wife. She looked like Audrey Hepburn, but that marriage only lasted a matter of months, I believe."

"What happened?" I asked, surprised. Judy had not mentioned another wife.

William didn't want to elaborate on it, but he said that Van could be "whacked out" at times.

"I knew your father, too," Tania said, walking into the room with a plate of pastries she had made for us. "We all went to Lowell High School together. I have to be honest: I didn't like him at all. He was a braggadocio, always talking about his accomplishments, but he never had anything to show for it."

William smiled at her, stroking his full gray beard. "Tania is very direct," he said.

Listening to William, I noticed that he used a very formal way of speaking. He had told me that Van had impeccable grammar, and I could see why they would have enjoyed talking with each other. William was a great conversationalist. One would never know he was foreign by listening to him speak, in his crackly, soft voice.

"Let me show you something in my office," he said, slowly getting up and maneuvering his way across the living room. I followed him down the corridor and up some more stairs before he showed me into a room lined with even more built-in bookcases. These shelves held books about criminology, forensics, murder.

"That's where I work," he said, pointing to a computer on his desk. "Your father studied forensics, too, you know. I tried to talk him into working with me a few times, but he was determined he was going to find treasure in Mexico."

He removed a book from one of the shelves. "I want you to see this. It was a gift from your father. It's extremely rare, one of my prized possessions. He brought it back from Mexico."

Realizing I was about to touch something my father had once touched, I reached for it almost reverently.

"Be careful," William said. "It's from the sixteenth century."

As I cautiously flipped through the pages, I noticed it was written in Spanish.

"Do you know what it's about?" I asked.

"Of course," William said. "This book was written as a guide to teach the Aztecs how to administer the sacraments. The Spanish were trying to spread Catholicism during that period, and they needed to ensure that the Aztecs fully understood the rituals of the religion."

Noticing the unusual pink coloring of the cover, I said, "This is strange."

"I'm not so sure it isn't human skin," William said. "It certainly isn't cow or goat, which is what they used to use. I've often wondered about that."

I studied the book for a while, wishing I had the nerve to ask him if I could buy it, but I could tell by the way he handled it so carefully that it really meant something to him.

"Van always brought us presents from Mexico. Tania has a beautiful bracelet around here somewhere that he gave her."

"Can I see it?" I asked.

"I'll ask if she knows where it is."

When I left that day, I had a clear understanding of why my father had liked William. He was one of the most dignified and intelligent men I had ever met.

Over the next five years, William and I kept up a constant correspondence, and I would visit him three more times. After my second visit, he asked me to call him Uncle Bill and began signing his e-mails "UB." As our relationship progressed, he opened up even further, sharing tidbits about my father along the way. Sometimes his memories were good—drinking ale at Schroeder's, hanging out at the Tonga Room. Other times, his memories haunted me.

Like the time he showed me a small wooden cube decorated with carvings of anguished faces trying to escape the depths of hell.

52

Throughout 2006, I visited San Francisco often, hoping to uncover more information about my father's life. Because of William, Judy, and the Best family, I had starting points, places to look.

I began to retrace my father's steps again through the Bay Area. This time I had a different perspective. This time I knew how cruel Van could be.

I visited Grace Cathedral and, as my father had once been, was awed by the beautiful music that flowed through the pipes on the walls. My eyes were drawn to the floor next to the organ, which was decorated with a circle that had a cross in the middle, and I shuddered. It looked like the symbol the Zodiac used to sign his letters.

I gazed at the magnificent paintings that depicted scenes from the Bible. Judy had told me that Van had once said he was in one of those paintings. I examined them carefully and noticed a man dressed in robes whose face did bear a slight resemblance to Van, but I realized this had been just another of the stories he told to impress people.

At city hall, I asked for a copy of Earl Van Best Jr.'s marriage license to Mary Annette Player. The receptionist informed me that two licenses appeared on the screen.

"Which one do you want?" she said.

Two? There should only be one, I thought.

"Both of them," I said.

I noticed that he had married Mary Annette Player on August 19, 1957. I also discovered that Van had remarried after Judy—to a woman named Edith Kos. And then I saw the date of that wedding: 6/6/66.

I visited the Avenue Theatre, where my father had played the organ. The old theater now housed the Channels of Blessing Church, but the original AVENUE sign still jutted out from the front of the building, reminding visitors of its historical significance.

While I was there, I called Lieutenant Hennessey on his cell phone to see if he would like to meet me for lunch. During our occasional calls, we had discussed getting together sometime soon.

"I'd love to, Gare, but I'm building a wheelchair ramp for my father's home. He doesn't get around very well anymore," Hennessey said.

"I'd be happy to come over and help," I volunteered. "I'm pretty handy with a hammer."

"That's real nice of you, but I couldn't let you do that. That would be asking too much. I appreciate it, though. I hope you enjoy your day."

After I hung up the phone, I decided to take a walk along the Bay to clear my head. Seeing some of the places my father had frequented had given me an uneasy feeling, and I wanted to do as Hennessey had suggested and enjoy my day. As I watched the planes take off and land on the airstrips across the water, I thought about my father's love of music and how Zach and I had both inherited some of his musical talent. I played guitar and sang in a band at local venues around Baton Rouge, and Zach had been playing the guitar since he was very young. It was the one good thing my father had given us.

At some point during that walk, I had a strange thought. Throughout the sixties, the underworld of San Francisco was joined in a brotherhood of music; Charles Manson himself had attempted to score a record deal with Terry Melcher, the previous owner of the Polanski-Tate house. I wondered if my father had known Manson or any of his "family" members. I knew investigators had wondered whether there might be a connection between Zodiac and the Manson clan.

When I returned home, I decided I would try to contact some of the members who were still alive. This was a surreal undertaking. Before Judy came into my life, I would have never thought to search for murderers and try to contact them, and now here I was. When I told Loyd and Leona what I was doing, they were appalled.

I didn't even consider contacting Charles Manson, because he just plain scared me. But I had stumbled across the fact that Bobby Beausoleil was residing at the Oregon State Penitentiary. I read about how he had killed Gary Hinman. After discovering a website through which I could send an e-mail to an inmate, I thought it might be worth a shot.

On September 10, 2006, I sent Beausoleil an e-mail asking if he had ever run into Earl Van Best Jr. in the Haight in the sixties. I was shocked when I received his response on October 14.

Beausoleil informed me that Van had jammed with his band,

the Orkustra, in a warehouse on a few occasions. "Quite a few musicians drifted in and out of our little circle, and he was one of them. I can't tell you where he went after that—or for that matter where he came from. What I can tell you is that he played a mean Hammond organ."

He signed the letter "Bobby."

In just a few lines, my suspicions had been confirmed.

A few months later, I returned to the Bay Area and called Hennessey from my office in Benicia, this time to ask if the DNA comparison had yielded any results. "We're years behind on backlog, Gare. Who knows when it will be," he said.

Discouraged, I hung up the phone. Being patient was harder than I had thought it would be. Had he not sent me the request form, I might have wondered if he'd even submitted my DNA sample. The following year, I learned that Hennessey had been moved from his position as head of homicide into the special investigations division.

One afternoon in late 2007, as I browsed through the Zodiackiller.com website, reading police reports about the murders, I stumbled across an open letter a retired San Francisco homicide detective had submitted in 2006.

The detective, Michael Maloney, star number 2014, had served with the SFPD for more than thirty years. He had always had a special interest in the Zodiac case and had been assigned, along with his partner, Kelly Carroll, to the cold case in 2000. Maloney was not your run-of-the-mill police officer and had a reputation as a rebel. While Maloney once said that he "did not want the Zodiac to follow him into retirement," the bitterness he felt about not being able to pursue the case obviously had.

When the Zodiac case was closed in 2004, the *Los Angeles*

Times had quoted Hennessey as saying, "The case is being placed inactive. Given the pressure of our existing caseload and the amount of cases that remain open at this time, we need to be most efficient at using our resources." Hennessey had added that the case would be reopened if a promising lead emerged.

Maloney, in his letter, did not seem to agree with Hennessey's position. He wrote, "The Zodiac case will not be solved until the current San Francisco Police Dept.'s manager in the homicide section is transferred. He [Hennessey] closed it [the Zodiac case] and ordered one of the most informed and capable police inspectors in the SFPD, Kelly Carroll, to return the case to the file and never respond to questions about it in the future from anyone, forever. And, rather than re-assign the case to another team, Hennessey put the case to bed after the first significant lead advancement in 30 years."

Maloney went on to explain: "My partner and I were the first team to be able to apply forensic DNA techniques to the Zodiac case. We were the first team to solve a cold case, 25 years old, with DNA. We know what we do, and we did it well. We could have torn that case apart with DNA testing."

I couldn't believe what I was reading.

Maloney continued, "When Hennessey is removed, the case will be opened again. DNA testing will eventually be cheaper. When that happens, the case will become very exciting because enough DNA tests will be made to really draw some conclusions, such as did the same person touch or lick all of the envelopes? If not, how many other DNA traces are we dealing with? Does this mean others were involved? Is there similar DNA in possession of other police jurisdictions connected to the case? What DNA exists on the Paul Stine shirt? I don't believe there isn't any on a shirt involved in a bloody murder. Sweat has lots of DNA."

As I read, I remembered that I had spoken with Kelly Carroll once. I had called him several years after Butler had quit communicating with me. Carroll had informed me that the case was closed. "I can never speak to anyone about this case ever," the detective had said. I recalled that Carroll had not seemed too happy about that. The conversation had struck me as odd, even then.

When I finished reading the letter, doubts about whether Hennessey had submitted my DNA resurfaced. Three years seemed like a long time to wait for a DNA result for a serial killer case, especially this one. Why had Hennessey met with me so many times if he had ordered his detectives not to follow any lead they received about the Zodiac? Why had he sent me the DNA request out of the blue? Had Hennessey wanted to be the one to solve it, or had he simply been toying with me? Or maybe something else had happened. Maybe Harold Butler or Earl Sanders had discovered what he was doing and had ordered him to back off the case.

I ran through all the possibilities in my mind, and the last one seemed the most believable. My instincts told me Hennessey was sincere. I decided I would ask him.

The next time I visited Benicia, I called the SFPD from my hotel.

"Hennessey has retired," I was informed.

I sat back in my chair, realizing exactly what that meant. My DNA was possibly sitting somewhere in a lab, where it could remain untested forever.

I dialed Hennessey's cell phone and left a message for him to call me.

He didn't call.

I waited a few days and e-mailed him. I had to verify that I knew him by answering a few questions before the e-mail would go through.

He did not respond.

I waited awhile and e-mailed him again.

Nothing.

I called him one last time before I gave up.

I knew something had happened. My thoughts circled back to Butler and Sanders. They had been such good friends of Rotea's. They would not want the world to know that Rotea had been married to the Zodiac's former wife. But I had no proof. I remembered Hennessey had once said, "Do you suspect a cover-up?" I had laughed and said, "Of course I do."

"Well, we'll get to the bottom of it then," Hennessey had responded.

I remembered that Hennessey had told me Butler had refused to let him see my father's file. The lieutenant had been forced to go through CLETS for information about my father's arrests. Why wouldn't Butler give the head of the homicide division a case file that had been requested? Had my father ever been a suspect in the case? What had been so heinous that we were not allowed to see inside that manila folder?

Now I would never know.

I went back to the website, trying to find some contact information for Maloney, only to discover that he had died of a heart attack in early 2007.

Damn.

I had finally found someone who might have some answers, who had said publicly that he suspected a cover-up, and I would never be able to talk to him.

53

Deciding that I had better start thinking like a detective, I went back to the Zodiac murders. I read every police file I could find on the Internet, noticing that, although the men had been attacked and sometimes killed, it was the women who seemed to be the main target of the killer's rage. I had read numerous books on serial killers and what drives them, and I knew that many were sexual sadists. I found it interesting that none of the women had been sexually assaulted. These murders had not been about control.

They had been about rage.

Revenge.

Operating under that theory, I printed out photos of the female victims and laid them side by side across my desk, next to a picture of Judy. As I picked up each photo and compared it with a picture I had of my mother when she was sixteen, my hands begin to shake.

Every one of them resembled Judy in some way.

I resolved to learn everything I could about the Zodiac victims, hoping that would lead me to another epiphany. As I got to know more personal details, the horror of what my father had done became more and more real.

One afternoon, I recalled what a detective had once told me about solving any crime: "You always go back to the source." With that in mind, I printed out all of the Zodiac letters and began studying them. I hoped my answers might be buried somewhere in those letters.

As I read through them and got to the quotes from *The Mikado*, I could hear William's voice in my head. "We knew every word of that opera."

When I read about Zodiac's "slaves for the afterlife," I remembered William's slave box. "Your father was obsessed with it," he had said.

All of my father's obsessions ran through those letters—his Anglophile pretentions and British way of speaking, his admiration for LaVey, his knowledge of weapons and military training.

But when I got to the letter postmarked April, 20, 1970, my heart began pounding. In that letter, Zodiac had written, "My name is" and included a cipher with thirteen characters. I wrote down my father's name—Earl Van Best Jr.

It had thirteen characters.

Excited, I did some more research and discovered that none of the prime suspects in the Zodiac killings had ever had thirteen characters in their names. I began to review the 408 cipher, the one that had been sent in sections to three different newspapers (see next page).

Zodiac had said that if this cipher were solved, the police would have him.

I found a version on the Internet where the decoded message had been typed above the Zodiac's cipher. I approached the three sections of the cipher as if they were a seek-a-word puzzle, looking at a particular letter and then looking vertically, diagonally, and across for my father's name.

I saw it right away, plain as day. It was in the section of the cipher that had been sent to the *San Francisco Examiner*: EV Best Jr.

I couldn't believe what I was seeing. Detectives—professional and amateur—had spent years searching for the killer's name in those ciphers.

But they had not been armed with the Zodiac's real name.

When they had a suspect, such as Arthur Leigh Allen, they had not been able to find the name of the suspect hidden among the symbols and letters.

As the sun disappeared into the horizon outside my window, the magnitude of what I had just discovered slowly sank in.

My father really was the Zodiac.

I remembered when I had first seen the "Wanted" poster on A&E three years earlier. I had set out to disprove my suspicions to myself. Back then, everyone, including Judy, had thought I was crazy.

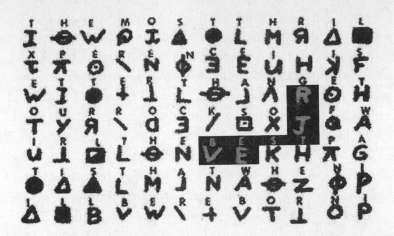

I had thought I was crazy.

But there it was in black and white. "In this cipher is my identity," Zodiac had written.

DNA or no DNA, I finally had something tangible that proved my father was the Zodiac.

54

It had now been five years since Judy found me. Throughout that time, we had experienced many ups and downs in our relationship as I tried to understand her role in all of this. I had spent a lifetime wondering about my identity. In her own fashion, Judy had helped me discover who I was, but I had learned that she was not always a reliable source of information relating to my past, and that she wanted to protect my brother, Chance, and the life she had led with Rotea.

She was my mother. I loved her. And she loved me, even

though I drove her crazy forcing her to remember things she wanted to forget. She had made it clear that she wanted to put her past behind her. I couldn't do that. Not long after I had discovered my great-grandfather's name on the Horry County Historical Society website, I had written letters to everyone I could find named Best living in Horry County, explaining that I had been adopted and asking if anyone knew Earl Van Best Sr. or his son. I received a response from a man named Robert Armstrong, who said he was the executor of the estate of my grandfather's wife, Eleanor. He wrote to tell me that my grandfather had been the pastor of the small Christian church he had once attended. "He was my mother's pastor, and I became quite friendly with him. He passed away several years ago (sorry I don't know the date)," Armstrong wrote, explaining that he had been asked to be executor because he worked in a bank.

He said that my grandfather had attended Asbury Theological Seminary, in Wilmore, Kentucky, and did have a son, although they had been estranged. "My poor memory suggests he was an alcoholic," he wrote, referring to Van. "He apparently died in Mexico and is buried there with apparently not even a marker on his grave. He had remarried to a lady in Austria and left 3 children in Austria, who, if we are on the right track for you, would be half-sister and half-brothers to you."

Armstrong listed the name Guenevere Obregon, Van's daughter, along with her address and e-mail address. "She had or has two brothers, Oliver and Urban. She apparently had been a judge in Austria," he continued.

I read the rest of the letter barely comprehending what I was reading.

My father was dead, buried in Mexico in an unmarked grave?

My grandfather was dead?

I read the letter over and over, letting feelings of loss, of sorrow, wash over me. In the beginning, I had fantasized about meeting my father. I had imagined sharing a cup of coffee with him, going out to dinner, telling stories, as I had done with Judy.

Laughing together.

For my whole life I had imagined the kind of man he would be.

That could never happen now.

According to Armstrong, my grandfather had been a military man, an honorable man. I felt a sense of pride rising up through my grief.

I sat there for a while, my thoughts jumbled. Why had the woman at the Social Security Administration hinted that my father was alive? Why hadn't Butler told me he was dead? Did he know?

And then it hit me—"He remarried to a lady in Austria and left 3 children . . ."

I had a sister and two brothers.

I had to find them.

I called Judy immediately, thinking she should know that Van was dead. Instead of saying the words, I read the letter to her.

She laughed.

She laughed even harder when I got to the part about my siblings in Austria.

"Sounds just like your father to go off to Vienna and have children, then wind up being buried in Mexico," she commented sarcastically.

I hung up the phone, disturbed by Judy's reaction. She had sounded relieved, almost happy, that my father was dead. I could hear it in her voice, in her laughter.

I went to my computer and wrote a short e-mail to Guenevere Obregon, explaining that I had been adopted and reciting what Armstrong had told me.

I got no response.

Thinking that maybe she no longer used the e-mail address

Armstrong had given me, I wrote her a letter and mailed it the old-fashioned way. I included photographs of myself and expressed how excited I would be to meet her.

A month passed by.

Nothing.

Losing hope that I had the right address, I typed her name into my search engine. A document titled "Republic of Austria, Independent Federal Asylum Review Board Activity Report" appeared on my screen. I clicked on it.

Jackpot.

Guenevere was a judge, a *magistère* on the board. I was impressed. I couldn't wait to talk to her, to ask her about her memories of our father. I wondered if she had been motivated to help criminals seek asylum because of Van's criminal past.

Three hours later, I found the phone number for the board.

I dialed the number over and over, my inability to speak German hampering my progress.

Finally, I reached a woman who recognized the words "Guenevere" and "*magistère*."

"Yes, yes, but no, she is not here. She is on, how do you say, maternity?" she managed.

I gleaned from the woman that Guenevere had been on maternity leave for two years.

"Do you have a telephone number for her?" I asked, crossing my fingers.

"No. Call back Monday. Maybe someone can help you then."

I called back the following Monday and reached a woman who said, "You are looking for Guenevere, yes?" before informing me that she was her secretary.

"Yes," I said, trying to keep the excitement out of my voice.

"She is on maternal leave and is at home expecting a baby."

"Can you get a message to her?"

"Sure," the woman replied.

"Ask her to telephone Gary Stewart. Tell her that I am her brother in the United States." I gave her my office number.

She giggled in surprise. "Oh, her brother. Okay, Gary, I will tell her, and I hope that she will call you back. Good-bye."

I hung up the phone feeling like I had just exhausted my last chance, but excited that Guenevere would get my message.

My change of mood was obvious when I walked into my office that morning. Phillip Schmidt, a close friend and co-worker, noticed immediately. "What's got you in so early this morning, sunshine?"

I had not yet told anyone in the office about my father. Everyone knew about Judy, but I had not mentioned that I was looking for Van. I told Phillip that I had learned I had two brothers and a sister in Austria. The phone, which usually rang nonstop, had been strangely quiet while we chatted. We were still discussing what I should do next when the phone rang. It was 9:30.

Phillip reached for it. "Delta Tech, this is Phillip. May I help you?"

I could hear a female voice and saw Phillip's confused look. He was having trouble understanding what the woman was saying. Finally, he heard "Gary" and covered the mouthpiece with his hand.

"I think it's your sister," he said.

I just stood there, suddenly petrified.

"I'll leave you two alone," Phillip said, handing me the phone. As the door closed behind him, I said, "Hello," much too cheerfully, my voice shaking.

"Hallo, I'm looking for Gary Stewart," a heavily German-accented voice said in perfect English.

Gripping the handset, I said, "This is Gary speaking."

"This is Guenevere. What's this about you being my brother?" I could tell she was smiling by the sound of her voice, and I let go of the breath I had been holding.

Our conversation lasted forty minutes. Guenevere asked why I thought we were brother and sister. I explained that I had been adopted and what Armstrong had told me.

Guenevere told me that she had a baby, Karl, who was two, and her second child was due in March. She explained that she had moved from the address where I had sent the letter because she and her husband needed a larger home for their growing family. She had not received the e-mails because she had not been to her office.

My heart soared. She had not been ignoring me.

I told her about my family, both families, and repeated the information I had sent her in the letters.

"Can you tell me about our father?" I asked.

"I didn't know our father," she said. "He abandoned us when I was a baby."

Her words shot through me. Van had done the same thing to my siblings that he had done to me. I knew well the sadness she must have experienced when she learned that.

"So is our father's criminal past the reason why you devoted your life to helping those like our father seek asylum?" I asked, my voice full of empathy.

There was silence on the other end of the phone.

"What do you mean, 'our father's criminal past'?" Guenevere said, the tone of her voice no longer cheerful.

I knew I had just misstepped. "I just assumed, if you worked for the asylum board, that our father might have been running from something in the U.S."

"My career has nothing to do with my father," Guenevere said coldly. "It's just what I went to university for, that's all."

As we said our good-byes and exchanged contact information, I knew I had stuck my foot in my mouth. I hoped I had not done too much damage, but the Guenevere who said good-bye was not the friendly Guenevere who had greeted me.

That evening I wrote a letter apologizing for springing such a surprise on her and sharing with her everything I had learned about Van to date, including all of the misinformation my friend at the Department of Justice and Harold Butler had provided.

She wrote back, disputing my facts. She said that her father had never been arrested in the United States. "You wrote that the police officer told you my father was arrested again in 1996 in California. This is totally absurd because my father died in the year 1984 in Mexico." She went on to say that after suffering so much hardship, she, her brothers, and her mother had closed the chapter on her father and his family in the States for good. "We do not want to have anymore ties to my father's side of the family and so we do not want you or anyone to interfere in mine, my brothers, or my mother's lives. We all ask you to respect our wish. Of course we wish you and your family all the best for the future."

I could have kicked myself for being so stupid. Of course no one would want to find out that they had a brother and then be immediately told that their father was a criminal. I had assumed that, because she was my sister, she would automatically relate.

I wrote Guenevere another letter, trying to explain myself, and received a response that was more amicable.

"Imagine how I felt," she wrote, "when you told me on the phone: I am your brother, your father had a relationship with a minor and he was a criminal too . . . I felt and still feel like I've been run over by a truck without any warning!"

She asked to see my birth certificate so she could be one hundred percent sure that I was her brother, and she asked for time to absorb everything. "If all of this is true, it would be a shock for my mother, who is not in good health."

She said that my father had "suffocated" in Mexico and her mother had traveled there to say good-bye for all of them. "He is buried in an unmarked grave because the wife of my grandfather did not want to fly him over to the States to give him a proper funeral."

She went on to say that she had never met my grandfather. "We never got one small toy from him, and when I was 11 years old I was sent to an international camp in the States where he could have visited me, but he did not want to see me. Or when I finished law school and was chosen by the dean of the Rutgers Law School to work as a university assistant there for a year, I wanted to visit his wife, Eleanor, but she did not want to see me either."

Guenevere concluded that she did not understand why it was so important that I have contact with her, but that she would need proof and she would need time.

She signed the letter "Gueny."

That gave me hope.

I gave her the time she needed. Over the next few months, I tried repeatedly to get my original birth certificate from the state of Louisiana and eventually took my case to court, but to no avail. My birth records were sealed, and that was that.

As the months went by, I began to lose hope that I would ever hear back from Guenevere, although I had written and explained that I was doing my best to get my birth certificate from the state.

Finally, after seven months, I retrieved from my mailbox a letter with a stamp marked ÖSTERREICH. My heart skipped a beat as I tore open the envelope.

The letter wasn't from Guenevere.

It was from Edith, her mother.

With a feeling of foreboding, I went inside and sat down to read the letter.

My father's third wife wrote that it was natural for children who have been adopted to want to find their birth parents, but that few can deal with the reality of what they find. She pointed out that the things Harold Butler had told me about Van had been wrong, that her husband could not have been in prison in 1996, because he had died in 1984. "This is for me a fact, or you telling me I was standing on the wrong grave. If my children are missing some small detail about their father, they can ask me," she wrote. "Stop stressing my children and upset me. Just STOP IT, since you are not the only one, who wants after 30 years, to be related to me (how practical fly to Europe and have a stay in Vienna)." She then informed me that people can choose their friends, but not their relatives, and wished me "the great fatherly family" her children never had.

I sat there, stunned, a thousand thoughts running through my head. Guenevere must have told her mother everything about me. Gueny had sounded so lighthearted in her last letter. Edith clearly didn't want to hear anything about a child from a former marriage.

Tears streamed down my face as I realized that I had to let this go.

55

As 2008 began, my efforts to get my birth certificate were ongoing, but I had not been successful. I had even brought Judy with me to the Office of Vital Statistics with proof that I knew who my real mother was, and my request was still turned down.

As soon as I received the letter from Edith, I realized why the Social Security Administration had no indication that my father was dead: Edith had gone back to Austria without reporting his death. Although I did not have the exact date, I decided to file a report so there would be a record in the United States. I guessed he had died in August 1984. I was wrong.

I was finally able to get my father's official report of death through the U.S. Department of State. According to the report, my father had died in a hotel—Hotel Corinto—in Mexico City. "Asphyxiation by blockage of major air passages by passing gastric matter."

I knew what that meant. He had choked to death on his own vomit.

Dr. Aurelio Núñez Salas had performed the autopsy.

Van had died on May 20, 1984, and had been interred at the Panteón San Lorenzo Tezonco, in Mexico City.

I hopped on a plane. I had to go see the man who had haunted my thoughts and dreams for the past five years.

As I sat in the Hotel Corinto, in downtown Mexico City, I felt as if I was experiencing déjà vu. It was here in this very hotel that my mother and father had stayed in 1962. I knew that because Judy had described a nine-story hotel with a swimming pool on top. This tall structure, near the Monumento a la Revolución in Plaza de la República, was the only hotel that had a swimming pool on the ninth floor. Here was where my mother and father had shared the most romantic time in their relationship.

Here their honeymoon had begun.

And here, in the same hotel, their story had ended.

As I sat down at the bar, with its mirrored walls and blue back-lighting, lined with bottles of Crown Royal and Jack Daniel's and tequila of every variety, I wondered how many times my father had sat in this same spot, maybe this same seat, looking at the man who stared back at him from those mirrors. I wondered what he thought of that man, if he ever really understood what he had allowed himself to become.

And I wondered what his thoughts were just before he died.

The irony of it all struck me: the man who had hurt so many died choking on his own vomit.

It seemed fitting, in a way.

I shook my head to clear my reverie, ordered a drink from the bartender, and casually said, *"Mi padre murió aquí."*

An old woman sitting on a stool nearby stared at me for a long moment and then nodded her head. "Ah, bambino Van Best."

I tried to ask her how well she had known my father, hoping to hear some stories about his life in Mexico, but she did not speak English, and my feeble efforts to speak to her in Spanish were fruitless.

Finally I gave up and headed to the ninth floor.

I sat in one of the poolside chairs and looked at the incredible view of the city, with Popocatépetl, the second-highest mountain peak in Mexico, looming forty-three miles in the distance. The sometimes active volcano, or "smoking mountain," is often referred to by the locals as "El Popo" or "Don Goyo."

I imagined my mother frolicking in the pool and my father laughing at her antics. She had been so young then, only fourteen, and her playfulness must have been catching. She had been so beautiful, and Van had looked at her lovingly, ignoring the other guests, who must have been giving him strange looks, wondering about their relationship—was he her husband or her father?

The sun was setting over the mountain, and I watched until it disappeared. Finally I got up and headed back to my hotel, the Sheraton Maria Isabel. I had not wanted to stay at the Hotel Corinto. That would have been too much.

The next morning I called the concierge and asked if I could hire a driver for the day. I had important business and needed someone reliable. At 9:45 a.m., a short, white-haired Mexican who introduced himself as Sergio met me in front of the hotel.

"Señor Gary?" he said.

"*Sí*," I replied.

"I understand you have a very special request today?"

"*Sí, señor*," I said, shaking his hand. I had explained to the concierge that I wanted to find my father's gravesite.

"Well, then," he said, in his heavily accented voice. "Let's not keep your father waiting any longer, my friend."

Although the San Lorenzo Tezonco cemetery was less than fifteen miles from the heart of the Zona Rosa, the drive was lengthened considerably by the construction and endless traffic through the community of Iztapalapa, one of the most dangerous neighborhoods in Mexico City.

"I don't drive through here, *señor*," Sergio informed me. "Never in my life. In all my years, *señor*, I have never had one request like this one. I feel very honored to take you to see your father for the first time in Mexico City."

The trip south from the ancient city of Tenochtitlan—the name given to the area by the Aztecs before it became Mexico City—took nearly two hours. I thought we had reached our destination when I began to see wooden vendors' shops with tin roofs that offered beautiful flowers, crucifixes, and monuments, including La Catrina, for the poor peasants visiting the final resting places of their loved ones. My thoughts drifted back to William's remark when I first told him I wanted to visit my father's gravesite.

"Be sure not to go on Día de los Muertos," he had warned.

"What is that?"

He had explained that in Mexico, people believe that on the Day of the Dead—November 1—and the days surrounding it, their dearly departed have divine permission to visit earth. There is a festival that takes place over the course of three days, during which the living welcome the souls of the dead with offerings of flowers, specially prepared food, candles, photographs, and incense. It is a peaceful and happy occasion to keep the memory of their loved ones fresh in the minds forever.

"But it's not for outsiders," William said. "And you don't want to run into any of those spirits who may have stuck around."

I was still thinking about that when we drove into the cemetery. Black letters on a small sign made of plywood announced our arrival at Panteón Civil San Lorenzo Tezonco. My gaze fixed on that sign—the symbol for the last stop in my father's miserable life.

My stomach began churning as we drove in.

"Here we are, *señor*. I'm so sorry. It is a very, very poor place."

I looked around and saw what he meant. My father was buried in the poorest cemetery in the worst neighborhood in all of Mexico City. I began to feel everything decelerating, like a slow-motion action scene in a movie where the silence drowns the senses. Everything seemed surreal. Breathing became difficult. Although I had experienced fatigue on my first day in Mexico City, due to its 7,500-foot elevation, this had nothing to do with that. This was stemming from the reality that I was really here in this place.

With my father.

As I watched for the cemetery's administrative offices, Sergio slowly drove up the divided, tree-lined boulevard.

"Turn right," I said when I saw an old brick office tucked behind a grove of mesquite trees. He pulled into a parking space in front of the building while I dug through my Swiss Army backpack for my father's death report and birth certificate.

Once inside, Sergio spoke to an elderly woman sitting in front of a typewriter and explained why we were there. She instructed us to walk around the counter to the far end of the building and go through a small door.

Inside the office, another elderly lady sat at a desk, and a middle-aged man attended to some filing. The back wall was lined with file cabinets, but it was a particular black double file cabinet with white doors that immediately caught my eye. It was labeled "1980–1984."

When Sergio explained to the second woman why we were there, she pointed to this file cabinet.

I pulled out a large book marked "1984" and began flipping through the pages, checking each name. When I turned to May 23, I saw my father's name as it had been recorded for the last time. Sixteen people had been buried there that day—eight children and eight adults. My father was number fifteen, between Francisca Quintero Cruz and Fernando Lecuona Armaz. There was a blue check by his name. I couldn't help but wonder if that was because he was American.

I called the man over. He wrote the plot number down on a small piece of paper and then muttered something to Sergio.

Sergio put his arm around me. "His name is Alejandro. We will follow him, *señor*. He will take us to your father."

As we walked out of the office, I struggled to keep it together. I had waited for years to get to this place, had experienced so many heartaches and frustrations since I had learned this man's name. Now that I was here, I wondered what I was doing, why I was doing this.

I headed toward Sergio's van, but he took me by the arm. "No, *señor*. We will walk. He says it is not too far."

I battled with my emotions as we walked into a small, tree-lined area with dirt pathways leading to what had once been a beautiful old stone chapel. The chapel walls had crumbled around the windows and doors, and the roof had collapsed—a casualty of an earthquake that had devastated Mexico City in 1985.

Thunder, a short distance away in the mountains, rumbled as dark clouds filled the sky. I tried not to look ahead, because I could feel we were getting close, and the closer we got, the more difficult it became for me to breathe. I reached into my pocket to pull out a handkerchief and wiped my eyes. Suddenly everyone stopped.

At first I didn't want to look, so I stared at the flowers adorning graves as far as the eye could see. I noticed litter and debris lying on the ground. I couldn't help but think of my grandfather, buried at the glorious Arlington National Cemetery, among the patriotic faithful in peaceful, hallowed ground.

I thought about Gertrude, whose grave I had visited not long before, in San Bernardino. She had lived through the deaths of the only three men who had ever loved her, their deaths coming in rapid succession in 1984: the commander, her first husband, in March; her second husband, John Harlan Plummer, in April; and her son in May. I had sat cross-legged at her grave and talked with her for the first time. She had died alone in a mobile home in 1986. There had not even been an obituary written.

I knew somehow that she had suffered like the rest of us in her own way. Sitting there, I had poured out my heart to her, but when I left, I didn't say, "I'll be back." I didn't say, "I hope you're happy and at peace." I simply told her that I loved her and that I was so sorry that she had not been able to accept love when it had first been offered to her. That had cost so many so much.

As I looked around, I couldn't help but be happy that my grandfather had not lived to see his son buried in a pauper's grave. This would have been unbearable for such a proud man, who had preached about the joy of heaven at so many of the dignified funerals of his parishioners.

Finally, I noticed that Sergio and Alejandro were standing between two marble grave markers that faced a small lump of barren ground. Alejandro whispered something to Sergio, reverently removed his straw hat, and placed it over his heart, then bowed his head.

"He is here, *señor*." Sergio pointed to the unmarked mound of earth at our feet.

For a moment I couldn't speak.

I stood there, silent in the presence of my father.

Again I looked around at the memorials on the other graves, placed there carefully by indigent family members who would forever miss their departed ones. Most of the tombstones displayed beautiful crosses, paving the way for their loved ones' entrances to heaven. And then I looked at the mound of earth that had never been visited by anyone except Edith. There was no cross here.

Finally I asked Sergio to ask Alejandro if I could leave some pictures on the grave. One was of me and William, and the other showed me, Judy, and Zach.

"The pictures will be blown away in the wind and will be litter by the end of the day," Alejandro replied to Sergio in Spanish. "But I can dig a hole over the spot where his padre's heart would be, and I can put them there."

Alejandro placed his hat on the ground. He dug a hole about sixteen inches deep, right over my father's heart. Stepping back, he bowed as I knelt down and placed the pictures in the hole. After he covered the photos with dirt, I handed him and Sergio fifty pesos each.

"*Un momento, por favor*," I said.

Alejandro replied in perfect English. "Take all the time you need, *señor*."

Sergio said he would wait by a nearby willow tree.

I realized that for the first time since the day he had left me in the stairwell, I was alone with my father.

I knelt down, trying not to let my anger get the best of me. I loved this man in some inexplicable way. He was my father. We were bound together by an invisible, unbreakable rope, yet I hated him so much for the things he had done. I looked up and asked God to help me say the right things. I prayed the way Leona had taught me. I asked God for forgiveness for my father. I asked Him to have mercy on Van's soul. And I asked God to forgive me for the anger I felt about what my father had done—not only to me but to so many others as well.

As I looked down at the ground, I saw my tears striking the dirt that covered my father. It occurred to me that Van had hated to hear me cry.

Right then, I let go.

I poured out my heart to him—all the pain, all the anger.

And then the forgiveness Leona and Loyd had instilled in me.

As I walked away, I noticed the storm clouds retreating behind the volcano. *"Adiós, mi padre,"* I whispered, wishing with all my heart that he could have been the man I wanted my father to be.

Wondering how long I had been there, I looked down at my watch. I realized it was May 17—the anniversary of the day Earl Van Dorne Best had died and Gary Loyd Stewart had been born.

56

In 2002, when Leona and Loyd first met Judy and Frank, I had been in a state of pure happiness as we sat at the table sharing a meal. I had felt so blessed to have not one but two beautiful mothers. As time went on and I began to search for my father, I often worried about how all of this would affect my adopted parents. They had been so good to me, and I didn't want to hurt them through my search for my father.

I had always realized how much the strength of my mother and her extraordinary faith had shaped my life. But one year, around Father's Day, I began to recognize how much the search for my identity had strengthened my love for Loyd, how much he had quietly supported me in his own way. Father's Day had never meant as much to me as it would now.

When we were children, my sisters and I would always sign the card my mother had bought and give it to him before going to church. As we got older, everyone in the family would pitch in to buy Dad a nice gift—a barbecue pit, a new television— and we would each give him our own personalized Hallmark card. This year, there was no Hallmark version that could say the things I wanted to say to my daddy. By 2009 I had a better understanding of what Father's Day really meant, so I made my own card:

Daddy,

Today, I had to go down to the City Court Building on St. Louis Street to take care of some business down there. As you know, parking is always a problem downtown, but I found a space on the corner of America Street and St. Charles that charges five dollars for the entire day. I parked there and went to take care of my business.

You know, now that I have spent so much of the past years researching my past and finding all of the complicated details about my abandonment on North Boulevard, that area of town has become a favorite place of mine. I guess in my heart I wish Van had really tried to leave me at the First Presbyterian Church there, but I know and have now accepted that I may never know the real story about what happened on that cold March day. What I do know is that this area of town, Beauregard Town, is now very special to me. In my heart and mind, it is a sacred and holy place. Every time I get a chance I try to drive by or park my truck and walk by the old Lytle apartment building. I do this quite often. There's just something about the place that draws me there, back to my beginnings.

But something different happened to me today. When I exited the parking lot on America Street, I turned left and drove three blocks, then turned left onto St. Joseph. As I drove north, I saw the courtyard where Van must have carried me into the back of the apartment building. I stopped there for a minute just to wonder and daydream and listen to what God was trying to tell me. For so long now, I have wondered just what Van might have been thinking and what was in his heart.

Did he love me? Did he care? Did he cry? Was he sorry for what he was about to do? All these things have been in my heart and on my mind for so long. As I sat and cried and listened, I got my answer. It doesn't matter what Van did or what he felt. There only one thing that matters about what happened that day. What matters is what God did.

For four and a half hours, I was alone.

But Daddy, now I see I was never alone.
Today, I realized that the moment Van placed
me on that floor and walked away from
his crying son, someone very special was
watching over me. I'm sure as Van slipped
out of that building hoping not to be
discovered with his evil heart, he might
have looked back or maybe even shed a tear.
I don't know. But I do know that God saw
the whole thing. He knew that this child
was alone, unprotected, and He wrapped me
up in His love and protected me until Mrs.
Bonnette came home from work.

Maybe Van didn't shed a tear, but I bet
God did when He witnessed the actions of
this father abandoning his only son. I just
think it breaks God's heart to look upon
evil. I think as God watched Van exiting
that building, His displeasure with Van
fueled His heart to find the perfect father
for this child. I believe that in those
hours, God calmed me and sat with me there
on those cold and lonely steps, comforting
me and making His plan for my life.

I know that as God babysat me that day, He
decided this child had to be given to someone
very special, someone with His heart. That
must have been when God hand-picked you to
be my father. He knew that it would take a
special kind of love to heal the scars left
by the biological father, and there was only
one person suited to fill that role.

```
I just wanted you to know how grateful I
am that God made the right choice by giving
me you. I love you with all my heart.
Happy Father's Day


Gary
```

My dad didn't want to read the card in front of everyone who'd gathered at his home that Sunday afternoon, so he went into his bedroom. In a few minutes, he emerged with tears streaming down his face. He told me that card was the best gift he had received in his life. He wrapped his arms around me in a big hug and whispered, "I love you, Gary."

I will never forget that moment.

Three years later, on June 16, 2012, the day before Father's Day, my mom and dad got up to their usual routine. Mom made Dad's coffee and then returned to her bedroom for her daily devotional time. Dad took his coffee to the computer room, as he called it, where he read the Bible every morning.

When Dad finished reading, he put on his old work tennis shoes and his sweat-stained ball cap. "Okay, hon. I'm ready," he called out to Mom, letting her know it was time to work in the garden.

As they walked out the back door onto their new brick-paved patio, Dad looked around at the sunny blue sky. Before he even closed the door, he began to sing, to thank God for the beauty of the day.

Oh, Lord, my God.
When I in awesome wonder
Consider all
The worlds thy hands hath made.

Interrupting, Mom did what Mom sometimes does. She couldn't help herself. It was too early in the morning.

"Loyd, shush. Not so loud. You're going to wake the entire neighborhood."

Dad just smiled. "Well, they need to hear it," he said.

"How great Thou art!" he sang louder, bending over to pick up a brick that was holding down a tarp he had used to protect the flower beds from recent heavy rains. He stood up with a brick in his right hand and looked toward the sky.

In that instant, the Lord called my daddy home.

Before his beautiful sweet, sweet shell of a body hit the ground, his spirit had already soared to heaven, his voice still praising his God.

I have no doubt that God took him this way because He knew how much my father hated good-byes. In reward for a life so well lived, he had been spared a long illness and the pain of having to say good-bye to his loving wife and family.

As I was writing his obituary on Father's Day, I wanted people to know what a wonderful man he was, how funny and kind and loving. I forgot to mention that he had been a deacon for many years at Istrouma Baptist Church. That had been one of his proudest accomplishments. I had been so focused on describing the kind of husband, father, and grandfather he had been that I forgot something that was so important to him. I'm sure he got a big chuckle out of that.

Istrouma Baptist Church was packed on the day of his funeral service. Hundreds of people whose lives he had touched in one way or another filled row after row or stood in line to say their good-byes to this fine man.

As I stood before all of those people, I proudly told the story of his life—how this simple man had made such a difference in the lives of his wife, his children, his grandchildren.

In the days after the funeral, I couldn't help but think about the differences between my two fathers—the one who had abandoned me and the one who had raised me as his own. I wondered what my life would have been like if I had grown up with Earl Van Best Jr. instead of Harry Loyd Stewart as a father. I know I would not have become the man I am today, the man Loyd taught me to be through his words and through his actions.

Yes, my biological father was a child rapist and a serial killer, but my real father, the man who loved me, who worked so hard to give me a good life, is in heaven, still watching over the son he so lovingly took into his home and into his heart.

57

It has been twelve years since Judy found me, and I have to say that it was one of the most significant days of my life. The wounds we inflicted upon each other over these years are healing, and we visit as often as we can. I recognize now how hard all of this must have been on her. I understand that she was still a child when she gave birth to me, and I cannot hold her responsible for the actions of another. I can't blame her for not wanting to remember things. I wouldn't want to remember such things, either. Five years ago, Judy started the Tucson Adoption Reunion Support Group, her way of making amends through counseling and advising other adoptees. The work she has done through this group has helped change many lives.

In January 2010, Tania called to inform me that William had passed away. I was very distressed by his loss, because we had become very close. I could always count on his honesty, no matter how much the details might further convince me of my father's sins. In the few years I knew him, he had become like an uncle to me, Uncle Bill.

Soon after, I went to visit Tania to offer my condolences. While I was there, the conversation turned to my father.

"You know, I didn't like him," she said. "I didn't ever want to say this in front of Vsevé, but your father dropped by unexpectedly in the late 1970s or early 1980s. Vsevé was away on a business trip, and I didn't want to invite Van in, because he looked very disheveled, dirty even. Anyway, he looked bad. I think he wanted money, but his pride wouldn't let him ask me. Finally I let him in, and he began to brag like he always did about the things he had done in his life. Then he suggested that I should leave Vsevé and run off with him. Your father was a sick man."

Harold Butler passed away on June 21, 2012. Any lingering hope I had of discovering everything he knew about my father died with him. Butler, like so many others, took his secrets to his grave.

To this day, I have never seen my original birth certificate. After I went to court, Judge Pamela Johnson ordered the Office of Vital Statistics to give me a copy. When I went to pick it up, the clerk looked at the judgment and shook her head. "That's not how we do things here in Louisiana." Ignoring the court order, she refused to give me the document. I'm still fighting to get it.

On May 19, 2011, I sent a letter to all of Louisiana's state senators, urging them to support Louisiana Senate Bill 155, which would have allowed adult adoptees access to their original birth certificates. The bill did not pass.

In a last, desperate attempt, I copied Guenevere on the letter. I added a note that simply said, "I'm still trying."

I received an e-mail from her the same day. It read:

"Hi. You have misunderstood something: in respect to us we

do not care about your birth certificate because we have already made it clear that we do not wish to meet you or have contact with you. Gueny."

Despite that disappointment, I am blessed with the family I have. I had lived most of my life beleaguered by an identity crisis—my inability to cope with not knowing who I was. Just as He did with Loyd, God knew that it would take a very special person to be able to understand me and love me unconditionally, and He gave me my beautiful wife, Kristy, in 2007. She has patiently supported me while I've gone through this journey to find my father and myself. She has been my rock, and, together with the rest of my family, we will help Leona get through this trying time. After sixty years of marriage, the loss of her Loyd has been tremendous, and she doesn't really know how to live without him. Her faith is strong, but I know she is now patiently waiting for God to reunite her with the love of her life.

About the time that Judy and I reunited, I began keeping a journal, hoping to be able to express my feelings on paper so that one day Zach would be able to tell his children his father's story. At the time, I didn't know where the narrative would lead, but I documented every step of the journey.

Over the years, I had shared the story of the Ice Cream Romance and my discoveries about my father's past, including the possibility that he was the Zodiac, with my close friends. They seemed fascinated by my story and suggested that I write a book. But I'm not a writer; my journal was filled with ten years of research and all the emotion I experienced during that time. I began looking for someone to help me. Since I could not count on the SFPD to test my DNA, I thought maybe a book containing all of the evidence I had gathered would push the stalled wheels of justice forward.

One morning in March 2012, I was sitting in the office of a

friend and business associate, Earl Heard, publisher of *BIC* business magazine, telling him a little about this story and explaining that I was looking for someone who could help me write a book. I knew that Earl had published several books and thought he might be able to point me in the right direction. At that moment, his receptionist informed him that Susan Mustafa was on the phone. Earl got a big grin on his face and said, "Man, do I have the writer for you. This must be a sign."

When I spoke with Susan on the phone, I could tell that she thought my story was interesting, but she became skeptical when I got to the part about the Zodiac. "I would have to see your evidence," she said firmly. "I'm not willing to put my reputation on the line unless I believe what I'm writing."

That weekend, she went to the beach in Biloxi, Mississippi, and read my journal, filled with all the evidence I had accumulated through the years.

When she came back, we met at Hebert's Coffeehouse, in Baton Rouge, and she agreed to help me write my book. She informed me that we would have to figure out a way to get my DNA compared with the Zodiac's.

Susan called George Schiro, a forensic scientist at the Acadiana Crime Lab, and explained what we wanted to do.

"Is it possible to get a definitive match with only four markers?" she asked.

"Yes, but it will be easier if we have the son's and the mother's DNA."

"Can you do the profiles?"

"No," George said. "Our work has to come through the police."

George recommended that Susan speak with Dr. R. W. "Bo" Scales, director of Scales Biological Laboratory, in Brandon, Mississippi. "Tell him you're a friend of mine," he said.

Susan called Dr. Scales the following day. She left him a message telling him that George had suggested she call. The doctor called her back that afternoon.

"Any friend of George's is a friend of mine," Scales announced, in his jovial voice.

"Well, I don't know," Susan said. "You haven't heard my crazy request."

"I've been doing this for more than twenty years. I've heard it all," he said.

"Okay, then. I need you to compare a DNA profile from a mother and a son to extract the father's profile."

"How old is the child?" Scales asked.

"Forty-nine," Susan said, and laughed.

"And where's the father?"

"He's dead."

Dr. Scales started laughing and suggested that maybe they start the conversation over.

"Here's the deal," Susan said. "I need this profile to compare against the profile of a serial killer. Police only have four of the killer's markers in evidence. The San Francisco Police Department swabbed the son for DNA eight years ago, and we have not received any results. We'd like to get the father's profile so that it won't cost a law enforcement agency to run the tests. All they would have to do is look at it and compare."

"Who's the serial killer?"

"Um . . . the Zodiac."

"Really?" the doctor said, incredulous.

"Really," Susan said.

Dr. Scales explained to Susan the process of obtaining DNA and arranged to have the samples submitted. In a matter of weeks, Judy and I had been swabbed, and Dr. Scales had generated my father's DNA profile.

In the meantime, Susan began doing her own research.

She sent a request for Van's criminal records, complete with dates, charges, and case numbers, to the SFPD. Ten days later, she got a letter in the mail informing her that all of Earl Van Best Jr.'s files had been destroyed.

That same month, Susan began discussing this book with her New York literary agent, B. G. Dilworth. B. G., who was not very familiar with the Zodiac case, began reading about it online. He knew from Susan that I had found my father's name in the 408 cipher, and he was curious to see the other Zodiac ciphers that had not been decoded. He pulled up some images of the ciphers on his computer and at random began studying the 340 cipher, looking for my father's name.

He began by looking for the name Best. He located a backward *B* in the middle of the cipher and then looked for a neighboring *E*. There was an *E* below the *B*, but no *S* beneath it. It was a dead end. He spotted another *E* in the column to the left, but it wasn't adjacent to the *B*. Looking in the next column, he found an *S*, and then a *T* in the next. He realized that he had found Van's last name spelled backwards and wondered if his full name would be there. He looked in the column on the far right and found an *E*. Working his way from right to left backwards across the cipher, he found the name, Earl Van Best Junior. Van had put one letter of his name in each column.

To assure himself this was not a coincidence, B. G. used the same method to try to find his own name. It wasn't there. He then looked for names of friends and relatives and then for more common names like Jane Brown and Mary Smith. He couldn't find any first and last names in the same sequence, let alone a name that consisted of four words.

For more than forty years, the 340 cipher had stumped the best cryptologists in the world. In hindsight, it seems so simple—a child's word-search game—but the main reason B. G. was able to solve it was because he knew the Zodiac's name.

Susan called me as soon as she got the news. "B. G. found your father's name in the 340 cipher," she said, excitement ringing in her voice as she explained how he had discovered it.

I hurried to my computer to pull up the cipher. I had not paid much attention to it before. I had found my father's name in the 408, and that had been enough for me. With the cipher on my screen, I followed her instructions about how to find it.

"Oh, my God! It's there!" I said, trying to grasp the magnitude of what I was seeing. The backward *B* stood out to me. My father had always insisted his name was in the ciphers. I realized that was a clue, his arrogant way of telling the world his name was in the 340 backwards.

"Hang on a minute and let me print it." As soon as the page came through my printer, I grabbed a pen and began circling the letters. "That's incredible," I said when I was finished.

"The odds that your father's name could be in two different ciphers must be astronomical," Susan said.

"I know," I said, sinking back into my chair, still staring at the cipher. His name in the 408 had not been a fluke.

58

"Hey, Gary, do you have any handwriting from your father?" Susan asked me one day. "A letter he wrote to your grandfather or something like that?" By this time we had been working on the book for more than a year.

"I wish I did," I replied.

Her question bothered me, as though I was forgetting something I should have remembered. A nagging feeling persisted throughout the day, until finally I went into my office and began

ROINUJTSEBNAVLRAE

EARLVANBESTJUNIOR

pulling out boxes filled with papers, letters, and other memorabilia, spreading them across my desk and floor.

Hours later, I pulled a document from one of the boxes. It was Judy and Van's marriage certificate.

"Van filled out all the paperwork when we got married and hired witnesses to sign the certificate so that he could marry me when I was fourteen," Judy had told me. "He lied to the minister about my age."

I could not believe what I had found: my father's handwriting from 1962.

My heart almost stopped as I stared at the document. I had studied the Zodiac letters enough to immediately recognize that my father's handwriting was very similar to the Zodiac's.

And there was more. Beneath that document, I discovered the licenses from my father's marriages to Edith Kos and Mary Annette Player. Each had my father's signature.

I called Susan to tell her what I had discovered. "We need to find an expert to compare the handwriting," I said.

After a few weeks spent researching forensic document examiners, Susan and I decided that Michael N. Wakshull of Q9 Consulting, author of *Line By Line: Forensic Document Examination—A Strategy for Legal Professionals*—had the necessary experience and credentials to fulfill our request.

Susan called him. "I'm a true crime writer, and I'm researching a cold case," she said after she introduced herself on the phone. "I need a handwriting expert to determine whether a fifty-year-old marriage certificate matches the handwriting of a serial killer."

"Which serial killer?" Wakshull asked.

He was surprised when Susan replied, "The Zodiac." Wakshull lives near Riverside, where Cheri Jo Bates was killed, and remembered the Zodiac case very well.

Wakshull was intrigued, but leery.

"All we have is a marriage certificate and three signatures on a marriage license. Will that be enough?" Susan asked.

"I don't know. I'm at a seminar this weekend," he said. "Can I call you on Monday so we can discuss the case? E-mail me the samples so I can look at them, but I have to tell you it's highly unlikely that I will agree to take this case. I'm not going to put my reputation on the line unless I'm certain."

The following Monday, after reviewing what Susan had sent him, Wakshull called and agreed to compare my father's handwriting with the Zodiac's.

For almost two months we waited anxiously for the results.

Finally, on December 9, 2012, we got our answer.

Wakshull had generated a sixty-five-page report, complete with comparative exhibits and analysis, and had concluded that he was virtually certain that the person who filled out the marriage certificate was the writer of the Zodiac letters. He explained that he couldn't say he was absolutely certain, because the rules of his profession do not allow him to make that determination without original documents. "Strong probability" and "virtually certain" were the strongest words he could use to encapsulate his professional opinion.

As I stared at the exhibits he'd generated, I got chills. He had overlaid my father's handwriting onto the Zodiac's, and the results were stunning.

I had that final piece of evidence—forensic evidence that would stand up in a court of law.

A few weeks later, Wakshull sent another exhibit. He had decided to overlay my father's face onto the two pictures in the Zodiac sketch to see how closely they matched. The result was indisputable.

When Susan finally told him my whole story, he went a step further. He noticed that the signature on the Cheri Jo Bates letters—the *Z* with the squiggly top line—looked like an *E* and a *V.* He compared the *E*'s from Van's signature on his marriage licenses against the squiggly line and got another match.

By this time, he was getting just as excited as we were.

"You realize you are going to have to defend your findings," Susan told him.

"I would defend them in a court of law," Wakshull responded, and he put it in writing.

There was only one thing left that bothered me. I had found copies of Zodiac's fingerprints online, taken from the Paul Stine crime scene, and I had noticed that Zodiac had a scar running across his right index finger. Van's fingerprints on his booking sheet after his arrest for child stealing had the same scar, but it was running in the opposite direction. It finally hit me that crime scene technicians would have put a piece of paper over the bloody print and then laid that onto another piece of paper, reversing the print.

Susan and I began to search for a qualified expert to compare the fingerprints. We decided on Lieutenant Bob Garrett, a former detective and crime scene investigator and an expert in fingerprint identification, crime scene reconstruction, crime scene investigation, and digital imaging. He agreed to look at our samples but said it was unlikely that he could make a match with a bloody fingerprint.

A few days later, he informed Susan that a match could not be made because of the blood on the print.

"But what about the scar?" Susan asked.

"A scar is a starting point. You can't make an identification from a scar," Garrett replied.

Later that afternoon, he e-mailed Susan an exhibit showing five fingerprints: the original bloody print from Zodiac, the bloody print reversed, the bloody print with the scar highlighted,

Van's print, and then an overlay of the bloody print and Van's print.

Susan called me immediately. "Check your e-mail. You've got to see this."

The scars were identical—same angle, same length, same width.

Susan called Garrett back. "Can I have your permission to use this exhibit in the book?"

"Yes, as long as you make it clear that I could not make an identification," he said.

Susan promised that we would.

Fifty-one years.

That's how long I've waited to learn the truth about my life.

And I still don't have all the answers.

It has been almost ten years since I was swabbed for DNA at the San Francisco Police Department. I have never heard back from anyone in the SFPD with the results of my DNA comparison, and I have not heard from Lieutenant Hennessey since 2006.

I'm not sure why he suddenly stopped communicating with me, and I still find it troubling. We had become friends. He had promised to "get to the bottom of this." He had said he would give me the "closure" he wanted for me and my family—"one way or the other."

I believed him.

I still believe him, even with all of the evidence to the contrary.

Through the years, I kept coming back to this, wondering if I had done something to upset him, wondering if someone at the SFPD had discovered he had requested the DNA comparison and put a stop to it.

As we were putting the finishing touches on this memoir, someone asked me whether Hennessey knew I was writing a book. That question prompted a memory.

I had not told him. Back then, this book was still in its infancy. I had planned to ask for his blessing when I got the results of the DNA comparison, I had made a commitment that I would not share with anyone what he was doing for me, and I did not want to publish a book without his approval. I felt I had kept that commitment.

But at the time—2006—Judy and I were in a very good place for the first time in a while. I had finally come to understand that her strong instinct for self-preservation would generally trump my need for the unabridged truth, and I had accepted that. I told her I was going to write a memoir about my experiences, which would include the Ice Cream Romance and my journey to discover the truth about my identity. She seemed excited and wanted to help. She suggested that we write an adoption/reunion story together and explained that she had friends in the literary world who could help bring it to life.

My mother didn't know that my memoir contained so much more than the adoption/reunion aspect of our story.

Feeling confident that Judy would keep its contents confidential, I sent her my manuscript.

At the time, the book ended with me in Hennessey's office being swabbed to compare my DNA to the partial Zodiac profile. Included was the DNA request form.

After she read it, Judy immediately became disenchanted with the whole "book thing," as she called it, and responded to my manuscript with a chapter she had begun writing for our adoption/reunion book.

In the chapter, she explained how proud she had always been of Rotea and how disappointed she was that Harold Butler and

Earl Sanders had not helped her more when I was first trying to find my father. "Actually, I talked to them both," she wrote, "explaining that I didn't have any details of Gary's father. I wasn't even sure of his full name, and we needed that plus his birth date, birthplace, and Social Security number."

She went on to explain that Harold had refused to share the contents of the file with us. "We both e-mailed and called Harold on various occasions, but he was firm that he was not going to reveal anything further. I was so disappointed that my good friends had chosen to take this position. Finally, after much angst over the situation, I rationalized that they were not trying to protect Gary and me—they were probably trying to protect Rotea Gilford's reputation."

"I had no idea that Gary had begun discussions with the lieutenant in charge of homicide, John Hennessey," she concluded.

It was then that my mother must have realized I wasn't going to quit—that I had gone around Butler and Sanders to find the truth.

It was soon after I received that letter that I learned about Hennessey's having moved from his position as head of homicide into special investigations. It didn't seem suspicious at the time, because he had asked me to be patient, and I had assumed that I would hear from him when the results came back.

Seven years later, I continue to wonder why I didn't hear from him, but the questions I have are different.

By revealing to my mother that Hennessy had requested the DNA comparison, had I unwittingly betrayed his trust?

Did my mother call her friends to let them know Hennessey had put in the DNA request?

Why hasn't available DNA evidence provided to the SFPD been fully investigated?

The fact remains: Judy married Van, the Zodiac. Judy married Rotea, the homicide detective. Did this remarkable coincidence have anything to do with Butler's and then Sanders's responses to whatever was in Van's file? Were Hennessey's efforts to help me find the truth about my father shut down? Or were they simply set aside in the face of the SFPD's crushing workload and the long history of false Zodiac leads?

I don't know for sure. What I do know is that I have not heard from my friend John Hennessey since I sent Judy that manuscript.

I have weighed the pros and cons of publishing this book for years, considering what could happen from every angle. One thought keeps coming back to me: the surviving families of the Zodiac victims deserve to know who committed these horrible acts.

I talked with my son, Zach, about it, being very honest about what I thought could happen if people didn't believe me. "You could be ridiculed," I told him. "Some of your friends might say some very mean things about your dad and your grandma Judy. And those who believe me could give you a very hard time about being the grandson of a serial killer."

"Dad, really, you are such a worrier. I'll be okay. I can handle it. You do what you have to do," he had said, giving me a hug. "Whatever happens, we can deal with it."

I have never been more proud of my son than in that moment.

When I talked to Judy, she seemed less certain, but she assured me that she would support me in whatever I decided to do. We will deal with the fallout together. We have been through a lot, and I have faith that our relationship will survive. When I was young, if Loyd suspected we were telling fibs, he was fond of saying, "The truth will set you free." I hope that will be the case for both of us. Through this book, I have handed the SFPD their killer. I've given them motive, means, opportunity, a forensic handwriting match, identical scars, and my father's name embedded throughout the Zodiac ciphers. And I have a DNA profile of my father waiting for comparison.

It will be interesting to see what happens.

I know without a doubt that God has led me to this place. I believe He intended for me to share this story, leaving out nothing that I've discovered along the way. I have fulfilled that responsibility with all that I am and all that He made me to be. I know that no matter what happens, He will watch over all of us and protect us, just as He so lovingly protected the baby in the stairwell.

The Zodiac abandoned me so long ago.

Maybe now I can abandon him.

In Loving Memory of Sheryl Lynn Stewart

December 6, 1959–January 7, 1961

and

Harry Loyd Stewart

December 21, 1931–June 16, 2012

ACKNOWLEDGMENTS

There are so many people who helped shape my destiny and who assisted me in learning about my past and that of my parents: Detectives Fournier and Jonau, who searched for the parents of the abandoned baby; Mary Bonnette; who found me; Lieutenant Hennessey, who believed me; William Lohmus, who came to love me and whose knowledge of my father seemed limitless; the Best family, who filled in the gaps and welcomed me with open arms; and Sergio, a stranger who was there for me during one of my most painful moments. A special thank-you to Michael Wakshull, Dr. Bo Scales, Lisa Hobbs Birnie, Max Davis, and Judy Riffel. I am eternally grateful to each of you.

I would like to thank my mom and dad, Loyd and Leona Stewart, for opening their hearts and their home to their adopted children—first Sheryl, then Cindy, and finally me. Thank you for treating us like we were your own. There was never a question that we were loved completely and as much as if we had been born to you. Thank you for raising me in Istrouma Baptist Church and making me attend services even when I didn't want to go. Your faith in God was the best example a son could have and instilled in me the faith, courage, and strength to face all of the challenges placed before me as I followed His plan for my life.

I would like to thank Judy Gilford for the gift of life she gave to me. Our journey together has not been an easy one, but I wouldn't trade it for anything.

To Susan Mustafa, who took the complex, patchworked story of my life and, with her creative writing brilliance, produced this book. Thank you. You are now officially the fourth and last of the adopted children in the Stewart family. And to my agent, B. G. Dilworth, thank you for your hard work and dedication to this project.

To Michael Signorelli: Thank you for your belief in us. To Jennifer Barth at HarperCollins: Thank you for the countless hours you spent working with us to make this book the best it could be. Your contributions helped turn what was an incredible journey into a riveting narrative.

I also want to thank the two people I love most in this world: my wife and my son. You believed in me even when I didn't believe in myself, when I questioned why God was taking so long to reveal the truth to me. You lifted me up and encouraged me through my discoveries, through my heartaches, through my disappointments, and you celebrated those times I was the happiest. Without you, this book would never have happened. To my beautiful and precious Kristy and my pride and joy, Zach, I am because you believed in me, and I love you dearly.

Finally, and most important, I am so thankful to God for this life He gave to me, for rescuing me, delivering me, and redeeming me from whence I came.

I will always miss you, Daddy, until I see you again!

—GARY L. STEWART

When I first read Gary Stewart's journal that became the foundation for this book, I couldn't believe what I was reading. I knew immediately that this would be a challenging project—so many stories, so many years, a romance and a serial killer case, all rolled up into one story that begins with a baby being abandoned on a stairwell. As I researched Gary's life and got to know him personally, I became more and more impressed with the character of this man who had persevered through this heart-wrenching journey to find his identity. Thank you, Gary, for choosing me to be your co-author. Any writer wants to find that one story that begs to be told. For me, this story was the one, and I am honored by your belief in me.

To my husband, Scott, thank you for putting up with all the nights I sit at my computer burning the midnight oil. Your understanding of what it takes to write a book makes what I do possible, and your critiques of my work have become invaluable to me. Your love and your friendship always make my world such a happy place to be.

I have been blessed in this life with so many wonderful people—my mom, "B-Bunny," whose strength and courage inspire me every day; my sisters, Bridget and Cathy, who always have a multisyllabic word handy when I need one; my children, Angel, Brandon, Gasper, and Jonathon, who make every day of my life worthwhile; and my granddaughter, Isabella StellaMaria, who has melted my heart since the day she was born.

Dr. Joseph Mirando, thank you for being my mentor and my friend, and for being so brutal with your red pen that I finally learned how to write.

Judy and Bob, thank you for welcoming me into your incredible family. Knowing both of you has been my privilege.

And to my wonderful friend Sue Israel; my manager, Mike Kinnamon of Music Central Management; and my agent, B. G. Dilworth—thank you for everything you do to help make my dreams come true.

—SUSAN MUSTAFA

TIMELINE

July 14, 1934
Earl Van Best Jr. is born in Wilmore, Kentucky.

September 7, 1949
Van enrolls in Lowell High School, in San Francisco, and meets William Lohmus and Bill Bixby.

August 19, 1957
Van marries Mary Annette Player.

January 4, 1959
Mary Annette files for divorce on the grounds of extreme cruelty and inhuman treatment.

October 1961
Twenty-seven-year-old Van meets thirteen-year-old Judy Chandler.

January 5, 1962
Van marries Judy in Reno, Nevada, without her mother's permission. The next month, Judy's mother has the marriage annulled.

February 22, 1962
Van is arrested for the rape of a female under eighteen years old. He is released on bail. Charges are later dismissed.

February 12, 1963

Earl Van Dorne Best, son of Earl Van Best Jr. and Judy Chandler, is born in Southern Baptist Hospital, in New Orleans.

March 15, 1963

Van abandons his son on a stairwell in an apartment building in Baton Rouge.

April 19, 1963

Judy and Van are arrested in New Orleans. Judy is charged as a runaway, and Van is charged as a fugitive of California.

May 17, 1963

The state of Louisiana grants custody of Earl Van Dorne Best to Loyd and Leona Stewart.

August 13, 1963

Van is sentenced to one year in state prison, suspended, and four years' probation for the rape of a female under eighteen years old.

October 23, 1963

Van is arrested on fraud charges. He is sentenced to three years in state prison. In November, he is charged with two additional counts of fraud by wire and sentenced to ninety days in Atascadero State Hospital. Upon his release from Atascadero, he is sent to San Quentin.

January 21, 1964

Loyd and Leona officially adopt Earl Van Dorne Best, and his name is legally changed to Gary Loyd Stewart.

July 12, 1965

Van is paroled from prison.

June 6, 1966

Van marries Edith Kos.

October 30, 1966
The Zodiac kills Cheri Jo Bates in Riverside, California.

December 20, 1968
The Zodiac kills Betty Lou Jensen and David Faraday on Lake Herman Road near the Benicia water-pumping station in Benicia, California.

July 4, 1969
The Zodiac kills Darlene Ferrin and shoots Michael Mageau at Blue Rock Springs Park, in Vallejo, California.

July 27, 1969
Manson Family member Bobby Beausoleil kills music teacher Gary Hinman after holding Hinman hostage in his home with the help of Susan Atkins and Mary Brunner.

July 31, 1969
The Zodiac sends the 408 cipher in three sections to the Vallejo *Times-Herald,* the *San Francisco Examiner,* and the *San Francisco Chronicle.*

August 9, 1969
Manson Family members Charles "Tex" Watson, Patricia Krenwinkel, and Susan Atkins kill Sharon Tate, Jay Sebring, Abigail Folger, Wojciech Frykowski, and Steven Parent.

August 10, 1969
Charles "Tex" Watson and Patricia Krenwinkel kill Leno and Rosemary LaBianca at Charles Manson's behest.

September 27, 1969
The Zodiac kills Cecelia Shepard and wounds Bryan Hartnell at Lake Berryessa, in Napa County, California.

October 11, 1969
The Zodiac kills cabdriver Paul Stine in San Francisco.

November 8, 1969
The Zodiac sends the 340 cipher to the *San Francisco Chronicle*.

March 22, 1970
The Zodiac gives Kathleen Johns and her child a ride in what Johns would perceive as an attempted kidnapping. They escape from his vehicle.

April 1970
Judy Chandler meets SFPD detective Rotea Gilford.

October 20, 1973
Richard and Quita Hague are killed in San Francisco, the first victims in the Zebra murders, a series of racially motivated killings that end in April 1974.

January 1974–September 1975
The Black Doodler kills fourteen gay men in San Francisco. He is never caught.

June 19, 1974
Rotea Gilford and Judy Chandler are married.

November 18, 1978
In Jonestown, Guyana, 909 people die in a mass murder/suicide orchestrated by Jim Jones of the Peoples Temple.

November 27, 1978
San Francisco mayor George Moscone and City Supervisor Harvey Milk are killed by Dan White in city hall.

March 28, 1984
Earl Van Best Sr. dies and is given a military funeral at Arlington National Cemetery.

May 20, 1984
Van dies in Mexico City.

March 13, 1998
Rotea Gilford dies in San Francisco from complications resulting from diabetes.

May 1, 2002
Judy Gilford contacts Leona Stewart, looking for her son.

June 1, 2002
Gary meets his mother.

April 6, 2004
Judy meets with former San Francisco chief of police Earl Sanders to discuss Van's criminal file. The Zodiac case is officially closed in San Francisco that same day.

June 16, 2012
Gary's adoptive father, Loyd Stewart, passes away.

December 9, 2012
Forensic document examiner Michael N. Wakshull determines that the handwriting on Van and Judy's marriage certificate matches that in the Zodiac letters.

BIBLIOGRAPHY AND RESOURCES

BOOKS AND STUDIES

Amburn, Ellis. *Pearl: The Obsessions and Passions of Janis Joplin*. Grand Central Publishing, 1993.

American Bible Society. *Holy Bible: King James Version*. American Bible Society, 1980.

Aquino, Michael A. *The Church of Satan*. Church of Satan, 2013.

Best, Earl Van, Sr. "State and Religion in Japan: A Survey of the Attitude of the Japanese State Toward Religion with Emphasis upon the Missionary Movement in a Totalitarian Society." Kennedy School of Missions, Hartford Seminary Foundation, April 1942.

Bugliosi, Vincent, and Curt Gentry. *Helter Skelter: The True Story of the Manson Murders*. W. W. Norton, 1994.

Carlsson, Chris, and Lisa Ruth Elliot. *Ten Years That Shook the City: San Francisco 1968 to 1978*. City Lights Foundation Books, 2011.

Connell, Richard. *The Most Dangerous Game: Richard Connell's Original Masterpiece*. CreateSpace Independent Publishing Platform, 2011.

Douglas, John, and Mark Olshaker. *Mind Hunter: Inside the FBI's Elite Serial Crime Unit*. Pocket Books, 1996.

———. *The Cases That Haunt Us*. Pocket Books, 2001.

Graysmith, Robert. *Zodiac*. Berkley, 2007. First published 1986 by St. Martin's Press.

———. *Zodiac Unmasked: The Identity of America's Most Elusive Serial Killer Revealed*. Berkley, 2007.

Guinn, Jeff. *Manson: The Life and Times of Charles Manson.* Simon & Schuster, 2013.

Hodgson, Godfrey. *America in Our Time: From World War II to Nixon—What Happened and Why.* Vintage Books, 1976.

Howard, Clark. *Zebra: The True Account of the 179 Days of Terror in San Francisco.* Richard Marek Publishers, 1979.

Kelleher, Michael D., and David Van Nuys. *This Is the Zodiac Speaking: Into the Mind of a Serial Killer.* Praeger, 2001.

Kurlansky, Mark. *1968: The Year That Rocked the World.* Random House, 2005.

LaVey, Anton. *The Satanic Bible.* Avon, 1976. First published 1969 by Avon Books.

Murray, William. *Serial Killers: Notorious Killers Who Lived Among Us.* Canary Press, 2007.

Magee, David. *Infinite Riches, The Adventures of a Rare Book Dealer.* Paul S. Eriksson, Inc., 1973.

Newton, Michael. The *Encyclopedia of Serial Killers: A Study of the Chilling Criminal Phenomenon, from the "Angels of Death" to the "Zodiac" Killer.* Checkmark Books, 2000.

Our American Century and Editors of Time-Life Books. *Turbulent Years: The 60s.* Time Life Education, 1998.

Parker, RJ. *Serial Killer Case Files.* CreateSpace Independent Publishing Platform, 2013.

Perry, Charles. *The Haight-Ashbury: A History.* Wenner, 2005.

Roland, Paul. *In the Minds of Murderers: The Inside Story of Criminal Profiling.* Chartwell Books, 2009.

Sanders, Ed. *The Family.* Da Capo Press, 2002. First published 1971 by E. P. Dutton and Co.

Sanders, Prentiss Earl, and Bennett Cohen. *The Zebra Murders: A Season of Killing, Racial Madness, and Civil Rights.* Arcade Publishing, 2006.

Schechter, Harold. *The Serial Killer Files: The Who, What, Where, How, and Why of the World's Most Terrifying Murderers.* Ballantine Books, 2003.

Schiller, Lawrence. *The Killing of Sharon Tate*. Signet, 1970.

Selvin, Joel. *Summer of Love: The Inside Story of LSD, Rock & Roll, Free Love, and High Times in the Wild West*. Cooper Square, 1999.

NEWSPAPERS AND PERIODICALS

Daily World (Opelousas, La.)
"TWO PERSONS WERE KILLED in the headon collision Saturday Morning." January 8, 1961.

Edwardsville (Ill.) Intelligencer
"Murderer Terrorizes Bay Area." October 16, 1969.

Indiana Combat Veteran (Indianapolis)
"State Chaplain Best Succumbs to Death." Vol. XXXVII, no. 3. May/June 1984.

Los Angeles Times
"Zodiac Kills Fifth Victim." October 16, 1969.

"Zodiac's Trail, a Confusing Crime Pattern." May 8, 1970.

"Zodiac Threatens to Kill Reporter for S.F. Newspaper." October 31, 1970.

"Evidence Links Zodiac Killer to '66 Death of Riverside Coed." November 16, 1970.

Morning Advocate (Baton Rouge, La.)
"Tot Abandoned Here Is Put in Hospital for Observation." March 18, 1963.

Napa Register (Napa County, Calif.)
"School Bus Is Target." October 17, 1969.

"'Zodiac' Jangles Nerves of Napa County People." October 18, 1969.

Oakland (Calif.) Tribune
"TROUBLE, Jail Parts Child Bride, Husband, 28." August 1, 1962.

"Ailing Child Bride, Spouse Disappear." August 31, 1962.

"Car Gives Clue in Child Bride Hunt, Bulletin Out for Arrest of Pair in 2nd Elopement." September 1, 1962.

Press Democrat (Santa Rosa, Calif.)

"Masked Man Stabs Couple; Links to Vallejo Killings?" September 29, 1969.

"Coed Stabbing Victim Dies." September 30, 1969.

Press-Enterprise (Riverside, Calif.)

"RCC Coed, 18, Slain on Campus." October 31, 1966.

"'Zodiac' may have killed Riverside Co-Ed, paper says." November 16, 1970.

"Detectives hope to find Zodiac's handwriting in City College records." November 24, 1970.

Register-Guard (Eugene, Ore.)

"Murder Suspect Free Because Gays Silent." July 8, 1977.

Reno (Nev.) Evening Gazette

"Pretty Coed Slain, Watch Single Clue." November 1, 1966.

San Francisco Chronicle

"He Found Love in Ice Cream Parlor." August 1, 1962.

"Ice Cream Romance: Child Bride Gone Again." September 1, 1962.

"Statewide Hunt for S.F. Child Bride." September 2, 1962.

"Love on the Run: Ice Cream Romance's Bitter End." April 20, 1963.

"S.F. Couple Held: Ice Cream Romance Ends on Bourbon Street." April 20, 1963.

"Ice Cream Parlor Lover: Senator's Letter to Judge Doesn't Help." August 14, 1963.

"Friends Quizzed in Slaying of Teen Pair Near Vallejo." December 22, 1968.

"Police Seeking Teens' Slayer." December 23, 1968.

"Woman Slain, Friend Shot." July 6, 1969.

"Coded Clue in Murders." August 2, 1969.

"A 'Murder Code' Broken." August 9. 1969.

"Cabbie Slain in Presidio Heights." October 12, 1969.

"The Boastful 'Slayer': Letter Claims Writer Killed Cabbie, 4 Others." October 15, 1969.

"Zodiac: Portrait of a Killer." October 18, 1969.

"Fear Rides the Yellow Bus." October 21, 1969.

"Dare by Brother of Slain Man." October 23, 1969.

"Zodiac Halloween Threat, Reporter Warned, Zodiac Threat on Halloween Card." October 31, 1969.

" 'I've Killed Seven,' the Zodiac Claims." November 12, 1969.

"Zodiac 'Legally Sane,' Cops Sure Clues Will Snag Him." November 13, 1969.

"Urgent Appeal by Belli to Zodiac." December 29, 1969.

"Zodiac Sends New Letter: Claims Ten." April 22, 1970.

"Gilbert and Sullivan Clue to Zodiac." October 12, 1970.

"Police Confer on Zodiac Killings." November 19, 1970.

"Zodiac Writes Again, 17 Dead." March 16, 1971.

"Zodiac Mystery Letter, the First Since 1971." January 31, 1974.

"Zodiac Ends Silence: 'I Am Back With You.' " April 26, 1978.

"Feinstein Says Toschi's Being 'Crucified.' " July 14, 1978.

"Latest Zodiac Letter a Fake, 3 Experts Say." August 3, 1978.

"Files Shut on Zodiac's Deadly Trail." April 7, 2004.

San Francisco Examiner

"Man with 'Child Bride' Arrested." July 30, 1962.

"Their Idyll at End—Jailed Mate Sobs for Bride, 14." August 1, 1962.

"Indictment in Child Bride Case: Girl, 14, Tells Story to Jury." August 7, 1962.

"Cops Halt Elopers' 3rd Flight." April 20, 1963.

"Jail for Man Who Married Girl, 14." August 14, 1963.

"Vallejo Mass Murder Threat Fails." August 3, 1969.

"Salinas Teacher Breaks Code on Vallejo Murders." August 10, 1969.

"Zodiac Manhunt Centered in S.F." October 23, 1969.

"Rotea Gilford, Former Deputy Mayor, Dies at 70." March 16, 1998.

San Francisco News–Call Bulletin

"Bride of 14—With a Sundae Kind of Love." August 1, 1962.

"Sundae Bride Hunted." September 1, 1962.

State Times (Baton Rouge, La.)

"Seek Identity of Abandoned Child's Parents." March 16, 1963.

"Teen-ager May Be Mother of Abandoned Tot." April 19, 1963.

Tiger Times (Riverside Community College, Riverside, Calif.)

"Police Still Lack Clues in Murder." November 4, 1966.

Times-Herald (Vallejo, Calif.)

"Investigators Lacking Clues in 2 Slayings." December 22, 1968.

"Teenagers Slayer Still at Large." March 30, 1969.

"Police Still Hunt for Shooting Clues." July 8, 1969.

Times-Picayune (New Orleans, La.)

"Man Admits Abandoning Young Infant, Police Say." April 20, 1963.

Tucson (Ariz.) Daily Citizen

"Ice Cream Romance Ends in Jail." August 14, 1962.

Vallejo (Calif.) News-Chronicle

"Jealousy Motive Checked." December 23, 1968.

"Appeal Is Made for Help." December 26, 1968.

ZODIAC LETTERS

April 30, 1967: "Bates Had to Die." Joseph Bates, Riverside Police Department, Riverside *Press-Enterprise*.

July 31, 1969: 408 cipher. Vallejo *Times-Herald, San Francisco Examiner, San Francisco Chronicle*.

August 4, 1969: "This is the Zodiac speaking." *San Francisco Examiner*.

October 13, 1969: Paul Stine letter. *San Francisco Chronicle*.

November 8, 1969: 340 cipher. *San Francisco Chronicle*.

November 9, 1969: Zodiac threatens to bomb a bus. *San Francisco Chronicle*.

December 20, 1969: Letter sent to Melvin Belli.

April 20, 1970: "My Name Is" cipher. *San Francisco Chronicle*.

April 28, 1970: Dragon Card. *San Francisco Chronicle*.

June 26, 1970: 32-character cipher. *San Francisco Chronicle*.

July 24, 1970: Kathleen Johns. *San Francisco Chronicle*.

July 26, 1970: Zodiac's version of Gilbert and Sullivan's "I've Got a Little List," from *The Mikado*. *San Francisco Chronicle*.

October 27, 1970: Halloween card sent to Paul Avery. *San Francisco Chronicle*.

March 13, 1971: Blue Meanies. *Los Angeles Times.*
January 29, 1974: "The Exorcist." *San Francisco Chronicle.*
February 14, 1974: Symbionese Liberation Army. *San Francisco Chronicle.*
July 8, 1974: Red Phantom. *San Francisco Chronicle.*

GOVERNMENT AGENCIES

Baton Rouge Police Department Criminal Records Division
City and County Assessor-Recorder's Office, San Francisco
County Clerk's Office, Wilmore, Ky.
East Baton Rouge Parish Clerk of Court
East Baton Rouge Welfare Department, Department of Public
    Works, Baton Rouge, La.
Federal Bureau of Investigation
Indiana Department of Health, Hamilton County, Noblesville
New Orleans Police Department Records Office
Office of the Clerk-Recorder, San Jose, Calif.
Recorder-Clerk Division, San Bernardino, Calif.
San Francisco Police Department Criminal Court Records Office
U.S. Department of State, Washington, D.C.
U.S. Embassy, Mexico City
Washoe County Clerk's Office, Reno, Nev.

POLICE REPORTS

Baton Rouge Police Department
California Department of Justice, Bureau of Criminal Identification
    and Investigation
Federal Bureau of Investigation
Napa County Sheriff's Office
New Orleans Police Department
Riverside Police Department, Riverside, Calif.
San Francisco Police Department
Solano County Sheriff's Office, Fairfield, Calif.

Stanislaus County Sheriff's Office, Modesto, Calif.
Vallejo Police Department, Vallejo, Calif.

LIBRARIES

East Baton Rouge Parish Library
Long Beach Public Library, Long Beach, Calif.
New Orleans Public Library
Norman F. Feldheym Central Library, San Bernardino, Calif.
San Francisco Public Library

WEBSITES

https://diva.sfsu.edu
www.ancestry.com
www.dogpile.com
www.familysearch.org
www.horrycounty.org
www.latimes.com
www.newspaperarchive.com
www.pbs.org
www.rootsweb.com
www.sfchronicle.com
www.sfexaminer.com
www.sfgate.com
www.theadvocate.com
www.ussearch.com
www.youtube.com
www.zodiackiller.com
www.zodiackillerfacts.com

INDEX

Page numbers in *italics* refer to illustrations.

ABOUT THE AUTHORS

GARY L. STEWART earned his bachelor of science degree in electrical engineering from Louisiana State University and is vice president of Delta Tech Service of Louisiana. Ten years ago, Gary began writing a journal, chronicling every detail of his search for his father and his own identity. That journal served as the basis for *The Most Dangerous Animal of All*. Gary resides in Louisiana with his wife, Kristy, and son, Zach.

SUSAN MUSTAFA is an award-winning author and journalist. She is the co-author of *Dismembered*, written with Sue Israel, which chronicles the story of serial killer Sean Vincent Gillis; and *Blood Bath*, about the life and crimes of serial killer Derrick Todd Lee, written with Special Prosecutor Tony Clayton and Sue Israel. Susan lives in Louisiana with her husband, Scott.